JAVA WEDNESDAYS

For Gene
with admiration
for the beautiful
work you do.
Love
Jan

by the Java Poets Collective

10/09

The Troy Book Makers

Troy, New York

www.thetroybookmakers.com

Printed in the United States of America

Book and cover design by Melissa Mykal Batalin

To order additional copies of this title, contact your favorite local bookstore or visit www.tbmbooks.com

ISBN: 978-1-935534-12-9

With profound thanks to poet Cara Benson,
whose poetry workshop for the New York State
Writers Institute at SUNY Albany first brought us
together in 2006. We have been meeting once a
month ever since at Professor Java's Coffee Sanctuary
on Wolf Road, gently critiquing each other's poems
and supporting each other with good cheer.
We assembled this collection of poems
to share something of ourselves and the
fruit of our poetic endeavors.

Contents

JAVA
WEDNESDAYS

Deb Adler

Going Away

I seem to be provisioning my car
for a journey I didn't plan.
This has gone beyond the odd breath mint
or misshapen Hershey With Almonds bar
hiding under the seat.
Suddenly there is trail gorp
and beef jerky in the glove box,
jostled by bottled water.
And now (it's cold enough outside)
string cheese sprouts from the console.
I expect hard tack to appear soon,
along with Tang and pemmican,
in a scarred tin box in the trunk.

Someone is outfitting this expedition,
keeping secret its destination.
The map — probably unreadable
from being left out in the rain —
is in a place locked and buried,
although I have the combination here somewhere...

I'm willing to go. Traveling isn't so bad,
and I'm not unused to going alone.
But like the mechanic
who put on the snow tires wondered,
Why do I have to travel so far in the dead of winter?

Letter to Camp

How are you?
Things here are well.
The cats stay closer at night with you gone,
and ask for more pets at daybreak.
The birds have mostly left,
but the cardinals with their late brood hang on.
Did I tell you about
the hummingbird? Buzzing me,
disappointed that my sun-warmed hair
was not sweet, she scowled at me,
hanging scoldingly in midair,
before zooming off in search of something
that would keep its promise of food.

I wrote a poem, but I haven't finished the laundry.
Instead, I have dozed in bed,
thinking back through all the years of you.

Have I fed you enough worms?
Taught you about marauding cats?
Did I explain about what males to select?
Were the flying lessons sufficient?

That's all. Except that yesterday,
I bought a hummingbird feeder,
and learned to make pink sugar water.

Deb Adler

Making Ready

Heavy on my unwieldy shovel,
black mulch spills in ragged furrows, pre-zinnia.
When my giant's tool won't be lifted one more time,
my hands decide to claw the gritty stuff
to crooked, miniature mountain ranges.

I burrow in, amazed:
the heavy manure-smelling mound
is warm as a foal's flank in sunshine.
Is this what nurses seeds to life?

I'm no gardener. My weightless seeds may die,
mulched or not.
This spring, I'm awkwardly planting
as my mother (the rightful gardener)
dies off: her life is late fall.

Her ashes should lie where she gardened for years.
She would recognize this smell, this grit, this color.
I think the soil will recognize her, as well,
as the mulch outwarms
her cooling ash.

Discards

I never saw my husband dead.
They told me not to,
And took away the useful bits.

But when my sister died,
I saw what death had left lying on that bed:

The lollipop stick, the candy wrapper.
Hair caught in the brush.

The rumpled sheets after the lover has gone
For good.

Cara Benson

Perhaps You're Ugly, But All's Well

after John Ashbery

Pt. I

These niceties are a noxious bother.
Sky fishing is pondering the after
life. Squint, boy.
Hold your hand up to block the incoming
truth.

Ribbed corduroy workpants and I'll give notice, brother.
Sucker.
Inheritance. Fighting. Blood. Ignorance.

Swimsuit around my ankles;
the captain meandered.
Liars one, then
all.
Blue sky quitter. You think
anyone's loose change jangles like mine?

There is nothing so iconoclastic as a trend setter.
FIRE! – master. Run. Wash your hands of the bricks.
Always bring your own money (or ride).
I'm full. I'll never leave.
The garden blooms in silence.

Originally appeared in *EOAGH #4*
http://chax.org/eoagh/issuefour.html

Swipe

Standing on the dock in droopy
boxer shorts, my marmaduke sidekick

for immediate introductions, I
deliver my uppercut to American

pageantry. My irises dye violet –
my lungs do the dirty work – it is

a matter of matter to speak. HERE
i am. WOOOF me too. I pluck hair:

he loves me he loves me he loves me
and ask again later.

Originally appeared in *Forklift, OH*
Print Issue #19, Fall 2008

Post-it

Sitting at a conference table is much easier than the outsiders imagine it to be. There is coffee and water pitchers and little yellow pads. These elements are consistently comforting to finger the edges of during tense meetings. But the sitting is good. Welcome the sitting. And the people and the sitting and the pencils and the pens. People say things and some don't. It is okay to be someone who doesn't say anything yet. Do not worry unless you want to that you haven't said anything yet. Just caress the styrofoam cup in front of you. See how easy it is? So you are at the table and touching things. Better look up. At the head of the table someone has made some space on the table. This is unusual. You didn't know but the reactions up and down the sides of the table are a tip off. There is murmuring and lots of touching. The table sitter next to you has in fact has reached for your cup in his in anxiety and makes skin contact. You clear your throat you and pull your hand away. That you retract it is a sure a sign your hand that you own your place at the table. Table. The front of the room behind you with the sides to your left and right stare waiting. To turn the table which is written on the paper before you you you see in your handwriting so you see you speak. And what you now commission cannot be undone even if you wake asleep sweating with scream.

Lather Rinse Repeat

Stringy village dweller

unhung tumble dry –

the bumpy ride, what

unknown toward fast

toward us. Away as

it always is: never

and the same.

Joe Capobianco

A Poem to My Grandson
Who Is Not Quite Here Yet

You don't know that a lot of people are waiting for you.
Some of us playing games with names
ending with vowels
sounding Latino-Italiano,
but they all seem too serious
for a little boy,
no matter how big you grow up to be!

Grandma knits you blankets.
Aunts and uncles buy you books.
I don't know if you will have enough space
for all the things people will give you.

But after the gifts are unwrapped
and the books are read,
I want to see you
and look into your eyes,
tell you stories about places and people
from a long time ago,
even before your mother was a little girl.

But there will be plenty of time
for you to listen.
You must learn how to crawl,
talk, eat, play.
So later, we will talk,
just me and you.
We have plenty of time.

Boxes Sealed

Boxes sealed, floors swept.
Hands slide over closet shelves.
Last grasps for lost treasure among dust bunnies.
Little time for reflection
about tomorrows in a new place.

Drinks tinkle, friends mingle.
Polite chat and knowing smiles.
Squeezed hands substitute
for long winded goodbyes.
Open ended questions
about getting together next year,
maybe the track or SPAC.
But tomorrow will end
in a new place, won't it?

Front door opens, shadows emerge, voices
retreat onto the lane, hanging in the air.
The start of our new days
are born of old ways with old friends,
and the new place,
well, it can just wait.

Twins

I watched them parade down Main Street,
mother and daughter,
side by side, step to step.
Hands, arms intertwined.
Bags, parcels and a fat pretzel with mustard.
Heads dancing, sometimes in unison,
other times at odds.
Makes me smile.
Makes me jealous.

Catch up time, families, friends, jobs,
brought together in non-stop free flow,
more or less in agreement, perhaps punctuated differently.
Daughter with more exclamation marks;
youth always has such urgency.
Mom, more generous with commas,
keeping the flow of sentences
going through caveats, prepositions
and promises to do more and bigger next time.

They cross the street, gesturing at store windows,
designer-laden, earth-toned.
The wind catches them and for a moment
silence reigns on the street, but not for long.
The door opens, they escape the gale,
and I lean back on the bench,
baggage handler, car watcher,
invisible on Main Street.

Harrison Said

Harrison said,
"poets must learn to climb
the walls that surround their words."
Since I am winking at sixty,
I thought it was okay to cheat,
and brought a ladder to help see.

My ladder, being grey and gnarly
like me, leaned badly
and kept me wobbling side to side.
Someone dear to me said
it suited my climb through life,
shifting side to side,
never holding a straight line,
looking left to yesterdays,
right to tomorrows.
Generally missing out
on the moment, the day at hand.

At the top I liked the view.
It worked for me, for at least this piece,
until I fell. But perhaps tomorrow
I'll find a different ladder with straighter rungs.
Maybe I'll even look down
to see where I am standing
before I start to climb.

Maria DeLucia-Evans

just about

my tired hands rest softly at your
knee. our muscles defining you
and me like the way it once was—the way
we'd want it to be if we could
choose these things. you see,

maybe it *is* about living in the
past, celebrating imperfections
of time we can't turn back, as a
way to steady ourselves for
choices we make as we slip
forward. it's about that tapestry

hanging on the back of our soul,
fabrics of colors and textures
so intense you'd never want
to see it unravel, or fray at
the edges. those things we chose, or
things that chose us, a line now too
blurry to tell if it even existed.

no matter what, promise me you'll
always look back and revel
in what was. it's how the non-perfect
becomes perfect. just about.

Hallelujah Rain

You told me about hallelujah rain, and then played it for me.
With closed eyes, I heard soft hands plucking strings of steel.

And then I thought I felt it—that almost rain coating my
sticky body, cutting through air hanging thick around sweaty
beer bottles and shirts with no bras.

But sap fell from a tree, and I fell into you.

Tumbled into your arms, which hold me.

Fingers strum my body now, and we wait together,
praying hallelujah.

Maria DeLucia-Evans

19 weeks 2 days

there's a penis growing inside me.
I read this once in a poem written
by an expectant mother poet*, and now
as my belly grows tighter, stretches
forward, pushes on the zipper

of my pants, I wonder what's
growing inside of me. will I be let
into this club of birth motherhood?
I stretch my fingers over the crest of skin,
pushing down lightly, feeling the connection

to what I know is there. holding my breath
slightly, I imagine how weeks turn into
months turn into healthy babies of time.
this has been done over and over, I know,

but this is the first time I've done it, and this
is what they told me I couldn't do. the people
say, "oh thank god you're pregnant,"
and "you must be so relieved," as if my wholeness
was being left not whole.

and maybe I am relieved, though I'd never say
that aloud. instead, I whisper to my
unborn, *I'm so glad you're here* and
please don't leave me, I need you now.

* Dr. Barbara Ungar, Phd English Literature

El Viaggiatore (The Traveler)

She craved his letters. In the back room of a dress shop near the Piazza della Signoria, his proposal arrived. Standing at the port, wooden trunk beside her, she kissed her mother goodbye. Finality surrounded the lingering embrace. She would never return.

The ship that promised everything never made it to New York. She arrived in Boston, terrified he wouldn't find her. Unable to yet speak English, she could only sit, fingers gripped around a leather bag, and wait for Nicola. She wept when she finally saw him.

The journey from Boston to rural Pennsylvania ended in despair. The house he built for her on an income hammering railroad steel was gone. They stared at burnt ash, walked through rubble. Smoke thick in their lungs, they kept breathing. Life was rebuilt on a hope that did more than survive.

Fifty years have passed, and she stands now, lost in the middle of O'Hare. English announcements sound overhead, but age has left Italian in her mind. She travels alone, sent to live with her boy Alphonso; Anna, her eldest, is done trying to care for her. But she doesn't remember that. She doesn't remember why she's standing amidst the hurried crowds and muddled words. She clutches a cracked leather bag and whispers, *Nicola*.

Gwen Gould

The Poultry Fancier

Daddy raised Black Cochin Bantams in the backyard
on no more than a quarter of an acre,
but that was enough.

Our yard was part lawn, and part rocky outcropping
with a little space up behind the rock garden
for the chicken coops.

When he ran out of space there, he even
built a coop on a precarious ledge
over the fence.

Raccoons and weasels would get under the chickenwire floor
pull the chicken legs through the wire
and chew them off.

Daddy shot a raccoon once on a limb overhanging
the mill pond. Funny, I don't remember
seeing a gun anywhere in our house.

He loved those chickens. He would go out there
after dinner and fuss with them,
applying "Nu-Skin" to their wounds,

analyzing which were prize specimens,
and just watching them
like they were a TV show.

I think Mother thought he loved them more than her.
She would flick the lights on and off
to get him to come in, after her patience ran out.

Daddy didn't just raise chickens, he was a "poultry fancier,"
showing his chickens at the county fair,
winning prizes every year.

He sold chickens to other fanciers across the country,
even made up stationery with a picture
of a Black Cochin Bantam on the letterhead.

Every spring, Daddy hatched baby chicks in the incubator
in the basement. Before he sent them to a show
he washed his prize chickens

in the kitchen sink and dried them with a hair dryer,
until the green tinge on their shiny black feathers
glowed to match his pride.

Some years after he died, the grand championship
of the poultry show at the Dutchess County Fair
was in his name.

Mother was a special guest for the occasion.

9/11

Trumpet-shaped blossoms, luscious red
cascaded across my window,
bluish glass towers gleamed in the distance,
immense structures, disproportionate
to human scale, teeming with life.

Those disparate images evoked
feelings of wonder and dread.
If the giant towers should fall
would they crash through my window
on Nassau Street?

Vibrant flowers of the lipstick plant
drew my eyes from my imaginings,
unraveling my fears.

But one morning the bluish glass
reflected a missile of destruction
with captive human life in its belly, shattering
the gleaming image and the lives of all, forever.

...My lipstick plant and I had moved to the country.

I nurtured that plant for nearly five years,
I couldn't bear to let it die.
It no longer had the energy to bloom,
but the eerie image of the towers
still filled the spaces between the leaves.

The Conversation Stopper

"I'm angry," she said.

"I don't want to be criticized," he said.

End of discussion.

Scott Hicks

A Sprig of Lilac

If lilacs had not since bloomed by the dooryard
I would have stooped to break for you
the gentlest of sprigs and lay it to your tender breast

With this enveloping fragrant spring
cooling all the days of your disbelief
so that never again should you doubt
your utter importance to the object of your desire

The sweetness of spring now passed
followed by the grinding tedium of summer
yielding again to a most melancholic fall
finally healed by a paradoxically bright winter

The winter shall relieve the burdens of your heart
being the occasion of new freedom for your soul
and touched by your elegant grace
my sadness shall absorb that of yours

When come spring anew
stoop to break a living sprig for me
and take it to that pool of brine
casting it on the emerald glass

Then pray for me wherever I be
that my heart again be strong
that my soul be lifted down to peace
that I be but the gentlest of memories

Recurrent View

Graying, clapboard houses
other's homes tucked against wooded hills
having passed them time and again
always wondering, searching, puzzled
why I must recreate their story
why I grieve so the absence of their promise

Lights, voices, prayers, children's play, extinguished
cars, tractors, rusted wind mill blades
aspirations, dreams, visions, vanished
without even history's roll call
the stillness folds my heart
the howling wind poses my endless questions

King Simon

Regal cats at night you would think do explore
but my housemate saves himself for the morning light
awakening me with a faint nip and a peculiar roar

Sensitive to stirrings he has heard before
yet saving this new day of wonderment through sight
to acquaint me with his playground to explore

He springs to the piano's top with a shrug at the floor
gently pressing his face to the high window now bright
to the cardinal's lush red, he defers his growl and roar

His backwards look at me with eyes of ancient lore
bidding I follow his vertical jumps into flight
charting red squirrels sprinting for chestnuts to horde

Jaws quivering, body taut, nose against the pane as a bore
stretching time, his object soon loses its luster bright
his gallops creating for those still asleep a thunderous roar

For those above and below awakened for a day's chore
know once again Simon has begun his day of delight
only to find him later pleading permission to explore
curled up to my leg, the green mist of his lost ancestral lore

A Poet's Resignation

Life's promises now motionless lie
grasping for the quickening muse
passing in final review for the finger's pulsations
wanting to pummel the heart's hardening to stone

In the sun we once proudly stood
and strode the coolest of green valleys
fearing to speak for to shatter the gentlest of day's warmth
holding hope which gives breath without prefiguring

The summer, its own brilliant self-validation
as children we were consumed by its intensity
for we had been face to face with the first and last
and now, faltering, our audacious case melting away

Our most ambitious dreams eclipsed by evening's mist
as giants we lie, quivering from the loss of primordial life
knowing that if defiance, having failed us
yet so she, mistress of our last grasp for the muse
be not quenched in others

Nick Kling

Sentinel

I am Little Nose,
protector of my Valley.
In utter silence I stand,
unblinking granite vigilance.
A century of centuries
cannot blunt my will,
no protest uttered.

I defend against the deluge.
Created by one though I was,
I know its pitiless authority.
There was no leniency present,
carving me apart,
leaving fraternal twins
in place of one mighty thing.

I am Little Nose,
mother of resource, sister of Big Nose.
We took measure
of all that came our way,
gate keepers,
primordial locks on the river,
regulating all flow.

I have seen time.
I have watched breathers come
from noble embryo to the present.
Larger now,
they are little changed,
malleable tissue
swaddled in dense casing.

Flawless...and eternally flawed.
I am Little Nose,
perch for all that is divine.
Home to hawk and snake,
oak and briar.
Rattle and strike,
Rattle and strike,
their watchfulness mirrors mine.

They know truth.
We learned it together.
Only stone is clean.
It infects no life,
it caresses* no brothers,
it devours no thing.
It is unto itself.

*caress – native term for physical torture of captives, in order to extract
revenge, establish dominance, and capture their soul.

Nick Kling

I am Little Nose,
redeemer of the future,
guardian of Big Nose.
The torrent is inevitable.
Breathers cannot restrain it,
nay,
they summon the gush.

I alone bar the way,
diverting the embrace of desolation.
I will reach into the gorge,
extend rocky sinews beyond capacity,
Kanatsiohareke* caressed Huron,
I will caress waters.
I am Little Nose.

Only stone can keep us.

*Kanatsiohareke — Mohawk Indian settlement in Montgomery County,
   NY, east of the Noses, a pair of Adirondack foothill mountains..

Industry

The Breast? Red.   The Nest?

Brush'd away...an afterthought.

No Babies This Year.

Cecele Allen Kraus

Longest Day of the Year

Anna didn't speak, seemed not to hear.
Maybe she's deaf, they worried, until the doctor
described her brain damage.

She was born in late June. We didn't speak
of summer solstice, how the world turned to winter.
Night fell bleak on our circumstances.

Four o'clock flowers trumpeted around our porch
late afternoons. I sang, *we are climbing Jacob's ladder,*
played in the yard, watched the red flowers untwist

and flutter into night-blooms, then ravel their petals
in the dewy morning hours. I sang, *every rung goes higher,*
higher, pushed myself up into the sky.

Anna visits in a dream, giggling, and tells me
of her boyfriend at the sheltered workshop. My sister
Amelia returns too – her eyes pierce as she wards off danger.

Oldest sister, I dream a sod carpet, pull it back,
and find gorgeous flowers, roots entangled in pachysandra,
closing in light, opening in the turf's dark.

Oh trinity of sisters. Anna, small bud blooming in
her own light, Amelia, wild orchid in a desert, and me,
stooped gardener, seeking flowers wherever I can find them.

Will Eternity Find You Waiting

Lying on the backseat in the car
I watch the telephone wire droop and rise
from pole to pole, waiting for the exact point
where it falls lowest then rises
against a purple sky.

My family drives up on Sunday nights
to a Pentecostal church by the highway.
Unfinished, it rises only four feet or so
off the ground. I watch for that moment
a banner appears across its exterior:
Jesus is Coming Soon. We descend
into this never-finished basement.
I figure there is no reason to finish:
the end-time is near. Two light bulbs beam,
moths swarm. Inside people testify:
Jesus saved the waitress wearing a hairnet
from a wanton life; my mother sobs out
her sorrow; my father is healed of smoking.

Wanting to be like the waitress, I wear
a hairnet. Like Joash, youngest king of Israel,
I am eight years old. We sing, *Jesus breaks
every fetter,* and the preacher shouts,
Will eternity find you waiting?

Waiting for a Call

At thirteen I waited for my boyfriend's call.
Without it I'd surely die.
In that flimsy tract house universe
a girl was made for waiting.
I had not yet learned to howl,
did not even know I was alive.

When early in the morning I'm alive
I listen for my mother's calls.
Since she's gone I've learned to howl
though I know I won't yet die.
Alto is the tone for which I'm waiting,
her low song out in the universe.

Telephone calls in an email universe.
I remember pay phones, wires alive,
long lines of anxious people waiting,
making collect and coin calls
to friends and relations before they die:
each dime's clink invokes a howl.

A long time now I've known how to howl,
send my calls up through the universe.
Once your people start to die
the air electrifies, comes alive
with sending and receiving calls–
rushing rafts of words–then call waiting.

A tender thread snaps while we're waiting
and in this tensile world we freely howl
as voice mail receives our calls.
Invisible wires in a hit or miss universe.
We forgive sins of omission to stay alive
until we join the soul web when we die.

Call your grandmother or she'll die,
my mother warned, *all alone, waiting.*
Your calls keep her alive.
She taught me how souls howl
in a world of wire, in a universe
fragile with unmade calls.

A universe where everyone's waiting.
Death protested with calls and a howl.
Sometimes we die though still alive.

Suzanne DeMuth Myers

The Conversation

turning to look down the road at
the crunch of tires on the dirt track he said
I wonder when we'll hear from him
eyes downcast to the bowl
of half shucked peas in her lap
her gaze darkens
shoulders drop
don't know
she says

it'd been years
since he'd been in contact
there was that one time he'd just arrived at the door
hugging his way in
small gifts, a box of candy for her
a magazine for him
gone immediately to the kitchen
lifting pot tops on things simmering on the stove
I'm hungry he declared, *anything to eat around here*
he sat down at the worn table
a plate of steaming chicken and dumplings
was placed in front of him
thick slices of fresh-baked bread
a tub of soft butter
a glass of lemonade
coolness condensing on the outside of the glass
rivulets of water dripped down to the tablecloth
and disappeared

conversation was kept deliberately light
after consuming the plate of food
wiping the very last bit of gravy
from the edge of the plate with the bread
he'd said *I think I'll go see Henry in town*
I'll be back early though and we can catch up
he kissed her lightly on the cheek
glanced at the figure leaning against the doorframe
they hadn't seen him since

Oh there were snatches of information
another incarceration
barroom brawl they'd heard
a friend-of-a-friend had seen him
in Cincinnati they thought
but there'd been no conversation
no information
just the sighting
she thought about him all the time
fingering the heart shaped stone
he'd found at the creek when
he was four years old
innocent of what could happen
an instant of poor judgment
the turn of a phrase misinterpreted
or misrepresented
who could tell

when the old swing
hanging by shreds of cotton rope
swung in the wind
cracked against the gnarled maple
she'd suddenly start
look towards the door
and wonder
where is he tonight
warm, held safely
or in some darkened street
hands stuffed deeply into empty pockets
leaning into the wind hurrying
to who-knows-where
to do who-knows-what

Inspired by the artwork of Rainey Dewey Mulligan

Love's Embrace

Cool breeze
shifts and brings
the morning
mists rise
leaving the dew
upon the grasses
emerging buds
bursting
expectant
waiting
for the moment
the specific moment
to part
protective lips
and kiss the wind
with their
newness
surrendering
protectorate existence
to embrace
whatever may come
resigning
their autonomy
to chance
encounters which
may
or may not

Terry Royne

The Wrong Side

There is a stretch of former rail
just under two miles long.
My life has gathered round it
from childhood to this song.

We moved there in the winter—
the tracks so active then.
A tragedy had happened there
before we had moved in.

Three neighbor ladies set out
to drive to town that day.
The driver, Mrs. Tinkham,
on the tracks she did delay.

The train it hit the Tinkham car.
She died along with one,
the wife of Mr. Snyder
who'd already lost his arm!

(T'was an unrelated accident
something about a saw.)
The only surviving neighbor wife
was widow Van Daan next door.

The tracks were full of tragedy
potential and for real
and that's what drew us to them
tough boys and little girls.

My brother and his scary friends
played "chicken" with the trains.
We held our breaths and pleaded God
to save their shit-for brains.

Now we lived on the wrong side
where woods spread all around.
The tracks divided our neighborhood
between the country and the town.

The woods sloped down into a swamp
that later became the ponds.
Ferns and wild asparagus
curled out in springtime fronds.

There were frogs and tadpoles in the ponds
to catch and throw back in.
There was skating in the winter
when the ice was not too thin.

I never quite forgave them
when my parents moved away
to the "better" side of town.
It was a real sad day.

Deep Inside

"If you go deeply enough inside yourself, you are everybody."[1]
Am I now, then, too far outside myself?
Is the world too much with me
or is the inside too dense?

Am I now too far outside myself?
Busy with others' illnesses, their decay
or is the inside too dense?
Fogged with wine and fear.

Busy with others' illnesses, their decay,
Sitting sh'vah with survivors
Fogged with wine and fear;
hoping, in healing, to be healed.

Sitting sh'vah with survivors
We silently think of all the losses
hoping, in healing, to be healed
learn to love the wound, the scar.

Is the world too much with me?
We silently think of all the losses
learn to love the wound, the scar.
"If you go far enough inside yourself, you are everybody."

[1] Brenda Hillman, in a poetry lecture at
Geraldine Dodge Poetry Festival, Sept. 2008.

Fertility

In June, my daughter and I amble
down to her garden patch.
I hold Charlotte, her daughter, my grand girl.
Nikki and I plant.

Charlotte, ten months, just
starting to walk, must help.
We cut holes in the mulch-plastic.
She drops seeds into the earth.

Ruby is hidden deep inside
her mother's body.
None of us knows
she is there.

Late August and the garden is overrun
Eggplantandsquashand
pumpkinandcucumbers
weeds too, uncontained.

Ruby still hides in the safe water
of Nikki's nursing body
while Charlotte, accomplished
walker, helper

gathers in her solid small hands
a pumpkin, an acorn, a little hubbard
and drops them, one by one
into the harvest basket.

Jan Marin Tramontano

Elegy for Joseph

When we arrived at the apartment
it was as if he left to get the paper
his morning ritual—
make coffee or reheat yesterday's
drink it black with a teaspoon of sugar
have a slice of crisp Italian bread
shiny with chunks of marmalade
do the daily crossword puzzle.

Stopped by a short breathless sloshing
he stood gasping at the kitchen sink—
help came as before
when it had been all right
a short hospital trip and he'd come home
finish reading a murder mystery
play pinochle with friends in the building.

His apartment sits empty, yet so full of him
the way he tracked doctors appointments
and bank statements
an extra banana from dinner the day before
a book of crossword puzzles
the TV no longer blaring
John Wayne or Sherlock Holmes.

A silence bursts open
needing to fill up that space
with remembering—

> how he worked nights
> sometimes two jobs to make ends meet

> how the family gathered together
> at his table every Sunday
> often thirty in number

> how he walked home on
> a searing summer afternoon
> carrying a blackboard on his back
> for his children.

Now he is part of the restless earth
alive with tree roots and iris
lilacs and a carpet of grass
he lies under a weeping willow
its long branches sweeping the ground
tender runners strengthening its trunk
light filtering through its leaves
graceful and steady.

Flight

cowbirds and nuthatches
titmice and chickadees
queue up on the deep red leaves
and brittle twigs of the burning bush
swing on the feeders
eat the last of sunflower seed and thistle
peck at bits of apple

crows stand ready
a strand of black pearls across wire
waiting for the signal
when a singular shriek
becomes raucous refrain

with graceful precision
the birds take off
weaving in and around each other
in a dark, disappearing flutter

if they would take me with them
I would fall into place
shiver upward
into the cool air of a milky sky
push through diaphanous clouds
into the blue

Squid Boats in the Gulf of Siam
Inspired by a Stephen Hannock painting

there is no horizon
squid boats skim dark waters

without stars or moon to guide them
the blackness is complete.

fishermen shoot rockets
flashes of fire erupt to light their way

through stagnant air, they ease
their boats by degrees.

with faith
they glide past others on the night sea.

Acknowledgement: *Birds By My Window*:
Willow Tree Poems, November 2007

Amy White

Angus

Even your eyelashes lush and black
could break a heart. In the mornings
you lie down where the sun falls warm,
dappling the grass, large
red and black mounds of comfort
basking on your cuds.

For those who have lost their mothers young
to watch you with your calves
is to have another chance.

At first, like a doe, for a day or two, you stow
the slick warm pulsing thing
in high grass or thicket; then come
days, weeks, of nickering, cleansing
cradling with that large rough tongue;
your engorged udder, with its four plugs,
an upside-down feast, tugged at,
sucked.

Straight—backed monuments of muscle,
flesh, sturdy bone, for hours like stone
you stand as the afternoon wanes.

Soft hairs fringe your ears;
those straight lashes cover eyes
fabulously deep, kind, curious.

The sound of you breathing is as if
your large lungs were sunk deep within the earth,
a source, and when you mouth new hay
the world settles to the rhythm
of your soft chew.

Drawn to each other, a head rests on a rump;
at night you crowd together, touching,
and quickly the calves range and rout about
a jolly band, tomorrow's herd.

And, oh the shape of you!
How the large barrel of rib and tummy
hangs from the broad improbable hip
your central axle, whose awkward knobs
hold you up.

Selling the Farm

Clouds have descended to lie
with the valley. They rub
their soft bellies on the budding
grasses, harbor the bush in moisture.

The land delivers itself
– supine giant limbs spread
to sky to my eyes as I wake
in the weeping wet, startled

to have the vast spread of sky
the green earth laid out so,
a moment—despite a future
abandonment of meadow.

Ledbetter Island

1.
In the new light your son throws the boys
down. They cleave to his back, coil
around the thighs, the abdomen.
He slings them on the grass;
they topple, laugh, scream:
a great game of contact, fear, strength,
all under a windy generous sun.

I see your limbs, your sweetness cradled
by the lucid waters' salty lap,
your laughter. How you hugged
and threw your boys about. How at Christmas
you bought sweaters as gifts for everyone.

2.
Into my billows did you dive and bloom.
We swim with the phosphorescents, pelagic stars.
Day and night the salty granite talks to the sky, marshals the sea.
My armor, my fur, my calculations, where are they?
I lose myself inland to daisy, meadow grass, the woods.
All night we drift and sway, seaweed slathered.
Waiting for sleep with open eyes,
I go on loving you after we are dead.

About the Poets

DEB ADLER wrote her way through five states, a desert, the edge of the continent, her loves, and losses. She rode horses and waitressed, photographed and communicated corporately. She had belated twins. Luck brought her to these poetic midwives. Now, finally, there is a poet in her mirror.

CARA BENSON'S two poem books, *(made)* and *Protean Parade*, are forthcoming. Other work includes: "Quantum Chaos and Poems: A Manifest(o)ation" (BookThug), *Elders Series #7* (Belladonna), and "Spell/ing ( ) Bound" (ellectrique press). She edits Sous Rature (www.necessetics.com/ sous-rature.html), edited *Predictions* forthcoming from Chain and teaches poetry in a NY State Prison.

JOE CAPOBIANCO After four decades of writing for NY public agencies, Joe turned to poetry. He revisited family photos, rediscovered a grandfather's journal and figured out how to communicate with children (and grandchildren) about growing up in the Bronx. Poetry helped him survive retirement, open heart surgery and *REALLY* long Maine winters.

MARIA DELUCIA-EVANS is both a poet and playwright. She also dabbles in fiction and creative nonfiction. Her poetry and fiction have been published in on-line and print journals. She truly appreciates the continual support and critique from her fellow poets—as they inspire her to keep writing and revising!

GWEN GOULD is founder/conductor of the Columbia Festival Orchestra, a professional orchestra. She also founded the West Village Chorale and Diamond Opera Theater. Her published writing includes: poetry in online journals and *Chronogram Magazine*; a chapbook, *Luminations*; a photo/poetic memoir, *Gathering at Punk Point* and various newspaper articles about music.

SCOTT HICKS was raised in Tulsa, Oklahoma. He came east for graduate school at Yale in 1965, majoring in Philosophy of Religion and Social Ethics, and later completed an MSW at SUNY Albany. He has practiced psychotherapy in a number of settings and is currently working at NYS United Teachers.

NICK KLING writes prose about saints and rascals, equine and human, for his job as a Thoroughbred racing columnist. He uses similar subjects for his poetry.

CECELE ALLEN KRAUS The sights of her childhood move from Washington State to Alabama woke her to the play between self and place. Cecele's work appears in publications such as *Friends of Colombia,* newspaper for Returned Peace Corps Volunteers, *News and Reviews,* newsletter of her psychoanalytic institute, and other journals.

SUZANNE DEMUTH Myers Poetry, her vehicle of expression, often flows without warning onto the page. Wandering through each day ideas, thoughts, and emotions align themselves into a poem, then the bridge moves on. An educator, wife and mom, she also loves to create jewelry and explore the New Hampshire countryside.

TERRY ROYNE began writing poetry in her twenties. She writes of those universal themes – grief, loss, adoption, birth, neighborhoods, lovers, and high wire walkers. Pantoums are her latest favorite form and she produces a poem a month because of her beloved writing group who keep her working and usually honest.

JAN MARIN TRAMONTANO writes poetry and fiction. Her work appears in print and online literary journals. She has published two poetry chapbooks, a memoir, and completed her first novel. She is grateful for this group of generous poets who work hard together, have fun and share her love of mocha lattes.

AMY WHITE has worked as an inner city teacher, an educational consultant and a political journalist. More recently she's lived on a farm, raising animals and riding horses. She has kept journals and written poems since childhood, her devotion to language being second only to her love of her family.

Path to Progress:

Innovative Solutions for
Growth, Prosperity, and Security

Path to Progress:

Innovative Solutions for Growth, Prosperity, and Security

Charles Moore

Cover design by Philip E. Pascuzzo of *Pepco Studios*
Book design by Jessika Hazelton
Edited by Mike Piekarski

Printed in the United States of America on recycled paper
by The Troy Book Makers • Troy, New York • thetroybookmakers.com
For Green Mountain Press • Rensselaer, New York

To order additional copies of this title,
contact your favorite local bookstore,
visit www.tbmbooks.com,
or visit www.thepathtoprogress.com

ISBN: 978-0-9882613-0-3

Contents

THIS BOOK IS A PRACTICAL, science-based, truthful analysis of the current state of affairs in respect to our environmental and economic condition. The facts presented may lead some to feel that if our condition is so dire, why act? My intention, however, is just the opposite. Before we can grow the economy to benefit all, while living sustainably, an accurate assessment of our current situation must be taken. My background is in environmental science, and urban, regional, and transportation planning. This has trained me to look at the bigger, wider picture, such as the broad causes and effects of large redevelopments, suburban sprawl, inner-city decay, the loss of farmland, and all the associated environmental and societal consequences. I grew up in a small, old, working-class riverfront city in upstate New York during the height of inner-city abandonment and deindustrialization. My perspective has been shaped by those experiences and consequent education. The problems and solutions I pose come from a "planning" perspective.

I hope, after taking into account the full picture presented here, readers can embrace a growth-oriented economy that does more than simply acknowledge extreme inequality as an unfortunate byproduct. What can happen is growth that is shared by many and growth that improves the quality of life for many. Actually, it must. Our lives today are not confined to one town or community. We work in one town, live in another, and perhaps shop in yet another. At the same time, we use multiple jurisdictions for water and sewer services, roads, police, fire, EMS, and so on. Our air quality knows no boundaries. All the challenges we face are regional and multijurisdictional in scope. We cannot approach things from a "single municipality" mindset anymore—not in our modern, sprawling world.

The book is not cynical or contemptuous. It is a synthesis of information intended to motivate, educate, and inspire. It is a call to action. Optimistically, this book will make it easier for individuals to make a difference as it outlines nongovernmental programs for immediate change.

Acknowledgements

THERE ARE SO MANY PEOPLE to whom I am grateful, and all of them have influenced my thoughts, career, and world views. All of them spurred the discipline needed to bring this book to fruition.

From family discussions, or arguments, around the dinner table to late-night debates around the campfire, there was always an angle someone would bring up that you hadn't fully considered previously. With my two brothers, Paul and Sean, and saintly mother and father, Patricia and Paul, discussions were always lively and passionate. My parents led by example, and their unconditional love and sacrifice taught us that you cannot put a price tag on happiness or the most important things in life.

My sister, Bridget, actually took significant time off from her busy schedule to guide, inspire, and edit many of my thoughts. Her husband, Eric, always raised discussions to a higher level. At the same time, the many colleagues, friends, and committed professionals I have come across throughout my career have truly inspired me. From my local and state government coworkers to my private sector colleagues and military brothers and sisters I served with, my faith in the overall decency of humanity is steadfast.

Growing up in a declining Rust Belt city, long after many of the good jobs had left, I encountered many who stayed simply to make a difference. I owe many of these people a debt of gratitude, from the nuns in my small Catholic school to the staff at the local Boys and Girls Club to my neighbors and coaches, there remained intact a solid community to help steer unbridled, youthful energy. My lifelong friend, Tom Nardacci, a true man of action, constantly reminds me to never forget where I came from. Another lifelong friend, Tom Cardamone, showed me how to survive and get along with everyone.

I would be remiss if I neglected to mention the Local Government Commission and the annual New Partners for Smart Growth conference sponsors for providing me with the opportunity to attend conferences in 2011 and 2012. These conferences are truly inspirational and the best around for bringing together a diverse group of people with the same goals: creating vibrant, healthy, inclusive, and fair communities.

My editor, Mike Piekarski, provided consistent honesty; sometimes blunt, clear direction; and a thoroughness I wish I had. Any mistakes or oversights in this book can be traced to my own stubbornness. My mother-in-law, "Mimi," was integral to me getting the time to write. Last but not least, my beautiful wife, Jennifer, has allowed me the time needed to attend these conferences, countless local meetings, and to read and write. She is the glue that keeps my two angels, Emma and Charlie, and me happy and healthy. They motivate me every day.

Part One

Issues

As of January 2012, the world held seven billion people, up from five billion just twenty years before. The middle class in China, India, and Brazil is just taking off, which means those countries will desire the same resources Americans currently take for granted. If the rest of the world attempts to consume resources at the same rate as the United States, we would require five Earths. In 1988, Passionist priest and acclaimed cultural historian Thomas Berry wrote: "Our entire society is caught in a closed cycle of production and consumption that can [only] go on until the natural resources are exhausted or until the poisons inserted into the environment are fed back into the system. What benefit is worth giving up the purity of the air we breathe, the water we drink, the life-giving soil in which our food is grown?"

We already know that dozens of toxic chemicals can be found in our bodies of water, in the food we eat, in the air we breathe. Species are disappearing a thousand times faster than normal, and the planet has not seen such a burst of extinction in sixty-five million years, since the dinosaurs disappeared. Islands and nations are already building seawalls to keep out the rising oceans. By the middle of the twenty-first century, it is predicted that fourteen states will experience high or extreme water shortages due to global warming. Since 1982, America has paved, built on, and developed thirty-five million once-rural acres, as much land as is encompassed in New York state. Pennsylvania and upstate New York's urbanized land grew by 47 and 30 percent, respectively, between 1982 and 1997, while their populations grew by only 2.6 percent. Bruce Katz, vice president and director of the Brookings Institution's Metropolitan Policy Program, notes that between 2007 and 2030, "we will develop another 213 billion square feet of homes, retail facilities, office buildings, and other structures. That's double the amount of space in the United States today."

We are living in extraordinary times and are facing enormous challenges and tragedies on a vast scale. We are being increasingly buffeted by high-powered hurricanes, tsunamis, earthquakes, mudslides, wildfires, and acts of international terrorism, while dealing with increasing economic insecurity and growing inequality. Given these challenges, however, there is no greater moment of opportunity. Most leaders like to talk about responsibility, initiative, efficiency, and reality-based decisions. The fact is that the statistics on urban sprawl, oil consumption, water usage, and environmental degradation occurring alongside increased and continuous poverty and suffering suggest that responsible, reality-based decisions are not being made, nor have they been for a long time.

And while these environmental problems go unabated, corporate welfare is expanding, and poverty and inequality are increasing. The middle class is shrinking, struggling, and on edge. Harvard professor Elizabeth Warren wrote in 2009: "America today has plenty of rich and super-rich. But it has far more families who did all the right things, but who still have no real security. Going to college and finding a good job no longer guarantee economic safety. Paying for a child's education and setting aside enough for a decent retirement have become distant dreams. Tens of millions of once-secure middle-class families now live paycheck to paycheck, watching as their debts pile up and worrying about whether a pink slip or a bad diagnosis will send them hurtling over an economic cliff."

For the last thirty-plus years, public corporations have been run primarily for the purpose of creating vast wealth for its senior executives. In 1980, award-winning economist John Kenneth Galbraith noted that "the salary of the chief executive of a large corporation is not a market award for achievement. It is frequently in the nature of a warm personal gesture by the individual to himself." Alarm bells were raised then. How far have we progressed?

A system that cannot deliver the well-being of people and the planet is in big trouble. There is a spiritual hunger today in an age of plenty. Gus Speth, Vermont Law School professor and former dean of Yale's School of Forestry and Environmental Studies, said in a 2008 interview in *Orion* Magazine: "In the West, we're seeing that people's own sense of subjective well-being has not been going up with all of this growth that we've been experiencing. Per capita income goes up, but happiness doesn't, satisfaction with life doesn't. It's just flatlined for decades now. And there are certain pathologies that have increased; a sense of loneliness in our society, bipolar disorders, other problems, stress and disintegration of communities. This should be a time when we really can take this fabulous amount of wealth that we've generated and enjoy it, and yet we seem to be caught in a system where it's either up, up, and away or down, down, and out. And we seem to career from crisis to crisis—personal crises, national crises, and economic crises."

We can no longer put our heads in the sand. Bold action is necessary, and if the government is too gridlocked or uninterested, then we—as individuals, communities, corporations, and nonprofits—must act. Part of the American narrative has been to look forward, to continuously improve its vision of a country for the people and by the people. In 2009, Rebecca Solnit wrote in *Orion*: "Still, everything changes. And a logic that was tantamount to religion has collapsed, the logic that made it so hard to do anything about everything: poverty, injustice, environmental degradation, corporations run rampant, economic madness." That logic is so weakened now that it can never come back with the same force as it had in the past three or four decades.

My strategy for regional growth and prosperity has four key components: environment, economy, equity, and security. When these four issues are addressed simultaneously, growth and prosperity will be advanced in the most comprehensive, holistic way. Sustainable development, which in this case means both economically and environmentally, will occur while permitting more individuals to grow out of poverty and further stabilize the middle class, the backbone of America.

With clear frustration among many of the electorate as recently expressed in the Tea Party movement, it is obvious that many of the politicians are either out of touch, not concerned, or too bogged down in other issues to address wholeheartedly the serious problems discussed in this book. Following the solutions presented here, systematic and specialized growth can and will occur without governmental assistance. When results are realized, perhaps elected leaders will catch on to the positive role government can play in fostering sustainable regional development. They once did. Republican President Abraham Lincoln once said, "Through government, we should do together what we cannot do as well for ourselves."

This book is a synthesis of historic and contemporary literature explaining our environmental, social, and economic condition. Part One provides the background and context for understanding these interrelated issues. Part Two presents strategies for addressing those issues. The strategies are broken down into "regional planning" approaches and local or individual opportunities for action. Scattered throughout are quotes from leading experts and historical figures. I used only the most respected, highly acclaimed researchers, scientists, academics, and professionals to eliminate the possibility of incorrect conclusions. Once presented, the call to action should be clear.

According to one of the Harvard Loeb Fellow criteria, I am "seeking the improvement of the quality of life in cities and the natural areas that sustain them." Two thousand years ago, Roman statesman and philosopher Cicero wrote, "Freedom is participation in power." Martin Luther King Jr. wrote in the 1960s that "social peace must spring from economic justice."

The famous biblical lesson of Cain and Abel teaches us that we are our brother's keeper, that we have a responsibility to watch out for and care for one another. Working to help poverty-stricken communities, lowering illiteracy, improving schools, protecting the environment, and building sustainable communities are just a few strategies. Yet, of all those goals, the front line of battle is our cities. Winston Churchill stated, "We cannot be the leading community in the civilized world without being involved in its problems, without being convulsed by its agonies and inspired by its causes."

Our environmental and sustainability challenges in air, water, open space, and biodiversity, and our need for inner-city improvements meet at the city line. Professor Andrew Ross of New York University, in a 2011 article for *The New York Times* wrote, "The struggle to slow global warming will be won or lost in cities, which emit 80 percent of the world's greenhouse gases." There's no mystery why these issues are so pressing. For the last forty-plus years, we've had a government-subsidized mass exodus from the inner cities of America. This pattern cannot continue.

The Old Testament book of Jeremiah (29:7) says, "Seek the welfare of the city in which you live and pray to the Eternal in its behalf; for in its prosperity you shall prosper." Cities bring people together, and not just for trade, commerce, or protection. The invention of the written record, the library, the archive, the school, and the university are some of the most important achievements of cities. Urban historian and author Lewis Mumford wrote in 1961 that "the most precious collective invention of civilization was the city, second only to language in the transmission of culture ... through its durable buildings and institutional structures and even more durable symbolic forms of literature and art, the city unites times past, times present, and times to come." Could the decay of our inner cities be the canary in the coal mine? With graduation rates at an all-time low, is there a bigger national crisis? Seventeen of the nation's 50 largest cities had high school graduation rates lower than 50 percent, according to a 2008 report issued by America's Promise Alliance, an advocacy organization led by retired general and former Secretary of State Colin Powell. Award-winning author Christopher Hedges similarly wrote about this in his 2012 book *Days of Destruction, Days of Revolt*, noting that when we forget our neighbor, in the biblical sense, in the ghettos of Camden, N.J., or at the Indian reservations of Pine Ridge or in the coal mines in southern West Virginia, or in the produce fields, those forces will turn on us. "They went first, and we're next."

Cities are our cultural centers and in many ways reflect the future diversity of our country. They are still our government centers. Yet, they are disproportionally home to the poor because of transit access, walkability, and access to social services. City taxpayers are single-handedly paying for those enhanced services, from which the whole region benefits. "Urban firms and residents shouldn't have to pay a disproportionate share of the taxes needed to care for disadvantaged Americans," said Edward Glaeser, professor of economics at Harvard University. Furthermore, he noted that "suburban residents shouldn't get a free pass on the environmental damage created by a car-based, energy-intensive, low-density lifestyle." A level playing field is all that is asked.

Still, while many cities have been decaying and struggling for years, there is inherent in them a fantastic and underappreciated potential. In examining Glaeser's 2011 book *Triumph of the City,* David Brooks of *The New York Times* recognized that cities have become even more important in our modern age. In 2011, Brooks wrote:

> Humans communicate best when they are physically brought together. Cities magnify people strengths, Glaeser argues, because ideas spread more easily in dense environments. If you want to compete in a global marketplace it really helps to be near a

downtown. Companies that are near the geographic center of their industry are more productive. Year by year, workers in cities see their wages grow faster than workers outside of cities because their skills grow faster. Inventors disproportionately cite ideas from others who live physically close to them .... When you clump together different sorts of skilled people and force them to rub against one another, they create friction and instability, which leads to tension and creativity, which leads to small business growth. As Glaeser notes, cities that rely on big businesses wither. Those that incubate small ones grow.

Richard Florida reinforces this in *Who's Your City*, noting the importance of face-to-face physical connections and the importance of high-quality communities.

Depending on the source cited, (the U.S. Census Bureau or the United Nations), America will add between one hundred and one hundred forty million people by mid-century. As the population grows, leaders will be asked to make increasingly difficult land-use decisions. The Urban Land Institute's 2011 *Urban Plan* asked "Where and how will we, our children, and future generations live, work, shop, play and travel from place to place? How we choose to answer questions like this will determine how we accommodate growth without squandering valuable natural resources, sacrificing the livability of our neighborhoods or violating our sense of community."

At the same time, many professionals believe that oil shortages in the future could turn outer suburbs into slums. Along with heightened demand from developing countries, oil will become much more expensive as the difficulty of extracting it from deeper ground sources and from tar sands increases. A lifestyle completely dependent on fossil fuels would suffer drastically.

The 1987 United Nations report titled "Our Common Future" said, "We must meet the needs of present generations while not compromising the ability of future generations to meet their own needs." A full reading of the report reveals that sustainable development must include environmental, social, and economic elements. The document is the first of its kind to draw links among these concerns. It noted, "We are unanimous in our conviction that the security, well-being, and very survival of the planet depend on such changes now." Twenty-five years have passed since that statement was made.

Moreover, research shows that living in a society with wide disparities in health, wealth, and education is actually worse for all society's members. In fact, studies indicate that high inequality causes more crime, less happiness, poorer mental and physical health, less racial harmony, and less civic and political participation by the population as a whole. A 2009 U.S. Census Bureau report showed that the income gap between those at the top and bottom of our economy was the widest ever. In 2008, the richest one-hundredth of 1 percent, or fourteen thousand families, possessed more than 22 percent of America's entire national wealth, while the bottom 90 percent of the population owned 4 percent. Social Security statistics from 2010 showed that the top seventy-two wage earners in the United States made as much as the nineteen million lowest wage earners. Today's 400 richest Americans have more wealth than the bottom 150 million Americans put together.

Nobel Prize-winning economist Joseph Stiglitz noted in a 2011 *Vanity Fair* article, "An economy in which most citizens are doing worse year after year—an economy like America's—is not likely to do well over the long haul." Even the wealthy will come to regret it. This translates to shrinking opportunity, inefficiency in the economy, and less collective action for infrastructure, public improvements, education, research, and technology. "America's inequality," Stiglitz wrote, "distorts our society in every conceivable way."

Societies cannot thrive when disparities are so sharp. If we can address some of the issues of the inner city using a regional approach, we can tackle a multitude of social, environmental, economic, and health problems on many levels. A new, improved vision for the future must be embraced. Ralph Nader once wrote that we need to "think of wealth, for example, in terms of not just money or possessions, but also charity, health, happiness, and justice in a community."

After reading this book, you will see that the future can be shaped. It is only after acknowledging the interrelated challenges and understanding them that we can then take action, methodically and directly. Robert F. Kennedy wrote, "Tragedy is a tool for the living to gain wisdom, not a guide by which to live."

We are much more than a private, for-profit, free market, individualistic, capitalistic society. More than anything, we are a democracy. At least that is what the founders intended. The United States Constitution is one of the greatest political and economic accomplishments in human history. Yet many may not realize the evolutionary process that created it. It was not born out of a single revelation. The seeds for self-government were planted in the founders by reading Greek and Roman history. Cicero, writing nearly two thousand years ago, had an enormous influence on John Adams and Thomas Jefferson. The Magna Carta, first issued in 1215 England with subsequent amendments, was foundational to our Constitution. In upstate New York, the Iroquois Confederacy and its form of union and democratic government influenced Benjamin Franklin and his Albany Plan of 1754. This was the first attempt at uniting to defend against outside influences and to regulate trade and financial activities. Following the Revolutionary War, the Albany Plan was used to help write the Articles of Confederation, the precursor to our Constitution. Therefore, we know that the creation of a democratic government was an evolutionary process with myriad influences that took generations to perfect. As Yale Law professor Akhil Reed Amar wrote, "The adoption of the Constitution was the most participatory, majoritarian, and populist event the Earth had ever seen." Evolution, change, growth, and progress are integral to all humanity and life.

Similarly, scientific discoveries and new understandings of the natural world and our place in it led to changes and adjustments to our great faith institutions. Nicolaus Copernicus caused havoc when he proposed that the Earth was not the center of the universe in 1543. Galileo Galilei reinforced Copernicus' discovery in 1615. Charles Darwin finally solved the puzzle of evolution in 1859. Finally, in the 1920s, astronomers with the help of Edwin Hubble realized that the sun was not the center of the universe and that it was part of a galaxy that was only one of many billions. Life changes, people get older, institutions evolve, landscapes change, discoveries shed new light—and nothing stays the same. We see that, just as science evolves when new discoveries are made, religions have evolved after incorporating new scientific knowledge and understanding of the cosmos and our place in it. By no means does this diminish the relevance of religion or faith, which seek more to understand questions of why things occur and give meaning and direction to life rather than to solve the questions of who or what. As Andrew Delbanco of Columbia University wrote in his 2012 book *College: What It Was, Is and Should Be,* "Science tells us nothing about how to shape a life or how to face death...it not only fails to answer such questions; it cannot ask them". Yet, Catholic saint Albert the Great of the thirteenth century, who was revered as a "Doctor of the Church," Islamic philosopher Averroes, Jewish philosopher Maimonides, and pre-eminent "Doctor of the Church" and Catholic saint Augustine, all held that if religious teachings contradicted certain direct observations about the natural world, then we are obliged to re-evaluate either the interpretation of the scientific facts or the understanding of Scriptures. We acknowledge that there is a massive and rich history of religious universities and libraries, among the best in the world, for understanding our place on the planet both scientifically and religiously. The Renaissance humanists of the fourteenth and fifteenth centuries were practicing Catholics. These scientists formed the basis of "The Enlightenment" of the eighteenth century, also called the "Age of Reason," the cultural movement that led to the establishment of the United States and the move to reform society and advance knowledge. We must keep in mind these things when moving forward to improve our communities and democracy for future generations. As Albert Einstein said, "We cannot solve our problems with the same thinking we used when we created them."

President Franklin Roosevelt wrote in 1940, "Better the occasional fault of a government that lives in a spirit of charity than the consistent omissions of a government frozen in the ice of its own indifference." Improvement and action in this sense is always an honorable goal. FDR's famous cousin, President Theodore Roosevelt, once said, "In any moment of decision the best thing you can do is the right thing, the next best thing is the wrong thing, and the worst thing you can do is nothing."

The preamble of the U.S. Constitution, our country's greatest document and inspiration to countless others, states: "We the People of the United States, in Order to form a more perfect Union, establish Justice, insure domestic Tranquility, provide for the common defense, promote the general Welfare, and secure the Blessings of Liberty to ourselves and our Posterity, do ordain and establish this Constitution for the United States of America." Note the power of the words "justice," "liberty," and "promote the general welfare." This is the spirit of the U.S. Constitution; these enable us to form a more perfect union. As author, doctor, and attorney Paul Abrams argued in 2007, "justice" and "liberty," are required to ensure domestic tranquility and to provide for the common defense. Abrams wrote, "Indeed, 'justice' must be part of 'liberty' and conversely. Consider that my liberty (to use my property as I choose, or not to pay taxes for government services) intrudes upon your justice (not to have toxic waste migrate to your land, or for all of us to receive government services). That tension produces both justice and liberty as they can be practiced together. 'For our posterity' requires appropriate stewardship of human, natural and financial resources so that the 'blessings of liberty' are not only 'for ourselves.' 'Promoting the general welfare' becomes subject to those limitations."

In what has been called the "Four Freedoms" speech of 1941, President Franklin Roosevelt said: "There is nothing mysterious about the foundations of a healthy and strong democracy. The basic things expected by our people of their political and economic systems are simple. They are: Equality of opportunity for youth and others. Jobs for those who can work. Security for those who need it. The ending of special privilege for the few. The preservation of civil liberties for all."

If we address the issues presented in Part One of this book with the solutions outlined in Part Two, we will come much closer to achieving Roosevelt's goals, along with regional growth and prosperity. Our democracy, quality of life, and bonds to community, society, and family would become that much stronger. Helen Keller wrote, "The most pathetic person in the world is someone who has sight, but has no vision." There are plenty of opportunities for individuals, communities, and regions to act and make a difference. Whether you believe in more government support or less, Part Two will show how people with energy, passion, and interest can make a difference.

Chapter 1
Environment

"We have not inherited the earth from our parents;
we have borrowed it from our children."

—Native American proverb

HUMANS HAVE HAD ENORMOUS IMPACTS on the natural world. *Collapse*, by scientist Jared Diamond, demonstrated those impacts throughout humanity's history. Diamond identified five factors that contribute to collapse: climate change, hostile neighbors, the loss of essential trading partners, environmental problems, and failure to adapt to environmental issues. He also listed twelve environmental problems facing mankind today. The first eight historically have contributed to the collapse of past societies. Those are:

1. Deforestation and habitat destruction
2. Soil problems (erosion, salinization, and soil fertility losses)
3. Water management problems
4. Overhunting
5. Overfishing
6. Effects of introduced species on native species
7. Overpopulation
8. Increased per-capita impact

In addition, three more factors that Diamond said may contribute to the weakening and collapse of present and future societies include:

1. Anthropogenic (manmade) climate change
2. Buildup of toxins in the environment
3. Energy shortages

In sum, with our continual progress, modernization, and growth come serious consequences for the world's flora and fauna. It is not hard to see the effects wrought by mass extinctions, pollution, and clear-cutting. "It will do little good for any nation to seek its own well-being by destroying the very conditions for planetary survival. This larger vision is no longer utopian. It directly concerns the hardest, most absolute reality there is: the reality of the water we drink, the air we breathe, the food we eat" (Berry 1988, 43).

As James Gustave "Gus" Speth wrote in his 2008 book, *The Bridge at the Edge of the World*, since the 1600s, half the world's tropical and temperate forests are now gone. In 2005, the Millennium Ecosystem Assessment (MEA) reported that "forests have effectively disappeared in 25 countries, and another 29 have lost more than 90 percent of their forest cover." The rate of deforestation in the Tropics persists at about an acre a second, about half the wetlands and a third of the mangroves are gone, an estimated 90 percent of the large predator fish have disappeared, and 75 percent of marine fisheries are now overfished or fished to capacity. Twenty percent of the corals are gone, and another 20 percent severely threatened. Species are disappearing at rates about a thousand times faster than normal. The planet has not seen such a rate of extinction in sixty-five million years, since the dinosaurs disappeared. In fact, Berkeley scientists have warned that we may be grossly underestimating how many species could disappear. "The current rate and magnitude of climate change are faster and more severe than many species have experienced in their evolutionary history," said University of California at Berkeley professor Anthony Barnosky, lead author of a 2011 report on climate change and mass extinction.

In 2003, doctor and biologist Camille Parmesan at the University of Texas and economist Gary Yohe at Wesleyan University analyzed records of the geographical ranges of more than 1,700 species of plants and animals. They found that their ranges were moving, on average, 3.8 miles per decade toward the poles. Animals and plants also were moving up mountain slopes...and "because it's happening consistently on a global scale, we can link it to greenhouse gases changes," Parmesan wrote. An international team of scientists quoted in the science journal *Nature* estimated that 15 percent to 37 percent of all species could become "committed to extinction" by 2050 thanks to climate change (Zimmer 2011).

A 2002 United Nations report said that more than half the agricultural lands in drier regions suffer from some degree of deterioration and desertification. Joe Thornton, in *Pandora's Poison*, reported that persistent toxic chemicals can now be found by the dozens in essentially each and every one of us. The U.N. reported that there are more than 200 dead zones in the oceans due to overfertilization. The MEA reported in 2005 that the following rivers no longer reach the oceans in the dry season: the Colorado, Yellow, Ganges, and Nile, among others. As Thomas Berry wrote in 1988, "An exhausted planet is an exhausted economy" (p. 73).

Humans have had an unprecedented impact on the planet, not all of it good. A basic accounting is in order before we move forward. This is not to say that we have not recognized certain deleterious effects and attempted solutions or mitigation. That is not the case. Since the humble beginning of the environmental movement in the 1960s, there have been spurts and sputters of activity, interest, vital action, and critical successes, combined with gross inequities. Yet, time is almost out. As Speth, however, made clear in *The Bridge at the Edge of the World*, if society heads down a path of simply no growth in human population or the world economy while allowing for the unabated release of greenhouse gases and continuing to deplete ecosystems and release toxic chemicals at current rates, then the world in the latter part of this century will not be fit to live in. Yet, human activities are not holding at current levels. They are accelerating dramatically. With a rate of growth equal to pre-2007-'08 recession levels, the world economy will double in size in only fourteen years. We are, therefore, facing the likelihood of an enormous increase in environmental deterioration unless something changes dramatically.

Sir David King, former chief science adviser in the British government and highly respected among the world scientific community, believes that climate change is the most severe problem the world faces, bar none. In fact, carbon dioxide in the atmosphere is now at its highest level in at least 650,000 years. The concentration of another greenhouse gas, methane, is about 150 percent above preindustrial levels. Methane accumulates from cattle raising, rice growing, and landfill emissions, as well as the burning of fossil fuels. Atmospheric concentrations of nitrous oxide, an infrared trapping gas, are also up due to fertilizer use, cattle feedlots, and the chemical industry.

The U.S. National Academy of Sciences, national scientific academies from around the world and 97 percent of the world's climate scientists agree that climate change and global warming is a fact. According to the academy, "a strong, credible body of scientific evidence shows that climate change is occurring, is caused largely by human activities and poses significant risks for a broad range of human and natural systems." Further proof lies in the U.S. Climate Action Partnership, a collection of the nation's most prominent businesses (hard-nosed, profit-driven capitalists) and leading environmental organizations that have come together to call on the federal government to quickly enact strong national legislation to require significant reductions of greenhouse gas emissions. General Electric, Alcoa, Duke Energy, DuPont, Dow Chemical, Ford, General Motors, and Chrysler have all signed on to this partnership. The group issued a statement calling on the president and Congress to act, saying, "In our view, the climate change challenge will create more economic opportunities than risks for the U.S. economy" (Boehlert 2010). If that does not convince you, according to the National Oceanic and Atmospheric Administration (NOAA), 2010 was the hottest year in the hottest decaded ever recorded. The 2010 heat wave in Russia killed an estimated 15,000 people.

More recently, as distinguished scholar, author, and environmentalist Bill McKibben pointed out in a July 2012 piece in *Rolling Stone* magazine, not only was May the warmest on record for the Northern Hemisphere, not only was it "the 327th consecutive month in which the temperature of the entire globe exceeded the 20th-century average," but it was also followed by a June in which some 3,200 heat records were broken in the United States. In March 2012 alone, fifteen thousand U.S. temperature records were broken, mainly in the East and Midwest. According to the National Oceanic and Atmospheric Administration, July 2012 was the hottest month in the contiguous United States since record-keeping began more than a century ago. Physicist Richard Muller of the University of California at Berkeley, one of the leading skeptics on climate change, reversed himself and announced that his own careful research showed that the atmosphere is, indeed, warming rapidly. "I'm now going a step further: Humans are almost entirely the cause," he said.

The Intergovernmental Panel on Climate Change (IPCC) stated that the "warming of the climate system is unequivocal." One observable result of that warming is longer and more severe storms. The IPCC noted that more intense and longer droughts have been observed over wider areas since the 1970s. The frequency of heavy precipitation events has increased over most land areas, consistent with warming and observed increases of atmospheric water vapor. This will mean that the availability of fresh water will shift, with some areas getting much wetter, and others, much drier. Drought and flooding will most likely increase. Water stored in glaciers and snowpacks will decrease, thereby reducing water supplies to more than a billion people, leading to increased species extinction, coastal erosion, flooding, and wetlands loss.

A 2011 report by an international panel of marine scientists said carbon-related ocean effects include acidification, warming, and oxygen depletion, which may lead to global marine extinctions on a scale unprecedented in human history. "The combination of stressors on the ocean is creating the conditions associated with every previous major extinction of species in Earth's history. The speed and rate of degeneration in the ocean is far faster than anyone has predicted. According to one of the scientists, Professor Jelle Bijma of the Alfred Wegener Institute for Polar and Marine Research, 'the current carbon perturbation is unprecedented in the Earth's history because of the high rate and speed of change. Acidification is occurring faster than in the past 55 million years...' He also pointed out that, 'Most, if not all, of the five global mass extinctions in Earth's history carry the fingerprints of the main symptoms of global carbon perturbations'" (Rigg 2011). The difference, of course, this time is that human action is the culprit.

The IPCC also noted that the last time the polar regions "were significantly warmer than present for an extended period (about 125,000 years ago), reductions in polar ice volume led to 4 to 6 meters of sea level rise." As a result, invasive species will continue to wreak increased havoc on forests, crops, and towns. Due to the rise in sea level, there will be mass migrations and the displacement of millions of people as coastal cities and communities seek higher elevations.

"Climate change," said William Reilly, former adviser to presidents Richard Nixon and George H.W. Bush, "is to America what the German buildup in the 1930s was to the British—the threat that grows more menacing even as we determinedly pretend it is not there."

Again, however, as Lewis Mumford once said, "Trend is not destiny." That is, the future is not necessarily laid out before us. We can change it. We can still mitigate the deleterious effects our actions have caused. James Hansen, a NASA climate scientist, said that "the crystallizing scientific story reveals an imminent planetary emergency. We are at a planetary tipping point. We must move onto a new energy direction within a decade to have a good chance to avoid setting in motion unstoppable climate change with irreversible effects."

Water and Toxic Pollutants

In the Old Testament Book of Ecclesiastes, it is written that "all streams flow into the sea, yet the sea is not full. To the place the streams come from, there they return again."

According to the U.S. Environmental Protection Agency, "Water covers approximately 70 percent of the Earth's surface, but less than 1 percent of that is available for human use. The world must share this small amount for agricultural, domestic, commercial, industrial, and environmental needs."

On our current course, water supply issues will become increasingly widespread in the United States. Freshwater withdrawals per capita from surface and groundwater in the U.S. are twice that of the Organization for Economic Co-operation and Development (OECD), an association of thirty-three developed countries. A 2010 report commissioned for the Natural Resources Defense Council said that by mid-century, climate change will mean a high or extreme risk of water shortages in 14 states. "The study found that more than 1,100 counties—one-third of all counties in the lower 48—will face higher risks of water shortages by mid-century as the result of global warming. More than 400 of these counties will face extremely high risks of water shortages." At the same time, more and more privatization is occurring. "Investors are moving into a water-related market that is estimated to be worth at least $150 billion in the United States. 'Water is a growth driver for as long and as far as they can see,' a Goldman Sachs water analyst told *The New York Times* in 2006" (Speth 2008, 33-34).

Just one notable example of the deleterious effect we've had on our nation's waters is the Chesapeake Bay. Settlers once saw such abundance in the bay that it was said that one could practically walk across it on the backs of the fish. Yet, today, because the bay collects runoff from six states, the streams and rivers that drain into the Chesapeake are now contaminated with farm fertilizers, pesticides and animal waste; oils, gases, and wastes from urban streets; and sediment from cleared lands. The result is a bay close to ecological collapse. "The once abundant oyster reefs are crumbling, and the once extensive beds of sea grass that shelter and nourish spawning blue crabs are dying, smothered by sediments that accumulate as soils erode, having been exposed by deforestation and excessive tillage. Oyster and crab catches have declined to less than 1 percent of historic levels. Similar declines in fisheries are occurring in every region of the country" (Babbitt 2005, 9).

Therefore, as can clearly be seen, issues associated with water rights, development, and cleanliness will not be left only to the Middle East or Third World countries.

It seems that we have become unwilling guinea pigs in our homes and workplaces when it comes to toxic pollutants. Between the unprecedented levels of toxins in our waters and the seemingly safe amounts we allow into our bodies, we have not fully understood the consequences. "Samples of Canadians were tested for the presence of eighty-eight harmful chemicals; on average forty-four were found in each person. Blood and urine samples from a Toronto mother were found to contain thirty-eight reproductive and respiratory toxins, nineteen chemicals that disrupt hormones, and twenty-seven carcinogens. Researchers do not know the long-term health effects of living with the chemical cocktail, but it is known that many of these are dangerous in experimental studies, particularly in prenatal and neonatal contexts" (Speth 2008, 35).

"A subcategory of these chemicals is the endocrine disrupting substances (EDS)—the so-called gender benders. Many can disrupt natural hormone functioning in humans, leading to feminization, low sperm count and hermaphroditism" (Speth 2008, 77). These chemicals are showing up in our fish. The Associated Press reported in October 2006 that smallmouth and largemouth bass possessing both male and female characteristics are present in the Potomac River and its tributaries across the Maryland and Virginia region. More than 80 percent of all the male bass were growing eggs, said a study of the Shenandoah River in Virginia and in the Monocacy River in Maryland, both of which feed the Potomac. There is growing evidence that links these endocrine disrupters to breast cancer, infertility, low sperm counts, genital deformities, early menstruation, and even diabetes and obesity. Dr. Philip Landrigan of Mount Sinai School of Medicine said that a "congenital defect called hypospadias—a misplacement of the urethra — is now twice as common among newborn boys as it used to be." Endocrine disrupters are "in thermal receipts that come out of gas pumps and A.T.M.'s. They're in canned foods, cosmetics, plastics and food packaging ... Last year, eight medical organizations representing genetics, gynecology, urology and other fields made a joint call in Science magazine for tighter regulation of endocrine disruptors" (Kristof, 2012a).

Consider the number of deaths per year due to toxic and environmental contamination. Pollution causes 40 percent of deaths worldwide, said David Pimentel, a Cornell University professor. Pimentel and a team of researchers studied 120 published papers on the effects of population growth, malnutrition, and various kinds of environmental degradation on human diseases. They concluded that "air pollution from smoke and various chemicals kills 3 million people a year worldwide. In the United States alone about 3 million tons of toxic chemicals are released into the environment —contributing to cancer, birth defects, immune system defects and many other serious health problems" (Pimentel 2007). "In 2004 a test of the umbilical cord blood of a dozen randomly chosen newborns at a St. Louis hospital revealed a total of 270 toxic chemicals —with each infant averaging nearly two hundred: carcinogens, endocrine disrupters, substances which adversely affect neurological development or immune system functioning" (Gottlieb 2010).

Endangered Biodiversity

Aldo Leopold wrote in *A Sand County Almanac* "A thing is right, when it tends to preserve the integrity, stability, and beauty of the biotic community. It is wrong when it tends otherwise."

In 1998, ecologist Jane Lubchenco, in her address as president of the American Association for the Advancement of Science, drew the following conclusions: "During the last few decades, humans have emerged as a new force of nature. We are modifying physical, chemical, and biological systems in new ways, at faster rates, and over larger spatial scales than ever recorded on earth. Humans have unwittingly embarked upon a grand experiment with our planet. The outcome of this experiment is unknown, but has profound implications for all life on Earth."

Again, the Chesapeake Bay is a perfect example of the devastating effects humans have inflicted on the natural world. Millions of people traverse the bay every year. Known for its beauty and bounty, much of our nation's founding was enabled because of the abundance of life it produced. But that has changed, as one writer described it:

> Like so many of our natural resources, the Chesapeake Bay once seemed inexhaustible, its waters so vast and productive as to be beyond serious harm. Oyster reefs were so extensive they were mapped and marked as hazards on navigation charts. Blue crabs swarmed through huge fields of sea grass that covered the shallows, and spawning shad, herring, and striped bass crowded rivers flowing into the bay ... By the end of the nineteenth century the bay produced more than 20 percent of the seafood consumed in the entire country ... Then in about 1950, after centuries of production, the fisheries began to collapse. The oyster harvest, once more than thirty million bushels per season, declined to a mere twenty-five thousand bushels. The live oyster reefs crumbled into heaps of decaying shells. The beds of sea grass began to die off, shrinking to less than a third of their original expanse. On the hottest days of summer, crabs began crawling ashore to avoid suffocation in oxygen-depleted bottom waters. The striped bass today are so contaminated with PCBs that Maryland advises limiting intake to less than twice a month for adults and even less frequently for children. (Babbitt 2005, 116-117)

Habitat disappearance through land conversion and other human activities is now the principal source of the loss of biodiversity. The 2005 MEA said that current species loss is estimated to be about a thousand times greater than the natural or normal rate of extinction. In fact, many scientists believe we are on the brink of the sixth great wave of species loss, the only one caused by humans. The World Conservation Unit, which keeps the records on species, calculated that two of every five recognized species on the planet risk extinction, including one in eight birds, one in four mammals, and one in three amphibians.

In 1994, fifteen hundred of the world's top scientists, including a majority of living Nobel Prize winners, issued a plea for more attention to environmental problems: "The earth is finite," they stated. "Its ability to absorb wastes and destructive effluents is finite. Its ability to provide food and energy is finite. Its ability to provide for growing numbers of people is finite. Moreover, we are fast approaching many of the earth's limits. Current economic practices that damage the environment, in both developed and underdeveloped nations, cannot be continued with the risk that vital global systems will be damaged beyond repair."

Sprawl

The Project for Public Spaces, a nonprofit planning, design and educational organization, wrote that "if you plan cities for cars and traffic, you get cars and traffic. If you plan for people and places, you get people and places."

Over the past half a century, the United States consumed about five times more land than it had population growth (Johnson, 2011). According to a 2007 report, "Threats to the American Land" by the Yale School of Forestry and Environmental Studies, since 1982, the United States has paved, built on, and developed thirty-five million once-rural acres, an area the size of New York state. Each year, the United States is losing about two million acres of open space—six thousand acres a day—and about 1.2 million acres of farmland, with prime farmland disappearing 30 percent faster than average. The report detailed that an area of wildlife habitat the size of West Virginia is projected to be lost to development in the next twenty-five years. Furthermore, in a March 2006 *New York Times* article, Felicity Barringer wrote that, despite a "no net loss of wetlands" federal policy, tidal marshes, swamps, and other wetlands are disappearing at a rate of about a hundred thousand acres a year.

Globally, the World Wildlife Fund says that the world loses 36 football fields' worth of forests every minute, and the planet could lose more than 230 million hectares of forest by 2050. Humanity is exceeding Earth's ability to sustain life by 50 percent, the organization says, and human demand is "overshooting" the planet's ability to produce renewable resources and absorb carbon dioxide.

The WWF posited that Earth's governments need to seek a goal of zero net deforestation and forest degradation (loss of natural resources). If that goal is not achieved, "at our current rate of resource use, we will need two [some estimates say five] planets to live on by 2030" (Zelman 2011).

Speth wrote in his 2006 book *Global Environmental Governance* that from 1970 to 2003, there was a 53 percent rise in the miles of paved roads in the United States, vehicle miles traveled increased 177 percent, the size of the average new single-family home rose about 50 percent, and municipal solid waste per person increased 33 percent. According to data from the two nonprofit news magazines, *Grist* and *Mother Jones,* since 1970, electricity consumption per person rose more than 70 percent while 80 percent of all new homes since 1994 have been exurban (beyond suburban areas) and more than half the lots have been ten acres or more. The self-storage industry, which did not begin until the early 1970s, has grown so rapidly that its buildings now cover more than seventy square miles, an area the size of Manhattan and San Francisco combined. Social critic James Howard Kunstler wrote that suburban sprawl is the "greatest misallocation of resources the world has ever known."

The overconsumption of space, oil, utilities, electricity, money, and other resources has defined our expectation of the American Dream. Each American today occupies almost 20 percent more developed land (housing, schools, stores, roads) than 20 years ago, according to the Center for Environment and Population, a non-profit research and policy group based in New Canaan, Conn. By the late 1990s, 1.7 acres—the equivalent of about 220 parking spaces or 16 basketball courts—were developed for every person added to the population. At the same time, many Northeast and Midwest cities were decaying. In 1950, Cleveland's population was about 915,000; by 2005, it had shrunk to 452,208 (Nasser 2006).

According to Census Bureau estimates released in 2009, by 2032 the U.S. population will reach 364 million people because of increased birth rates and massive immigration. This can have a huge effect, as one writer explained:

> This means that the country will be adding the equivalent of Southern Florida's three urban counties (Miami-Dade, Ft. Lauderdale-Broward and Palm Beach) every twenty-four months!

21

The vast majority of the new dwelling units will be forced to connect to existing systems of water supply, sewage treatment, roads and schools, thereby adding to the regional deficits in terms of traffic congestion, strained utility systems, and overcrowded schools. A population of 1.2 million people will need 545,000 new dwelling units, will be flushing 1.1 million new toilets, standing under 800,000 new showers and pushing the buttons on 545,000 new garbage disposals. That will be quite a load on the existing water, sewer, and drainage systems. (Finley 2008, 54)

According to the National Household Travel Survey, suburban households in Greater Boston buy 85 percent more gas at the pump than households living within five miles of downtown. That amounts to about six tons of carbon dioxide emissions each year. Suburban households in Greater Boston also consume about 20 percent more electricity than city dwellers. This is responsible for an extra two tons of carbon dioxide emissions per household per year (Glaeser 2008).

"The average single-family detached home consumes 88 percent more electricity than the average apartment in a five or more unit building. The average suburban household consumes 27 percent more electricity than the average urban household. Gas consumption per family per year declines by 106 gallons as the number of residents per square mile doubles" (Newsom 2011).

Think of the massive land area and countless miles of infrastructure needed to support strip development, highways, and parking areas on the outskirts of cities. Contrast that with the waste or underutilization of neglected inner cities, the buildings, roads and infrastructure, not to mention the human potential. Neither of these conditions provides the best or fullest use of our resources. In our hypercompetitive, "flat" world economy, with increasingly scarce and in-demand resources, a society cannot afford such waste: economically, environmentally, or socially. When suburban sprawl is compared and contrasted with neglected and marginalized American cities, the view is striking. Most people would not consider walking or even driving through certain neglected or marginalized areas. When hosting visitors from out of town, people generally don't prefer to take them to see the outskirts of the region, with its endless subdivisions and strip malls.

"Certainly, no friend is taken on a tour of the freeways during peak hours of commuting" (Finley 2008, 93).

At the same time, our current governing methods encourage parochial thinking. "There are no financial incentives to either the central city or the suburban communities to tackle true cross boundary issues such as the social conditions in the inner city or the true costs of sprawl allowed by the [building of] suburban communities" (Finley 2008, 29).

"Before (former Vice President) Al Gore became the nation's leader (in) warning against global warming and climate change, he pinpointed sprawl as America's number one enemy" (Finley 2008, 30). In fact, a 2011 study in the journal *Environment and Urbanization* said that carbon emissions in cities are lower than in the car-dependent suburbs. "While cities have the highest emissions per square mile, suburbs have far and away the highest emission per person," the study said. A more thorough discussion can be found in a 2009 National Research Council report and a 2004 piece in *The New Yorker* by David Owen. In his article, Owen wrote, "Spreading people out increases the damage they do to the environment, while making problems harder to see and address" (Zimmerman 2011). Therefore, as Jess Zimmerman wrote in *Grist*, "Manhattan is one of the greenest places in America." New Yorkers emit a third of the greenhouse gas emissions of the typical American.

Along the same lines, a 2010 U.S. Geological Survey study showed how urban sprawl threatens genetic diversity: "Biologists from the U.S. Geological Survey and the National Park Service said that as urban development fragmented the Santa Monica Mountains into isolated 'habitat islands,' wildlife populations have become genetically isolated. They said animals are unable to cross urban barriers to breed with neighboring members of their own species. Urban sprawl in Southern California is limiting the genetic diversity of animal populations and possibly making them more prone to extinction." Scientists said they're "starting to see the same genetic isolation across multiple species in the same region, from invertebrates to vertebrates," although they don't yet know what effects will be on the rarer, more specialized, species in the region (Lee 2010).

Joel S. Hirschorn, Ph.D., in his 2005 book *Sprawl Kills,* dissected and explained the powerful forces and the human and financial costs of sprawl. Based on his background as chief scientist for the non-partisan National

Governors Association, he pointed out that "after 50 years of American housing and culture being dominated by sprawl, millions of citizens do not know of any other style of living. Sprawl kills is not a metaphor. It is fact. Sprawl actually does kill, in that it makes people fat, tired, depressed, stressed, more likely to die in auto accidents and succumb to very serious diseases! Most people do not recognize the impacts of the built environment on the quality of their lives" (Finley 2008, 30-31).

Benton MacKaye, "father of the Appalachian Trail," forester, and regional planner, wrote: "Just as industry plans out where it will next expand or open up a new plant, they would look at the future layout, which involves why and how they will locate there. The military would answer the same type of considerations, along with what they need and want. They would look at the geography and if it were favorable for a base or campaign." In his groundbreaking book, *The New Exploration*, he asked, Why should civilization or governments not plan for new communities and growth? Evidence today proves that the lack of planning and foresight is taking its toll. "Economists and social scientists have testified to the growing human, social, and financial costs of the trends that produce more and more homes, stores, industrial space, and commercial outlets spreading across the countryside" (Finley 2008, 27).

Suburban poverty. Poverty is spreading too. As Yonah Freemark wrote in the magazine *The Next American City*: "Though the poverty rate remains higher in central cities, the number of poor suburbanites is growing quickly .... Over the last ten years, more than two-thirds of poverty growth in the nation's metro areas occurred in the suburbs, and there are now 1.6 million more people living in the suburbs than in central cities." At the same time, whereas cities have institutions to assist many of society's most vulnerable, the suburbs do not (Freemark 2010).

"Although poverty rates remain higher in central cities than in suburbs [20.9 percent versus 11.4 percent in 2010], poverty rates have increased at a quicker pace in suburban areas." Seventy-three percent of suburban nonprofits are seeing more clients with no previous connection to safety-net-programs (Allard 2010).

Particularly hard hit are the nation's hundred largest metropolitan areas. "There, between 1980 and 2000, the number of suburban census tracts with poverty rates of 30 percent or higher grew 89 percent, and the number of poor residents more than doubled" (Briggs 2005, 28). Recent statistics reveal the continuing trend of poverty moving outward.

Urban policy. In his 2005 book *Cities in the Wilderness* (p. 115), former governor of Arizona and U.S. Department of the Interior secretary Bruce Babbitt wrote, "For fifty years, national urban policy has been a national suburban policy."

The Federal Housing Administration (FHA) and the Veterans Administration (VA) have backed millions of low-interest mortgages for single-family homes since World War II. In addition, government agencies Fannie Mae (the Federal National Mortgage Association) and Freddie Mac (the Federal Home Loan Mortgage Corporation) have supported trillions of dollars more in mortgage pools. The Federal Highway Administration (FHWA) spends approximately six times the amount of money on roads and highways as it does on mass transit. More than $126 billion in tax expenditures subsidize largely suburban-oriented home ownership in 2009 dollars. This includes $86 billion in deductible tax revenues (mortgage interest), another $25 billion in federal tax liability waived as a credit for state and local property taxes paid, and $15 billion a year as capital gains exclusions on home sales (Peirce 2011f). That contrasts with only about $6 billion a year in tax credits to subsidize largely city-oriented rental housing.

Governmental fragmentation. In his groundbreaking book, *Cities Without Suburbs*, David Rusk tackled the complex issues of sprawl, race, and development in America's cities. After thoroughly analyzing census data, Rusk came up with an explanation for why some cities are relatively healthy and growing and others are relatively troubled and declining. The author argued that "big box" regions implicitly facilitate greater racial and economic integration, while "little box" regions are characterized by greater racial and economic segregation. Big-box regions have less fragmented governments and are more metropolitan in scale as opposed to little-box regions in which many communities compete under the governance of fractured municipal authorities. Fractured government costs more, Rusk said, because it also means a fractured tax base. Development in one town drains vitality from its neighbors and increases the cost of providing public services. Only when little boxes are merged, or at least cooperate enough, to form big boxes do the communities stand a chance of providing modern services at affordable tax rates and attracting and controlling the kind of economic growth that is sustainable and beneficial to all, said Rusk. He contended that cities and suburbs together are integral components of regional economies. Consider that the New York City region was a bunch of little boxes until all the boroughs were combined—including the once-rural areas of Queens, the Bronx and Staten Island—to create the metropolis that soon became the capital of the world (Rusk 2003, 3).

Rusk wrote: "The 1950 census was the high-water mark for most of America's big cities ... Thereafter, Washington, Wall Street, Detroit, Hollywood, and Madison Avenue made middle class families an offer they could not refuse: a redefined American Dream. Sustained economic growth, cheap home mortgages, affordable automobiles, and federally subsidized highways—all touted on screens large and small—made that dream house with its own yard, quiet neighborhood, local school and nearby shopping possible for millions of families. Compared with staying put in many city neighborhoods, suburbia was a bargain. Urban America became suburban America" (Rusk 2003, 7-8). Many western states mitigated those effects through annexation, a perhaps unintentional yet beneficial governmental design left over from settlement patterns, to relieve some of the isolation created by suburban growth. Rusk said that to increase its population, a city must be "elastic," meaning it must stretch the edges of its rubber sheet to take in new territory. "It must become more elastic outward rather than upward" (through annexation)." Almost all metro areas have grown across the country, but "elastic cities expand their city limits; inelastic cities do not." Areas such as "Houston, Columbus, Albuquerque, Madison, and Raleigh grew through aggressive annexation of surrounding areas" (Rusk 2003, 9, 17). That contrasts with the city limits of Detroit and Syracuse, which did not change.

Rusk also detailed how racial bigotry shaped growth patterns. "Both racial prejudice and discriminatory public policies played a major role in the evolution of overwhelmingly white suburbs surrounding increasingly black and Hispanic inelastic cities," he wrote. There were other motivations, such as proximity to jobs, bigger yards, city taxes, and politics but, undeniably, racially motivated white flight was a major factor (Rusk 2003, 23). In addition, federal and state policy institutionalized discrimination through the redlining of black neighborhoods, in which interest rates for those areas were made prohibitively high for residents. Other times, those residents were simply denied mortgages in white areas. FHA and VA loans continued those policies. Federal regulations favored construction of single-family homes after World War II but discouraged the building of multifamily apartments. From 1934 to 1960, suburban St. Louis County received six times as much FHA mortgage money per capita as did the city of St. Louis. Per capita FHA lending in suburban Long Island was eleven times greater than in Brooklyn. As late as 1950, the FHA still encouraged the use of restrictive racial covenants two years after the U.S. Supreme Court ruled them unconstitutional. FHA's redlining continued overtly until the mid-1960s. The full extent of discrimination in mortgage lending was only revealed after passage of the Home Mortgage Disclosure Act (1975), and significant mortgage funds began to flow back into inner-city neighborhoods only with vigorous enforcement of the Community Reinvestment Act of 1977 (Rusk 2003, 24-25).

In his book, *The Regional Governing of Metropolitan America* (2002), David Miller used a rigorous statistical analysis that left some telling results related to governmental fragmentation. He found that:

- In terms of economic development, "centralized state systems and decentralized metropolitan region systems underperform empowered (strengthened) but more centralized metropolitan regions."
- "Too much diffusion of power in metropolitan areas serves to increase the probability of racial segregation and to deter those areas from taking advantage of economic expansion."
- "Gaps between rich and poor communities will always be a part of the metropolitan environment ... However, the distance between rich and poor should be minimized or, at least, kept from widening ... Indeed, competition feeds upon itself and makes the competitive more competitive and the non-competitive more non-competitive."

Economist Richard Voith of the Federal Reserve Bank in Philadelphia said that the decline of central cities affects the entire metropolitan region negatively in three ways: through amenities (cultural institutions, vibrant pedestrian districts, waterfront parks, libraries, and so forth), agglomeration economies (benefits that firms get from locating near each other), and social problems (Berensson 2011).

As outlined in an essay by sociologist, planner, and associate professor at Massachusetts Institute of Technology Xavier de Souza Briggs for his book *The Geography of Opportunity*, "Most of the conditions that make inner city America such a consistent nexus of social problems, for example, are orchestrated by social and economic forces operating at a metropolitan or larger scale" (Briggs 2005, 318).

Yet, challenges are not confined to the cities. Rapidly growing bedroom suburbs lack adequate police, fire, and emergency services—all volunteer forces with minimal or decreasing numbers of volunteers.

Suburbs have been drawing resources from central cities for decades. "Now, regions, fueled by the decentralizations of urban growth, have emerged as the dominant economic and demographic units, rather than cities. Economic clusters extend beyond, or completely outside of, long-established city business centers ... the lack of affordable housing in surrounding neighborhoods with higher-performing schools further isolates low-income city residents from quality public education. Finding housing near new outlying job centers is almost impossible, further isolating inner city residents when adequate transit is not available" (Briggs 2005, 290).

The outer-edge suburbs, or exurbs, have become the regions of population growth, employment growth, and wealth creation. According to 2012 analysis by the Urban Institute and researchers at the U.S. Census Bureau, the exurbs have been growing faster than the rest of the country even amid the housing bust and economic recession. Growth rates there outpace more densely populated areas as well as the nation as a whole. "Ninety-six of the 98 most populous metropolitan areas saw higher growth rates in the exurbs than in the metro area as a whole between 2000 and 2010," wrote Nate Berg of "The Atlantic Cities," an online journal. Many of the older areas, such as central cities and inner-ring suburbs, have been left behind, with growing concentrations of poverty, particularly minority poverty. To make matters worse, they're usually without the fiscal capacity to handle the result: joblessness, family fragmentation, and failing schools.

What is persistent and prevalent in sprawl is the segregation by race and income and unequal patterns of metropolitan development. With increased traffic congestion and disappearing farmlands and open spaces, the sense of community vanishes, not just for those in the inner city and inner suburbs, but for all families in metropolitan areas.

"There are also significant fiscal costs associated with urban sprawl. Spending on bridges, roads, sewers, and other public works escalates because of the high cost of extending existing networks and constructing new systems" (Briggs 2005, xiii). HUD reported in 1999 that in communities experiencing sprawl, road costs were 25 to 33 percent higher, utility costs 18 to 25 percent higher, and municipal and school district costs 3 to 11 percent higher than in sprawl-free communities.

"Genuine freedom could only happen within a context of economic security."
—Franklin Delano Roosevelt

"IT TOOK ALL OF HISTORY to build the seven trillion dollar world economy of 1950; today economic activity grows by that amount every decade" (Speth, 2008, x).

Based on pre-2007-2008 recession rates of growth, the world economy is projected to double in size by 2022. By 2011, world population swelled to seven billion from only one billion 200 years before. In addition, economic output has increased to seventy trillion dollars and will be $140 trillion by 2030 if we continue at the same growth rates. The threats discussed in the environmental chapter are a direct result of the economic effects of the modern, increasingly prosperous, world economy. Notwithstanding the greater good and the prosperity modern capitalism has enabled, it would be dishonest to take no notice of the immense destruction it has wrought on the environment. The results of an absolute commitment to economic growth at almost any cost must be acknowledged and understood. The world economy as a whole is still poised for unprecedented growth. But do we desire economic growth to no end? If the answer is yes, we should consider what was written by Bron Taylor, professor of religion and nature, environmental ethics, and environmental studies at the University of Florida and author of *Dark Green Religion: Nature, Spirituality and the Planetary Future*: "Ecologically maladaptive cultural systems ... eventually kill their hosts."

That corresponds to a 2011 statement released by the Bolivian legislature, which read in part, "Mother Earth is a living, dynamic system made up of the undivided community of all living beings, who are all interconnected, interdependent and complementary, sharing a common destiny." The Bolivian legislators were attempting to reclaim the indigenous wisdom previously abandoned: specifically, a connection to nature, a reverent respect for the circle of life, and the search for a way to limit resource-devouring, cancerlike economic growth (Koehler 2011).

The lawmakers must have recognized a startling fact: "Today's economic growth in affluent societies is not materially improving human happiness and satisfaction with life" and has turned out to be a very poor way to generate solutions to pressing social needs and problems (Speth 2008, 10). The World Health Organization calculates that one in four people in the United States suffers from chronic anxiety, a mood disorder, or depression. As author Christopher Hedges wrote in 2012, "when the most basic elements that sustain life are reduced to a cash product, life has no intrinsic value."

As we move forward, we should recognize that growth just for the sake of growth does not necessarily benefit mankind. Certainly, capitalism, wealth and economic gains have contributed extraordinarily to certain areas of our quality of life. But, to fully comprehend this fact, we also should consider another aspect. The United Nations' 1996 human development report reviewed the economic performance of many nations and found five types of growth as follows:

1. Jobless, by which the overall economy grows but does not expand opportunities for employment
2. Ruthless, by which the fruits of economic growth mostly benefit the rich
3. Voiceless, by which growth in the economy has not been accompanied by an extension of democracy or empowerment
4. Rootless, by which growth causes people's cultural identity to wither
5. Futureless, by which the present generation squanders resources needed by future generations.

Recognizing the colossal—and unprecedented—size of corporations in the modern day is essential to contemplating our future. According to *Global Inc. – An Atlas of the Multinational Corporation*, today there are more than sixty-three thousand multinational corporations. As recently as 1990, there were fewer than half that. Of the one hundred largest economies in the world, fifty-three are corporations. Exxon Mobil, in fact, is larger than 180 nations. Corporations are required by law, and driven by self-interest, to increase their monetary value for the benefit of their owners and shareholders, and there is pressure to show quick, and steadily growing, profits (Barnes 2006, 33-48). This is at times in conflict with or contradictory to the ideals of the U.S. government and the hope of ensuring justice, liberty, and freedom for all citizens.

Before the 2007-'08 recession, different estimates showed that General Motors was bigger than Denmark, DaimlerChrysler was bigger than Poland, Royal Dutch Shell was bigger than Venezuela, and Sony was bigger than Pakistan. They likely still are.

To keep the economy of the United States chugging along requires extraordinary amounts of nonrenewable resources. Recognizing that China, India, Brazil, and other countries are moving toward an Americanized "middle class" and expanding their economies, their need for nonrenewable resources will increase. In light of this, and perhaps most startling, is that in 2007 the United States consumed about twenty-one million barrels of oil a day, approximately the same as Russia, Japan, Germany, India, and China combined. What is the capacity and what will we need to consume in the next twenty, thirty, forty years to keep up?

Wealth and Well-Being

In the 1830s, Alexis de Tocqueville, in his book *Democracy in America,* wrote: "Among the new objects that attracted my attention during my stay in the United States, none struck me with greater force than the equality of conditions. I easily perceived the enormous influence that this primary fact exercises on the workings of the society."

"Conventional wisdom presumes that growing populations bring economic growth. But what drives wealth isn't how many people a place is adding, but how much more productive its workers are becoming," wrote renowned researcher Richard Florida on his "Creative Class" blog in 2011. Florida also wrote that there is no relation between population growth and productivity growth among states. Data, he said, showed that while the Sunbelt is growing in population, it is comparable to the Midwest in productivity. Florida looked at more than 350 metro areas across the U.S. and found that the five with the fastest population growth all saw their productivity decline. Atlanta's productivity fell by more than 12 percent, which put it in the same league with Detroit. His research indicated that there was "no statistical association whatsoever between population growth and productivity growth." Ultimately, he said, "America's economic winners are the places that have improved their productivity—something which doesn't turn on the sheer numbers of workers they have on tap, but rather how skilled and innovative they are."

For more than 50 years, epidemiologists Richard Wilkinson and Kate Pickett have studied inequality. In their groundbreaking 2009 book *The Spirit Level*, the epidemiologists concluded that greater equality makes societies stronger and that the weakening of community life and the growth of consumerism are interrelated. They found that almost every modern social and environmental problem—ill health, lack of community life, violence, drugs, obesity, mental illness, long working hours, large prison populations—is more likely to occur in a less equal society. The U.S. is currently seeing unprecedented levels of inequality.

As *The Spirit Level* noted, we've gone from a community, in most cases, to mass society. Social anxieties have risen so dramatically over the last half century that it could very well be explained by "the breakup of the settled communities of the past. People used to grow up knowing, and being known by, many of the same people all their lives ... Familiar faces have been replaced by a constant flux of strangers. As a result, who we are, identity itself is endlessly open to question ... And this vulnerability is part of the modern psychological condition and feeds directly into consumerism" (Pickett 2009, 42, 43).

In the USA, trust has fallen from 60 percent in 1960, to less than 40 percent in 2004. "Large inequalities weaken community life, reduce trust, and increases violence" said Pickett in *The Spirit Level* (2009, 45). Furthermore, we know that low-trust environments reduce the rate of investments and the overall growth of the economy. Very low-trust societies can be caught in a poverty trap, and high-trust societies exhibit higher rates of investment and growth. In other words, as economics writer Nancy Folbre of *The New York Times* wrote, "trust greases the wheels of economic development." Management guru Steven Covey argues that high-trust companies are more successful than others.

"As the economist Jack Hirshleifer explained in a classic article, 'The

Dark Side of the Force,' extreme differences in wealth and power among groups often lead to appropriation or exploitation rather than trade. Not surprisingly, humans have learned to be suspicious of those who have the capacity to do them harm. By this account, the powerless are less likely to trust the powerful than vice versa" (Folbre 2011).

Political scientist Robert Putnam of Harvard University said in his groundbreaking book *Bowling Alone*: "Community and equality are mutually reinforcing...Social capital and economic equality moved in tandem most of the twentieth century. In terms of the distribution of wealth and income, America in the 1950s and 1960s was more egalitarian than it had been in more than a century ... those same decades were also the high point of social connectedness and civic engagement. Record highs in equality and social capital coincided ... conversely, the last third of the twentieth century was a time of growing inequality *and* eroding social capital ... The timing of the two trends is striking: Sometime around 1965-1970 America reversed course and started becoming both less just economically and less well connected socially and politically."

In *Who's Your City?*, Richard Florida wrote about what he called a "Trick or Treat Index," which measures how confident parents feel about allowing their children to go door to door on Halloween. When he lived in Washington, D.C., not a single child would come to his neighborhood home on the holiday, but when he lived in Toronto, his neighborhood was mobbed with a diversity of youth. Florida also discussed the "Popscicle Index," something Catherine Fitts, the former assistant secretary of Housing and Urban Development, came up with. She describes it as the percentage of people in a community who feel that a child can leave home safely to buy a Popsicle. "The U.S. Census Bureau released a study which found that nearly half of all children in the United States live in places where their parents fear that neighbors may be a bad influence, and more than one in five children are kept indoors because they live in dangerous neighborhoods—a number that rises to 34 percent for African Americans and 37 percent for Hispanics" (Florida, 2008, 259).

John Steinbeck, in his book *Travels with Charley*, wrote, "A sad soul can kill you quicker than a germ." That relates to an interesting British study called Whitehall I, completed in 1967, that investigated the connection between male civil servants and what researchers assumed were high levels of heart disease, the so-called "executive's disease." Researchers assumed they would find the highest levels in the most "stressful" positions; instead they found the exact opposite. "Men in the lowest grade (messengers, doorkeepers, etc.) had a death rate three times higher than that of men in the highest grade (administrators)" (Pickett 2009, 75). Inequality affects us in myriad ways, something we are just now recognizing. The effects on personal dignity run deeper than perhaps previously recognized.

Along those lines, a baby born in the United States, the richest country in the world, has a 40 percent higher risk of dying in the first year after birth than a baby born in Greece, one of the poorer European countries. Greeks spend less than half per person on health care than do Americans, and Greece has six times fewer high-tech scanners per person than the U.S. In rich countries, there is no relationship between the amount of health spending per person and life expectancy. Most studies point to the simple fact that more egalitarian societies tend to be healthier. Moreover, the effect of subpar social conditions on health has been well documented. In a national survey conducted by the Robert Wood Johnson Foundation, four out of five physicians agreed that unmet social needs led directly to worse health. The truth is that we spend far more than any other industrialized nation on health care but experience far worse results such as in life expectancy and infant mortality, in which we are near the bottom of the list. The difference, however, is that spending on social services—such as rent subsidies, employment-training programs, unemployment benefits, old-age pensions, and family support that can extend and improve life—is significantly greater in other countries, and this largely explains the different health care results. Or, as Elizabeth Bradley and Lauren Taylor wrote in a *New York Times* article titled "To Fix Health Care, Help the Poor," "It is Americans' prerogative to continually vote down the encroachment of government programs on our free-market ideology, but recognizing the health effects of our disdain for comprehensive safety nets may well be the key to unraveling the 'spend more, get less' paradox."

According to Pickett (2009), "health disparities are not simply a contrast between the ill-health of the poor and the better health of everybody else. Instead, they run right across society so that even the reasonably well-off have shorter lives than the very rich. Likewise, the benefits of greater equality spread right across society, improving health for everyone—not just those at the bottom."

The *New England Journal of Medicine* in 2005 said that trends in childhood obesity are now so serious that they are widely expected to lead to shorter life expectancies for today's children. That would be the first reversal in life expectancy in many developed countries since governments started keeping track in the nineteenth century." *The Spirit Level* noted that more adults are obese in more unequal countries, and more children are overweight in more unequal countries.

Quality of Life

"I've come to understand that what the richest and strongest among us want for their families is what most all members of society want for theirs, too: a home, steady work, enough money for a comfortable life and secure old age, the means to cope with illness and other misfortunes, and the happiness of living freely as citizens without fear. A society whose economic system cannot make those opportunities widely available is in deep trouble, the dreams of its people mocked and denied" (Moyers 2010).

John Maynard Keynes, considered the father of macroeconomics and possibly the most influential economist of the twentieth century, looked forward to the day when the "economic problem" would be a thing of the past. In the *Economic Possibilities for our Grandchildren* in 1933 (p. 365-373), he wrote:

> The economic problem, the struggle for subsistence, always has been hitherto the primary, most pressing problem of the human race ... Thus for the first time since his creation man will be faced with his real, his permanent problem—how to use his freedom from pressing economic cares, how to occupy the leisure ... how to live wisely and agreeably and well ... When the accumulation of wealth is no longer of high social importance, there will be great changes in the code of morals. The love of money as a possession—as distinguished from the love of money as means to the enjoyment and realities of life— will be recognized for what it is; a somewhat disgusting morbidity,

one of those semi criminal, semi-pathological propensities which one hands over with a shudder to the specialists in the mental disease ... I see us free, therefore, to return to some of the most sure and certain principles of religion and traditional virtue—that avarice is a vice, that the exaction of usury is a misdemeanor, and the love of money is detestable, that those walk most truly in the paths of virtue and sane wisdom who take least thought for the morrow. We shall once more value ends above means and prefer the good to the useful.

In 1958, John Kenneth Galbraith, another widely influential economist of the twentieth century, wrote that "sooner rather than later our concerns with the quantity of goods produced—the rate of increase in gross national product—would have to give way to the larger question of the quality of life that it provided."

More recently, Nobel Prize-winning economist "Joseph Stiglitz's criticism of standard GDP measures which gauge levels of production and money income, but ignore what easily matters as much or more—the safety and quality of people's communities, social inclusion, educational opportunities and health, and controlling greenhouse gas emissions and other unsustainable burdens on the natural environment" led French President Nicolas Sarkozy in 2009 to "include happiness and well-being in France's measure of economic progress" (Peirce 2010a). In 2005, British conservative leader and future prime minister David Cameron said that gauging people's well-being is one of the "central political issues of our time."

Australian policy intellectual Clive Hamilton wrote in his 2004 book *Growth Fetish*:

Despite the high and sustained levels of economic growth in the West over a period of 50 years—growth that has seen average real incomes increase several times over—the mass of people are no more satisfied with their lives now than they were then ... In addition, the costs of economic growth, which fall largely outside the marketplace and so do not appear in the national accounts, have become inescapably apparent—in the form of disturbing signs of ecological decline, an array of social problems that growth has failed to correct, and epidemics of unemployment, overwork and insecurity. For the most part, capitalism itself has answered the demands that inspired 19th century socialism ... But attainment of these goals has only brought deeper sources of social unease— manipulation by marketers, obsessive materialism, environmental degradation, endemic alienation, and loneliness. In short ... in the marketing society, we seek fulfillment but settle for abundance. Prisoners of plenty, we have the freedom to consume instead of the freedom to find our place in the world.

"Prosperity and happiness are not correlated, and indeed prosperity, beyond a certain point, is associated with the growth of important social pathologies" (Speth 2008, 128-129).

McKibben, the author and environmentalist, wrote in 2007 that "our single-minded focus on increasing wealth has succeeded in driving the planet's ecological systems to the brink of failure, even as it's failed to make us happier .... Instead it had led us to becoming more thoroughly individualistic than we really wanted to be, increasing social isolation and undermining our sense of community."

Psychologist David Myers observed that at the beginning of the twenty-first century, Americans found themselves "with big houses and broken homes, high incomes and low morale, secured rights and diminished civility. We were excelling at making a living but too often failing at making a life. We celebrated our prosperity but yearned for purpose. We cherished our freedoms but longed for connection. In an age of plenty, we were feeling spiritual hunger. These facts of life lead us to a startling conclusion: Our becoming better off materially has not made us better off psychologically" (Myers 2004).

"GDP does not count the costs and benefits that occur outside the market. For example, a country can consume its natural capital, but that shows up in national income accounts not as capital depreciation but as income" (Speth, 2008, 138). As economist Robert Repetto wrote, "A country could exhaust its mineral resources, cut down its forests, erode its soils, pollute its aquifers, and hunt its wildlife and fisheries to extinction, but measured income would not be affected as these assets disappeared ... [The] difference in the treatment of natural resources and other tangible assets confuses the depletion of valuable assets with the generation of income ... The result can be illusory gains in income and permanent losses in wealth" (Repetto et al 1989, 2-3).

In short, "America's affluence is not being translated into outstanding environmental or social performance" as compared to the rest of the industrialized world (Speth 2008, 143). Cuba, for all its problems, troubles, and much lower income levels, has life expectancy and infant mortality rates almost identical to that of the United States (Pickett 2009, 217).

We must consider the people the market is intended to serve. As George Lakoff, professor of linguistics at the University of California, Berkeley wrote: "Markets are not provided by nature. They are constructed—by laws, rules and institutions. All of these have moral bases of one sort or another. Hence, all markets are moral, according to someone's sense of morality. The only question is, Whose morality? In contemporary America, it is conservative versus progressive morality that governs forms of economic policy. The systems of morality behind economic policies need to be discussed."

At the passing of the famous economist, one author wrote:

> What Galbraith understood, and what later researchers (including this author) have proved, is that Adam Smith's "invisible hand"— the notion that the individual pursuit of maximum profit guides capitalist markets to efficiency—is so invisible because, quite often, it's just not there. Unfettered markets often produce too much of some things, such as pollution, and too little of other things, such as basic research. As Bruce Greenwald and I have shown, whenever information is imperfect—that is, always—markets are inefficient; hence the need for government action .... Yet history shows that in every successful country, the government had played an important role. Yes, governments sometimes fail, but unfettered markets are a certain prescription for failure. Galbraith made this case better than most .... Galbraith knew, too, that people aren't just rational economic actors, but consumers, contending with advertising, political persuasion, and social pressures. (Stiglitz 2006)

Foreign students are catching on to these inconsistencies too. Richard Florida used an example of the diverse makeup of his master's level course at George Mason University. He wrote: "Whether they were from East Asia, India, Latin America, Europe, Africa, they all wanted to raise their children outside the United States. The educational systems were better, they said; their societies were less materialistic; and there was less pressure to work and far more time and consideration for family. And, they added, they would leave the United States even if it meant giving up money and long-term career prospects. There is a veritable world of options out there for people looking for a great place to raise their families" (Florida, 2008, 259-260).

Ray LaHood, secretary of the U.S. Department of Transportation under President Barack Obama, said: "Livability means being able to take your kids to school, go to work, see a doctor, drop by the grocery or post office, go out to dinner and a movie, and play with your kids at the park, all without having to get into your car. Livability means building the communities that help Americans live the lives they want to live—whether those communities are urban centers, small towns or rural areas."

America as a whole has experienced steady income growth over the last thirty years, yet fewer and fewer people are participating in it. Yes, there are large amounts of prosperity but not society-wide benefits one would imagine from such enormous amounts of wealth in circulation. In *America's Social Health: Putting Social Issues Back on the Public Agenda*, Marque-Luisa Miringoff and Sandra Opdycke show somewhat deteriorating social conditions despite huge growth in GDP per capita. The measure they used to create their composite index includes infant mortality, high school dropouts, poverty, child abuse, teenage suicide, crime, average weekly wages, drug use, alcoholism, unemployment, and so on. Something has to give.

The Index of Sustainable Economic Welfare (ISEW), created by World Bank economist Herman Daly and theologian John Cobbs in 1989, demonstrates that despite continuing increases in GDP, ISEW decreases at a certain level because "growth in GDP is outweighed by increased environmental and social costs, and growth can actually reduce welfare" (Speth 2008, 140).

The Genuine Progress Indicator (GPI), an improvement on the ISEW, reveals that Americans on average are no better off today than they were in 1970 even though GDP per capita has grown significantly during that period. Specifically, the GPI shows that since the early 1970s, growth's positive effect on the welfare of Americans has been far less than that suggested by GDP.

In an article in *Yes! A Journal of Positive Futures* in the summer of 2004, author David Myers discussed that in an American Council on Education survey of a quarter million entering college freshman, the proportion who said they considered it very important to become "very well off financially" rose in the 1970s and 1980s from 40 percent to 74 percent, while the number who said they considered it very important to "develop a meaningful philosophy of life" declined significantly.

Despite America's vast and unprecedented amount of wealth, the country is ranked 6th in global innovation-based competitiveness but 40th in rate of change over the last decade; 11th among industrialized nations in the fraction of 25- to 34-year-olds who have graduated from high school, 16th in college completion rate, 22nd in broadband Internet access, 27th among developed nations in the proportion of college students receiving degrees in science or engineering; 48th in quality of K-12 math and science education; and 29th in the number of mobile phones per 100 people (Friedman 2010).

"The Place and Happiness Survey" completed by Richard Florida and the Gallup Organization in 2008 identified the things that mattered most to people. Based on the more than twenty-seven responses received, Florida found that the two top items were aesthetics (parks, culture, nightlife) and basic services, which include schools, health care, affordable housing, roads, and public infrastructure. The survey covered dozens and dozens of specific community attributes.

Helena Norberg-Hodge, linguist, writer, and activist, reflected in *Ancient Futures* that after almost two decades studying the culture of Ladakh (a region in the northernmost reaches of India, north of the Himalayas), she came to believe that preserving a traditional way of life among the Ladakhis—extended families living in harmony with the land—would bring about more happiness than "improving" their standard of living with unchecked development. She admitted that she had assumed that "progress" was inevitable. "I passively accepted a new road through the middle of the park, a steel and glass bank where a 200-year-old church had stood ... and the fact that life seemed to get harder and faster with each day," she wrote. "I do not anymore. In Ladakh I have learned that there is more than one path into the future and I have had the privilege to witness another, saner way of life—a pattern of existence based on the coevolution between human beings and the earth. I have seen that community and a close relationship with the land can enrich human life beyond all comparison with material wealth or technological sophistication. I have learned that another way is possible" (Mortensen 2006, 111-112).

Poverty

Mohandas Gandhi once said, "Poverty is the worst form of violence." If that is so, the United States is a very violent nation. Now, of course, the poor of the United States generally can't compare to the slums of Bangladesh or the barren plains of the Sudan, but, as Robert Rector of the conservative Heritage Foundation wrote, "The poor man who has lost his home or suffers intermittent hunger will find no consolation in the fact that his condition occurs infrequently in American society; his hardships are real and must be an important concern for policy-makers." In fact, the condition is not so infrequent in America. One out of every six Americans (46 million) lived in poverty in 2010, an increase of almost three million since 2009. That was the highest number of people in poverty since the Census Bureau began keeping track in 1958. The poverty line as defined by the federal government for a family of four in 2010 was $22,314. For a family of three, poverty is defined as having an income of less than $18,310; for a family of two, it is an income of below $14,570. The federal government has determined that these amounts are required to sustain a minimum standard of living in America. In addition, more than a third of the U.S. population (103 million) in 2010 was living on a "low income," what the federal government cites as an income of less than $44,000 for a family of four. As of December 2011, the U.S. Census Bureau said that one in two people was poor or had low income. The reality on the ground is that half of the U.S. population is financially insecure and struggling at a scale not seen since the 1930s. Douglas MacKinnon, a former writer for Ronald Reagan, George Bush, and Bob Dole, cannot understand the silence on this issue. He wrote in *The New York Times* in March 2012, "We tend to punish, ignore or fear those who live in hopeless despair" and urged leaders to understand what this is like. "Learn about lives without heat, electricity, a phone, subway money or adequate medical care ... poverty remains one of the unsolved tragedies of our time."

MacKinnon, in his moving memoir *Rolling Pennies in the Dark*, wrote: "Poverty is not a state of mind. It's real. It's relentless. It's cruel. And if you don't figure a way out, it will eventually defeat you mentally. It will defeat you physically. And then, finally, when you think you can take no more, poverty will gleefully lead you to the edge of the abyss and dare you to jump. Tragically, many do."

What is poverty? Sister Maureen Joyce, former head of Catholic Charities of the Albany, N.Y., diocese, wrote that it is "a woman trying to escape domestic violence and changes her identity to reduce the risk of being tracked down by her abuser. But if she does, she will lose her professional credentials and will have difficulty making enough money to support her children. A man with lung cancer [who] accepts hospice services and inevitable death after he and his wife learn that his Medicare drug plan has reached a limit and won't cover recommended therapy. The couple can't afford the $710 per prescription." Poverty could be "a counselor [who] tries to get a child in a family with a three-generation history of homelessness to understand that constantly moving is not a normal way of life." Maybe it is similar to the plight of 8-month-old Shamal Jackson, who died in New York City from low birth weight, poor nutrition, and a viral infection from poverty and homelessness. It was never learned what brought him to that state. The mother and her son "slept in shelters with strangers, in hospitals, in welfare hotels, in the welfare office, and in the subways he and his mother rode late at night when there was no place to go. In the richest nation on earth he never slept in an apartment or house" (Edelman, 1992, 83). Edelman also wrote about an out-of-control kindergartener who fights and curses and never does his homework, whose mother has emotional and drug problems, and whose older brother—involved with violent crimes—teaches him how to smoke marijuana.

These are just a few examples of the millions of Americans who live in poverty. In Albany, a city near my hometown, 42 percent of the children live in poverty. Nearby, in Schenectady, N.Y., more than 40 percent of households pay more than 35 percent of their income on rent, which is defined as unaffordable by the federal government. According to HUD, "families who pay more than 30 percent of their income for housing are considered cost burdened and may have difficulty affording necessities such as food, clothing, transportation and medical care. An estimated 12 million renter and homeowner households now pay more than 50 percent of their annual incomes for housing, and a family with one full-time worker earning the minimum wage cannot afford the local fair-market rent for a two-bedroom apartment anywhere in the United States." Local social services agencies and nonprofits cannot come close to meeting the demand.

Jacob Riis, the Danish journalist who was the first to chronicle urban poverty beginning in the late 1880s, wrote that "the slum is the measure of civilization." Among industrialized nations, only Turkey and Mexico have higher rates of poverty than the U.S. According to civil rights icon Jesse Jackson: "Fifty million people lacked access to adequate food at some time in 2009. Nearly 18 million lived in households where one or more persons had to skip meals because of lack of food. Forty million received food stamp benefits each month. Fifty-one million lacked health coverage in 2009 ... and one in three African-American children now lives in families that have trouble providing for them." One in five families earns less than $15,000 per year. Sheldon Danziger, director of the National Poverty Center at the University of Michigan, said that "among rich countries, the U.S. is exceptional. We are exceptional in our tolerance of poverty." Interestingly, Danziger said that Canada has the same child poverty rate as the U.S., but after government taxes, benefits, and other social programs are factored in, its child poverty rate falls to 13.1 percent while the U.S. rate stays at 23.1 percent.

Of course, poverty is not confined to inner-city neighborhoods or the nonworking. Nationwide, among families with children, nearly half of all those on food stamps—47 percent—are working.

Lack of opportunity. Significant changes have led to our current situation. "In the early twentieth century the vast majority of both black and white low-income families were intact. The two-parent, nuclear family was the predominant family form in the late nineteenth and early twentieth century" for black families, and most woman-headed families were widowed (Wilson 1987, 63-64).

Professor William Julius Wilson, an eminent sociologist at Harvard University, has extensively studied this trend. Wilson has received 41 honorary degrees and was a MacArthur Prize Fellow from 1987 to 1992. He is a recipient of the 1998 National Medal of Science, the highest scientific honor in the United States. Wilson "makes the case that the focus should be on promoting work opportunities and alleviating poverty concentration rather than simply fighting racism or promoting punitive policies" (Venkatesh 2009). Wilson expounded on that theory:

> He argues that many years of exposure to similar situations can create responses that look as if they express individual will or active preference when they are, in fact, adaptions or resigned responses to racial exclusion ... Parents in segregated communities who have had experiences [with discrimination and disrespect] may transmit to children, through the process of socialization, a set of beliefs about what to expect from life and how one should respond to circumstances .... In the process children may acquire a disposition to interpret the way the world works that reflects a strong sense that other members of society disrespect them because they are black ... Three generations of black ghetto dwellers have been relying on welfare and sporadic work and doing so in isolation from the mainstream. It is folly to believe that some distinctive behavior, value, or outlooks have not arisen as a consequence. (Venkatesh 2009)

Therefore, as Wilson and countless other professionals have repeatedly pointed out, the benefits that jobs programs and vocational training have on the cultural front cannot be understated. Those employment mechanisms, however, are seriously underfunded. In *Why America Lost the War on Poverty – and How to Win It*, author Frank Stricker emphasized that most antipoverty approaches are futile without the presence (or creation) of good jobs. "Stated somewhat crudely, increasing employment will reduce the number of people who might promote or even condone deviant behavior. Change might not occur overnight, and it may not be wholesale, but it will take place" (Venkatesh 2009).

Writer Jason DeParle wrote that, based on "at least five large studies in recent years," Americans are less upwardly mobile than comparable nations:

> A project led by Markus Jantti, an economist at a Swedish university, found that 42 percent of American men raised in the bottom fifth

of incomes stay there as adults. That shows a level of persistent disadvantage much higher than in Denmark (25 percent) and Britain (30 percent)—a country famous for its class constraints. Meanwhile, just 8 percent of American men at the bottom rose to the top fifth. That compares with 12 percent of the British and 14 percent of the Danes. Despite frequent references to the United States as a classless society, about 62 percent of Americans (male and female) raised in the top fifth of incomes stay in the top two-fifths, according to research by the Economic Mobility Project of the Pew Charitable Trusts. Similarly, 65 percent born in the bottom fifth stay in the bottom two-fifths." (DeParle 2012)

At the most selective schools, 74 percent of the entering class comes from the quarter of households that have the highest socioeconomic status, and only 3 percent come from the bottom quarter. This illustrates the fact that the U.S. is more class-bound than the rest of the Western world.

New York Times columnist and Nobel Prize-winning economist Paul Krugman, in 2012, lamented the change in fortunes of a large segment of society:

Adjusted for inflation, entry-level wages of male high school graduates have fallen 23 percent since 1973. Meanwhile, employment benefits have collapsed. In 1980, 65 percent of recent high-school graduates working in the private sector had health benefits, but by 2009, that was down to 29 percent. So we have become a society in which less educated men have great difficulty finding jobs with decent wages and good benefits. Yet somehow we're supposed to be surprised that such men have become less likely to participate in the work force or get married, and conclude that there must have been some mysterious moral collapse caused by snooty liberals. And [political scientist Charles] Murray also tells us that working class marriages, when they do happen, have become less happy; strange to say, money problems will do that.

Unfinished work. We know that massive unemployment is bad for present and future generations and not just for the nonworking. If we learned anything from the 1930s, it was that governments cannot ignore this fact. In the belief that it is morally reprehensible in a country of such abundance, America greatly limited poverty during the twentieth century through federal legislation. More than 35 percent of all elderly persons lived in poverty in the 1960s. They were the poorest age group in 1959, with more than one in three poor. Yet, from 1959 to 1973, American federal programs cut poverty in half. Furthermore, with revisions to the Social Security Act in 1972 that indexed senior citizens' benefits to inflation, more than 1.7 million elderly persons were moved out of poverty in three years (Rusk 1999, 101). Today, if Social Security were taken away, 47 percent of seniors would be in poverty. In fact, senior citizens are the only age group that experienced a decline in poverty and an actual increase in income in 2009. This was possible because of Social Security and Medicare.

At the same time, the gap in wealth between old and young is at its largest ever. In 1984 when the Census Bureau started tracking the pertinent data, the age-based wealth gap was 10:1. By 2009, it had skyrocketed to 47:1. This can largely be explained by the boom and bust of the housing market, but it also highlights the fact that "over the past four decades, poverty rates for older householders fell by two thirds, while for younger householders they doubled" (Taylor 2011).

As we now know, however, the job was only partly completed. When we when look outside the senior citizen population, the picture is much dimmer. "The percentage of city populations living below the poverty level is well over 25 percent in the twenty largest cities" (Finley 2008, 59).

"In general, there has been little positive change in the plight of the poor for over a generation. The conditions poverty creates are dangerous, offensive, and infectious to America" (Finley 2008, 59). Most politicians, urban developer and planner William Finley wrote, pledge more police, cameras, and tougher sentencing, as if the prisons are not already overflowing. "Until the problems of these center city breeding grounds are addressed in a positive, creative, and uplifting way, they will remain a blight on the urban landscape and a black mark on our collective conscience."

In the summer of 1967, riots erupted across America, and many of the major cities' poorer sections were burned and looted. Over the first nine months of 1967, rioting broke out in 128 American cities, some of which required the services of the state police. Eight of those cities called in the National Guard. In the wake of Detroit's violence, Mayor Jerome Cavanaugh said, "It looks like Berlin in 1945." For many in America and the rest of world, the televised images elicited feelings of shock and revulsion. Viewers must have wondered: How could the beacon of the world, the country of freedom and opportunity, create such a violent and angry segment of the population?

The Kerner Commission, named after former Illinois governor Otto Kerner, was created by President Lyndon Johnson in 1968 to find out the answers to three questions regarding the riots of 1967: What happened? Why did it happen? and What can be done to prevent it from happening again? The commission found that the riots resulted from frustration at the lack of economic opportunity. Ultimately, the commission wrote, "To pursue our present course will involve the continuing polarization of the American community and, ultimately, the destruction of basic democratic values." The conditions that encouraged the riots were simple and obvious to those involved: the lack of economic opportunity and racism.

To illustrate, Detroit lost 134,000 manufacturing jobs between 1947 and 1963, just as some 200,000 black Southerners moved north to escape the Jim Crow laws and with the hopes of greater opportunities. As Joshua Zeitz wrote in *American Heritage:*

> The black newcomers, who were always the last to be hired and the first to be fired, faced job and wage discrimination while the industrial job base that had helped previous waves of migrants shrank. All told, by the mid-1960s black unemployment rates were at 10 percent in New York, 17 percent in Chicago, 20 percent in Cleveland, and 39 percent in Detroit ... The riots were the product of despair. Black Americans who worked hard and played by the rules were being systematically denied the opportunity to share in the affluence and abundance of postwar America. "They tell us about that pie in the sky, but that pie in the sky is too damn high," said one black rioter in Newark, New Jersey. In the aftermath of that insurrection, which took place only a few days before Detroit's (in 1967), the poet Amiri Baraka told a state commission that "the

poorest black man in Newark, in America, knows how white people live. We have television sets; we see movies. We see the fantasy and the reality of white America every day." (Zeitz 2007)

The Kerner Commission made a set of sweeping recommendations aimed at stamping out inequality, many of which were never implemented. In fact, data suggest that poverty is more concentrated in the inner cities than ever before. A key witness invited to appear before the Kerner Commission was Dr. Kenneth B. Clark, a distinguished scholar of the City University of New York. Referring to the reports of earlier riot commissions, he said: "I read that report ... of the 1919 riot in Chicago, and it is as if I were reading the report of the investigating committee on the Harlem riot of '35, the report of the investigating committee on the Harlem riot of '43, the report of the McCone Commission on the Watts riot. I must again in candor say to you members of this Commission—it is a kind of Alice in Wonderland—with the same moving picture re-shown over and over again, the same analysis, the same recommendations, and the same inaction."

The facts indicate, therefore, that the 103 million new Americans since 1968 have been denied the America that Robert F. Kennedy and Martin Luther King Jr. envisioned for them: a society more fair and just, where poverty is not endemic and where citizens could fully enjoy the fruits of their labor. The revolution that began in America in 1968 that looked toward the future for fulfillment of America's manifest destiny of a "city upon a hill" has fallen short. The reasons for the social unrest of those days have not been resolved. The saying goes that those who don't learn from history are bound to repeat it. Can that really be possible in our information age?

Martin Luther King Jr. said the social crisis in America was "inseparable from an international emergency which involves the poor, the dispossessed, the exploited of the whole world." He said that "social peace must spring from economic justice" and "injustice anywhere is a threat to justice everywhere."

Concentrated Poverty. In 2004, according to University of Minnesota professor Edward Goetz, research in the 1980s in Columbus, Ohio, showed that concentrated poverty has more to do with the exodus of the middle class out of central cities than with the movement of the poor into those areas.

Briggs, the sociologist and planner from MIT, wrote, "Low-income people of color who are concentrated in high-poverty neighborhoods are prey to economic disinvestment and political neglect, exposed to crime, and isolated from good jobs, quality education, health services, and even essential amenities such as supermarkets" (Briggs 2005, 300). Most or many inner-city neighborhoods lack basic amenities, such as banks, grocery stores, neighborhood parks, and cultural centers. The isolation associated with these communities is devastating, and the number of poor living in neighborhoods of extreme poverty (where at least 40 percent of the population is at or below poverty) has increased by one-third since 2000. Over the last decade, concentrated poverty nearly doubled in Rust Belt areas. Elizabeth Kneebone of the Brooking Institution said that "places that used to be solidly working class in the '90s have fallen behind after two recessions." These islands of economic desolation include dilapidated housing, crime and social strife that make investment extremely difficult. Troubles are heightened and poverty is reinforced. Places such as New Haven, Conn., where the number of poor people living in neighborhoods of extreme poverty jumped by half since 2000, or Detroit and Toledo, where one out of every four people is living in an extremely impoverished neighborhood, are not isolated incidents. The same is true for El Paso, Texas; Baton Rouge, La.; and Jackson, Miss. The loss of manufacturing jobs has eliminated much of the opportunity once available. Options are limited or nonexistent (Goodman 2011). "Very poor neighborhoods face a whole host of challenges that come from concentrated disadvantage—from higher crime rates and poorer health outcomes to lower quality educational opportunities and weaker job networks," wrote Kneebone. "A poor person or family in a very poor neighborhood must then deal not only with the challenges of individual poverty, but also with the added burdens that stem from the place in which they live."

"To be poor and Hispanic or poor and black is, in general, to be isolated from mainstream society" (Rusk 1999, 107). Echoing the "It Takes a Village" proverb, Rusk wrote in *Inside Game Outside Game* that it takes a family, a neighborhood, and school to raise a child successfully. He added that schools and neighborhoods need to be correspondingly stronger to compensate for weak families. "American society generally functions in a way that fulfills that formula for many poor white children ... However, those with the weakest families are consigned overwhelmingly to the weakest neighborhoods and the weakest schools. High-poverty ghettos, barrios, and slums are substantially the outcomes of the middle-class dispersion and disinvestment promoted by the sprawl machine. Such high-poverty neighborhoods themselves—and the neighborhood schools that struggle to serve them—become the poverty machine for the next generation" (Rusk 1999, 125).

"More than a third of black children live in poverty; more than 70 percent are born to unwed mothers; and by the time they reach their mid-30s, a majority of black men without a high school diploma has spent time in prison...Black children can't wait for Washington to get its act together (Herbert 2010c).

Khalil Muhammad, director of the Schomburg Center for Research in Black Culture, believes that this is a problem with social and institutional roots that must be addressed through the collective effort of society. It's been done before. He wrote in *The New York Times* in 2012 regarding the waves of poor white immigrants in the early twentieth century: "Violent white neighborhoods were flooded with social workers, police reformers and labor activists committed to creating better jobs and building a social welfare net. White on white violence fell slowly but steadily in proportion to economic development and crime prevention." In other words, collective effort worked, and that effort was never fully repeated for minority communities. Harvard economist William Ripley wrote at the turn of the twentieth century, "The [white] horde now descending upon our shores is densely ignorant, yet dull and superstitious withal; lawless, with a disposition to criminality." However, "they are fellow passengers on our ship of state and the health of the nation depends upon the preservation of the vitality of the lower classes."

Culture of deprivation. It should be noted that, "today, social scientists are rejecting the notion of a monolithic and unchanging culture of poverty. And they attribute destructive attitudes and behavior not to inherent moral character but to sustained racism and isolation" (Cohen 2010). Robert J. Sampson, a Harvard sociologist, has his own take on culture, what he calls "shared understandings." Sampson, who has studied inequality, said the dominant focus is on "structures" of poverty. "But he added that the reason a neighborhood turns into a 'poverty trap' is also related to a common perception of the way people in a community act and think. When people see graffiti and garbage, do they find it acceptable or see serious disorder? Do they respect the legal system or have a high level of 'moral cynicism,' believing that 'laws were made to be broken'" (Cohen 2010)? As Patricia Cohen noted in *The New York Times*, professionals in the poverty field have started to conclude that "programs that promote marriage without changing economic and social conditions are unlikely to work."

Geoffrey Canada, the man behind the enormously successful "cradle to college" Harlem Children's Zone and the Promise Academy, said: "Imagine growing up in a community where your cousins, your uncle, your father, everybody has gone to jail. That's been the normal experience. Now you're nine years old, and you're trying to figure out what it means to be a nine year old in Harlem. Well, pretty quickly you're going to come to believe that going to jail is no big deal" (Tough 2008, 264).

Politician and sociologist Daniel Patrick Moynihan's famous 1965 study, *The Negro Family: The Case for National Action*, concluded that the "pathology" of many ghetto families with high rates of illegitimacy, divorce, and single motherhood was the direct result of slavery and racism, and it was the responsibility of the nation as a whole to address the situation. Even conservative scholar and social scientist Charles Murray, along with William Julius Wilson, concluded that "the dysfunction of ghetto families was the result of decades—generations—of discrimination, isolation, and cultural decay, as well as one of the most cataclysmic shifts in the economy in American history" (Tough 2008, 33).

Referring to America, Galbraith wrote in *The Affluent Society (1958)* that "the survival of poverty is remarkable" and "a disgrace." Similarly, Michael Harrington, in *The Other America,* called poverty an "outrage and a scandal." According to Bill Barnes of the National League of Cities, a nonprofit advocacy organization, the 2010 U.S. poverty rate was the highest in the country since 1994. Even though the poverty rate was 22.2 percent in 1960, it dropped rapidly and significantly to 12.1 percent ten years later due to governmental intervention. Since 1970, the rate has been between about 11 percent and 15 percent. Barnes further noted that "even less attention is paid to the rural cities where the rate is 21.8 percent. This is the highest poverty rate of all major categories of places. The United States is far more affluent today than in 1960 or 1970."

As Finley, the developer, wrote: "It should be obvious that poverty is everyone's problem. It will not go away if ignored; only fester and get worse. It will never be obliterated unless regional, state, and national leaders accept the need for searching out solutions as their challenge." As David Brooks reported in *The New York Times* in July 2007, "You have to holistically change the environment that structures behavior" (Finley 2008, 134). Based on his decades of research, Rusk wrote that only a metropolitanwide community effort and funding will eventually save the people in the worst neighborhoods from generations of poverty and misery. "No center city should be shouldered with the sole responsibility of erasing their blighted and dangerous neighborhoods" (Finley 2008, 136).

A Center for American Progress report released in April 2007 titled "From Poverty to Prosperity: A National Strategy to Cut Poverty in Half" found that child poverty costs more than $500 billion a year in lost productivity and increased health care and criminal justice expenditures. Conversely, implementing the principal recommendations from the report could cut poverty in half in ten years and cost $90 billion a year. In response, the Center for American Progress Action Fund, the Coalition on Human Needs, and The Leadership Conference on Civil and Human Rights launched "Half in Ten," a campaign whose goal is to cut poverty in half in ten years. The Half in Ten website says, "Poverty is not intractable despite (inaccurate) common stereotypes. The U.S. poverty rate fell by more than 40 percent between 1964 and 1973. By rebuilding our economy, creating good jobs, investing in families, and ensuring economic security, we can replicate this success and move millions into the middle class."

"We should expect adults to work and young people to stay in school and not have children before they are able to care for them. We should also expect that jobs be available to those who want to work, that full-time work provide a decent standard of living, that all children grow up in conditions which let them reach their full potential, and that a nation of opportunity should also be a nation of second chances ... Economic opportunity has served as the foundation for citizenship and civic engagement throughout our nation's history...freedom and democracy are essentially meaningless for those who lack economic independence" (Center for American Progress 2007, 8, 10).

Instead of blaming the poor, Herbert Gans, award-winning scholar and author of *The War Against the Poor,* wrote:

> Standards of living, even for the very poor, have risen considerably in the last century, but rates of morbidity and mortality due to hypertension, heart disease, tuberculosis and many other chronic illnesses, homicide, and now AIDS, remain much higher among the poor than among working class and moderate income people, not to mention the higher income groups. Whether stereotyping and stigmatizing poor people as undeserving also exposes them to more illnesses and a shorter life expectancy is not yet fully known (although very possible). But even displaced workers who lose their jobs when their firms close begin after a period of unsuccessful job hunting to think that their unemployment is their own fault—and thus to treat themselves as undeserving. Eventually many become depressed and begin to share in the illnesses of the stigmatized. If the present erosion of jobs continues indefinitely and more people have to be banished from the labor force, they too will suffer more of the chronic illnesses of the poor, more dangerous lives, and a shorter life expectancy ... Only when Americans discover that labeling and blaming the poor only supply symptomatic temporary relief but solve nothing, can both undeservingness and poverty, as well as all the problems in their wake, be attacked. (Gans 1995, 102)

We must always remember that the enemy is ignorance. When a segment of society gives in to despair or hopelessness, there can be terrible consequences. Examples of this despair can be witnessed in those who lash out at the dominant cultural norms, show no respect for authority, and exhibit a blatant disregard for everyone. If we just look at the clear examples of this overseas, the translation is profound. Graffiti spray-painted on a small village school in Pakistan's Himalayan Mountains sums it up this way: "The time of arithmetic and poetry is past. Nowadays, my brothers, take your lessons from the Kalashnikov and rocket-propelled grenade" (Mortensen 2006, 241).

There is no difference between despair here or overseas. When that feeling sets in, when opportunity is inaccessible or at least perceived to be, consequences can be fatal. Greg Mortenson, author of *Three Cups of Tea* and *Stones into Schools,* was quoted in *Parade* magazine in April 2003, just as American ground forces were massing on the outskirts of Baghdad to assault the capital. He said: "If we try to resolve terrorism with military might and nothing else, then we will be no safer than we were before 9/11. If we truly want a legacy of peace for our children, we need to understand that this is a war that will ultimately be won with books, not with bombs" (Mortensen 2006, 301). We must remember that when addressing our own problems here at home. Increased police presence alone is not a substitute. To echo what John F. Kennedy once said, "Those who make peaceful revolution impossible make violent revolution inevitable."

Effect on children. There is no greater representation of innocence than that of a child. Children are our future, our hopes, our dreams, our inspiration, and also our most vulnerable. To have a child poverty rate of 20 percent, or one in five, in the wealthiest country on the planet is a tragedy beyond reason. The Annie E. Casey Foundation's "Kids Count" report, released in August 2011, revealed that childhood poverty rose dramatically in 38 states over the previous decade, reversing declines throughout the 1990s. And, according to a 2012 UNICEF report on child poverty in developed countries, "the U.S. ranks second on the scale of what economists call 'relative child poverty'—above Latvia, Bulgaria, Spain, Greece, and 29 others. Only Romania ranks higher, with 25.5 percent of its children living in poverty, compared with 23.1 percent in the U.S" (Knafo 2012). "Relative child poverty" is defined as a child living in a household where the disposable income is less than half of the national medium income. "The undeniable fact is that our children's future is shaped both by the values of their parents and the policies of our nation," according to the National Conference of Catholic Bishops Pastoral Letter of 1991.

In "A Thanksgiving Prayer to End Poverty in Our Lifetime," Marian Wright Edelman wrote: "What kind of nation, blessed to be the wealthiest in the world, lets one in five children be poor, with its children the poorest age group among us? This indefensible and preventable child poverty reflects a spiritual and values poverty far deeper than the eye can see and threatens the very meaning and future of America" (Edelman, 2009).

"A recent study by scholars at the Urban Institute focused on the dangerous effects of 'persistent poverty' so many children experience. It notes that nearly half of all children born into poverty will be persistently poor, meaning they will be poor for at least half of their childhoods. Further, it states that while just four percent of children born into non-poor families end up spending at least half their early adult years in poverty, 21 percent of children born poor will spend a significant amount of their early adulthood in poverty. These children have a range of worse adult outcomes than children born into higher-income families. Children who are born poor and live in persistent poverty are more likely to drop out of high school, experience teen pregnancy, and have unstable employment as young adults" (Edelman, 2010).

Conservative columnist David Brooks acknowledged this in a February 2012 article in *The New York Times*. "People who grow up in disrupted communities are more likely to lead disrupted lives as adults, magnifying disorder from one generation to the next," he wrote, adding that "social context is more powerful than we thought." Therefore, "this requires bourgeois paternalism: building organizations and structures that induce people to behave responsibly rather than irresponsibly and, yes, sometimes using government to do so. Social repair requires sociological thinking."

Professor Irwin Redlener of Columbia University's Mailman School of Public Health wrote in The Huffington Post in February 2012: "Today the necessity to address the economic challenges of profound poverty among children could not be more compelling. It is no longer only a matter of compassion and charity. Even the most hardened, empathy-challenged national leader needs to understand that children who don't fulfill their potential, or who lack a feasible path to educational attainment and economic productivity, may become serious liabilities with respect to U.S. prosperity—and influence—in the decades to come."

A 2010 Children's Defense Fund report, *Held Captive: Child Poverty in America,* stated that the nation is experiencing its highest child poverty rate since 1959. For poor children, though, poverty means more than lack of money. For them, it can be a life sentence of exile from the larger society. In Quitman County, Miss., the defense fund report's authors made a startling discovery: Enriching experiences for children are so meager and government aid so spotty that after-school tutoring and reading programs in Quitman and three other Mississippi Delta counties are financed by what is essentially foreign aid. That aid comes from the Bernard van Leer Foundation of the Netherlands, which focuses on children and families in "socially and economically difficult circumstances."

Betty Ward Fletcher, a member of a Jackson, Miss., consulting firm, was hired by the Dutch foundation to help it design a program in the state, called Children's Villages, to help youngsters age 5 to 14. "Some of its people wondered why it should be (operating) in the most affluent country in the world, but they decided the reality is, we have poor children in this country who are denied the opportunity to be all they can be." Fletcher spoke of one 10-year-old Mississippi boy who would consistently break into homes, steal food, play on the computer, and then leave (Cass 2010).

"Research shows that young people are strongly influenced by their peers. In neighborhoods and schools with high concentrations of delinquent youngsters, more youth get into trouble than would be expected given their individual backgrounds. Simply put, even 'good' kids can turn 'bad' if the setting they are in is heavily comprised of troubled youth and the social climate is negative" (Fischer 1996, 197). "Move a child from a chaotic and impoverished school to an ordered and affluent one, and more often than not that same child will learn more; he or she will become 'smarter.' Move a job seeker from a region with a 10 percent unemployment rate to one with a 3 percent rate and more often than not that same job seeker will land a better paying position. Move a family headed by working but poor parents from a society with minimal family support to one with family allowances, universal medical care, and other assistance, and more often than not the children in that same family will be healthier, do better in school, and contribute more as adults" (Fischer 1996, 207). Context matters.

The "King of Rock 'n' Roll," Elvis Presley, highlighted all too well the effects of generational poverty. In his 1969 comeback hit "In the Ghetto," he sings about a young boy growing up with nothing and then asks if we're too blind to see what is needed. "People, don't you understand/the child needs a helping hand/or he'll grow to be an angry young man someday."

Chapter 3
Social Equity

"The point is, ladies and gentleman, that greed,
for lack of a better word, is good.
Greed is right. Greed works. Greed clarifies,
cuts through, and captures the essence of evolutionary spirit."

—Gordon Gekko in *Wall Street*

THAT QUOTE IS HARDLY FICTION. Gekko's speech had been retooled from one originally given by convicted inside trader Ivan Boesky (Cowie 2010, 311).

Martin Luther King Jr. once said that any religion that is not concerned about the poor and disadvantaged, "the slums that damn them, the economic conditions that strangle them and the social conditions that cripple them is a spiritually moribund religion awaiting burial."

Economic growth has been pursued blindly, efficiently, and with devastating speed. By doing so, we accept vast social inequalities. "Social, moral and ecological ills were sustained in the interest of economic growth; indeed adherents to the faith proposed that only more growth could resolve such ills" (McNeill 2000, 334-336).

"We must realize that when basic needs have been met, human development is primarily about being more, not having more" (Speth 2008, 209). As the authors of *The Spirit Level* wrote:

Despite the modern impression of the permanence and universality of inequality, in the time-scale of human history and prehistory, it is the current highly unequal societies which are exceptional. For over 90 percent of our existence as human beings we lived, almost exclusively, in highly egalitarian societies. For perhaps as much as the last two million years, covering the vast majority of the time we have been 'anatomically modern' (that is to say, looking much as we do now), human beings lived in remarkably egalitarian hunting and gathering—or foraging—groups. Modern inequality arose and spread with the development of agriculture. The characteristics which would have been selected as successful in more egalitarian societies would have been very different from those selected in dominance hierarchies. (Pickett 2009, 205)

Robert Frank, an economist at Cornell University, wrote in his book *Falling Behind: How Rising Inequality Harms the Middle Class* (2007) that in 1998, even though the American economy was booming as never before, one family in sixty-eight had filed for bankruptcy—four times the rate in the early 1980s before the most dramatic rises in inequality. Frank also found that bankruptcy rates rose most in parts of the U.S. where inequality had risen most.

When referring to families in poverty, some self-righteously say "Get to work." But 55 percent of children living in poverty have at least one parent working full time, and the numbers are growing.

According to the Institute for Policy Studies and United for a Fair Economy, CEO pay is now 350 times the average worker's, up from 50 times the pay from 1960-1985. And what of senior citizens? What would happen to them if Medicare were repealed? Millions of Americans are just one layoff, one health crisis, or one family emergency from poverty's door.

According to data from the Economic Policy Institute, during the five years from 2000 to 2005, productivity—the measure of output of the economy per worker employed—grew by 16.6 percent. Over the same period, the median family's income slid by 2.9 percent. While productivity increased steadily during the last third of a century, median wages were stagnant or grew very little. Workers did not share fully in the economic gains produced by increases in productivity.

From 1992 to 2005, the pay of CEOs of major companies rose by 186 percent. The equivalent figure for median hourly wages was 7.2 percent.

Since at least the 1980s the U.S. has encouraged private wealth accumulation at the expense of parks, schools, infrastructure, and environment. Robert Kennedy pointed out that many of the things that make us healthier and happier are excluded from our measure of well-being:

the safety of our children in the streets, the quality of their education, the integrity of our politicians, the strength of our relationships.

Woodrow Wilson said, "If there are men in this country big enough to own the government of the United States, they are going to own it."

Krugman, the columnist and economist, pointed out that at the beginning of the Great Depression, income inequality was very high. Then, between 1929 and 1947, real wages for workers in manufacturing rose 67 percent while real income for the richest 1 percent of Americans fell 17 percent. Two major forces drove those trends: the unionization of major manufacturing sectors, and the public policies of the New Deal that were sparked by the Great Depression, which led to the rise of the middle class. Accordingly, "the growing spending power of everyday Americans spurred the postwar boom from 1947 to 1973. Real wages rose 81 percent and the income of the richest 1 percent rose 38 percent. Growth was widely shared, but income inequality continued to drop. Since around 1990 there has been a massive re-polarization of incomes in America between the wealthiest 1% of the population and everyone else" (Creamer 2009). The Center on Budget and Policy Priorities reported that "fully two-thirds of all income gains during the last economic expansion (2002 to 2007) flowed to the top 1 percent of the population. And that, in turn, is one of the chief reasons why the median income for ordinary Americans actually dropped by $2,197 per year since 2000."

Theodore Roosevelt once said "the citizens of the United States must control the mighty commercial forces which they themselves call into being." It doesn't seem as though we've been very successful. Scholar Les Leopold, the author of *The Looting of America*, wrote an article in The Huffington Post in 2010 titled "How to Earn $900,000 an Hour: The Rise of Wall Street Billionaires and the New Class War." He wrote that the top 25 hedge fund managers of 2009 each made $1 billion and paid only a 15 percent tax rate because their income is treated as capital gains (Leopold 2010). According to *AR* magazine, which follows hedge funds, John Paulson, a hedge fund manager in New York City, made $4.9 billion in 2010 alone.

"An imbalance between rich and poor," wrote Plutarch almost two thousand years ago, "is the oldest and most fatal ailment of all republics." Theodore Sorensen, former speech writer for President Kennedy, agreed. "If those who are left out, left behind, and left too little for their families to get by on resort to drugs or violence or crime, if their sense of desperation breeds contempt for a society in which they no longer have a vested interest, contempt for its laws and institutions, and in time contempt for human life itself, then the sense of community and common purpose essential to capitalism, democracy, and political and social stability are gone" (Sorensen 1996, 45).

We should heed the words of Franklin Roosevelt: "The first truth is that the liberty of a democracy is not safe if the people tolerate the growth of private power to a point where it becomes stronger than their democratic state itself. That, in its essence, is Fascism—ownership of government by an individual, by a group, or by any other controlling private power."

Segregation

Hubert Humphrey once said, "We must create a climate of shared interests between the needs, the hopes and the fears of the minorities, and the needs, the hopes and the fears of the majority."

According to the Kirwan Institute for the Study of Race and Ethnicity research, "In 1960, African-American families in poverty were 3.8 times more likely to be concentrated in high-poverty neighborhoods than poor whites. In 2000, they were 7.3 times more likely." That research presents examples of low-opportunity areas as compared to high-opportunity areas. For instance, in a low-opportunity area in Detroit in 2009:

- Fewer than 25 percent of students finish high school.
- More than 60 percent of the men will spend time in jail.
- There may soon be no bus service in some areas.
- It is difficult to attract jobs or private capital.
- It is not safe, and there are very few parks.
- It is difficult to get fresh food.

In a high-opportunity area:

- One hundred percent of students graduate, and 100 percent go to college.
- Most will not even drive by a jail.
- There is free bus service.

- It is relatively easy to attract capital.
- It is very safe, and there are great parks.
- It is easy to get fresh food.

In 2008, almost 40 percent of public school students were minority, roughly double the percentage during the 1960s. Most startlingly, the award-winning book *The Geography of Opportunity* noted that with a steady decline from the 1950s through the 1980s, black segregation in schools has actually increased to levels not seen in thirty years. "In the most segregated metropolitan areas, between district segregation represented less than 4 percent of all segregation in 1970, compared with an astonishing 84 percent in the year 2000. A growing share of black and Hispanic students, particularly in the big-city school systems, attend schools that are virtually all nonwhite, characterized by high student poverty rates, limited school resources, less experienced and credentialed teachers, less educated parents, high student turnover, overcrowded and disorderly classrooms, and a host of health and other problems" (Briggs 2005, 32).

"America's metropolitan areas are both very sprawling and very segregated by race and class, a pattern that is especially apparent when U.S. cities and suburbs are compared with those of Europe or other wealthy regions around the world" (Briggs 2005, 17). "Rising inequality is beginning to produce a two-tiered society in America in which the more affluent citizens live lives fundamentally different from the middle and lower income groups. This divide decreases a sense of community," wrote Wilson, the Harvard professor, in 2011.

Segregation rates among blacks and whites remain distressingly high in absolute terms, particularly in the Rust Belt cities of the Northeast and Midwest. As Brown University sociology professor John Logan described the decline, "It's at a rate that my grandchildren, when they die, will still not be living in an integrated society" (Briggs 2005, 24).

Sprawl has been devastating to inner-city families without the means to escape, and their neighborhoods. Decentralization, or job sprawl, the increased distance between local jobs and housing locations, accompanied the erosion of an economy characterized by heavily unionized, high-wage, blue-collar factory jobs concentrated in central cities. According to HUD, by the mid-1990s, about 70 percent of all jobs in the manufacturing, retailing, and wholesaling sectors—which tend to have many entry-level positions—were in the suburbs, and suburban job growth and business expansion continued to outstrip that in cities throughout the decade. Furthermore, many suburban jobs are inaccessible by public transportation (Briggs 2005, 34).

"The segregation of metropolitan areas by race and class shifted somewhat in the 1990s, bringing the risks long associated with inner cities into older suburbs as the latter became more racially and economically diverse. Poverty concentration declined in central cities, but the long-run trend, between 1970 and 2000, was one of wider class divide: segregation by income increased sharply for both blacks and whites" (Briggs 2005, 35).

Myron Orfield, drawing on his experience in the Minnesota State Legislature, suggested that central cities and at-risk suburbs represent a natural coalition because changing the fiscal inequities and race and class exclusion associated with our current development patterns are essential. "The key arena, says Orfield, is state legislatures, where the authority over local taxation, land use, transportation and infrastructure investments, and more are concentrated in America's system of federalism" (Briggs 2005, 319).

Recent gains in racial integration have been limited. Black-white segregation remains generally high in areas of the Northeast and Midwest. In those areas, there is slow population growth, and white flight from increasingly minority neighborhoods is still common.

After reviewing the 2010 Census data, Logan, the professor, wrote: "The result for black-white segregation is both surprising and disappointing. Black-white segregation reached its peak around 1960 as a result of the extreme ghettoization of incoming black migrants from the South in major cities of the Northeast and Midwest. Between 1980 and 2000 there were signs of progress, though it was slow—and slower in the 1990s than in the 1980s."

Change has come almost to a full stop. Even "in the least segregated metros, those with the smallest black populations, there has been an increase in segregation," Logan wrote. Regarding housing policy, he said that "another policy implication regards the enforcement of laws against discrimination in housing. These data alone don't tell us the causes of segregation, but they are an exclamation point in the debate on fair housing policy. It shouldn't be possible anymore for people to argue that this is a problem that is going away naturally, and all the hype about a postracial society is likely to deflate. Housing and civil rights advocates continually demonstrate that a significant source of segregation continues to be discrimination against minority home seekers. The new findings should reinforce their argument" (Baum 2010).

In 2011, *Salon* magazine featured a story on America's ten most segregated cities (population more than 500,000), After analyzing 2010 Census data, author Daniel Denvir wrote: "Decades after the end of Jim Crow, and three years after the election of America's first black president, the United States remains a profoundly segregated country ... We may think of segregation as a matter of ancient Southern history: lunch counter sit-ins, bus boycotts and Ku Klux Klan terrorism. But as the census numbers remind us, Northern cities have long had higher rates of segregation than in the South, where strict Jim Crow laws kept blacks closer to whites, but separate from them. Where you live has a big impact on the education you receive, the safety on your streets, and the social networks you can leverage."

Segregation is only decreasing slowly, "although the dividing lines are shifting as middle-income blacks, Latinos and Asians move to once all-white suburbs—whereupon whites often move away, turning older suburbs into new, if less distressed, ghettos" (Denvir 2011).

According to Denvir's article, Milwaukee was rated the country's most segregated city, followed by New York City, Chicago, Detroit, Cleveland, Buffalo, St. Louis, Cincinnati, Philadelphia, and Los Angeles. Like most of these deindustrialization-battered Rust Belt cities, segregated urban blacks were disproportionately hurt as jobs and the tax base suburbanized and moved away. Zoning ordinances, restrictive covenants, and the historic practices of realtors exacerbated problems. In addition, most or all of the above mentioned cities have much greater political fragmentation, meaning individual city jurisdictions and school districts as opposed to county-wide boundaries and school systems, which typically lessen segregation.

There is not enough land to just keep moving farther out to avoid racial integration. Meanwhile, the largest increases in poverty have been in the suburbs. Interestingly, Thomas Sugrue, a University of Pennsylvania sociology professor, wrote in a *New York Times* article: "In the Detroit metropolitan area, blacks are moving into so-called secondhand suburbs:

established communities with deteriorating housing stock that are falling out of favor with younger white homebuyers. If historical trends hold, these suburbs will likely shift from white to black—and soon look much like Detroit itself, with resegregated schools, dwindling tax bases and decaying public services." Using a historical perspective, Sugrue, in 2011 added:

> Blacks and whites alike wanted to own their own homes and gardens, find better schools for their children and live on safe streets. But unlike whites, blacks did not have the freedom to move where they pleased. Detroit had many all-white suburbs with affordable housing, but qualified black homeowners could not get mortgages to move there. Whites, meanwhile, benefited from enormous homeownership subsidies through the Federal Housing Administration and the Veterans Administration; blacks did not, at least until the late 1960s, when local, state and federal laws that forbade housing discrimination were passed. The private sector played its part, too: loans and mortgages to minorities or for houses in racially mixed or black neighborhoods were deemed "actuarially unsound," too risky an investment for lenders and builders. Even after the antidiscrimination laws of the late 1960s, real estate brokers surreptitiously maintained the color line in housing through "steering," in which they directed whites to "white neighborhoods" and blacks to minority communities or places undergoing racial transition.

Although it decreased overall, as revealed in an analysis of 2010 Census data, segregation is still pervasive and not necessarily voluntary. According to an article on segregation by Yale professor Douglas S. Massey and George Washington University professor Gregory D. Squires:

> More than 10 million families will lose their homes to foreclosure before the housing market "clears" according to Credit Suisse ... Meanwhile, research by a variety of organizations ranging from the Federal Reserve to the Center for Community Change reveals that subprime loans were concentrated in, and specifically targeted to, low-income, minority neighborhoods. As a result, foreclosures

have fallen heaviest on the most disadvantaged segments of society. To illustrate, when subprime lending peaked in 2006, just 18 percent of white borrowers received subprime loans compared to 54 percent of African Americans. An unfortunate irony, as the *Wall Street Journal* reported in 2007, is that over 60 percent of subprime borrowers had credit scores that qualified them for prime loans, underscoring the discriminatory nature of the marketing ... Discriminatory lending patterns do not happen by chance. As the National Community Reinvestment Coalition has reported, in recent years racial minorities and minority communities were deliberately targeted by predatory lenders for subprime lending. The more segregated a metropolitan area is, of course, the easier it is to find exploitable clients. Segregation creates natural pockets of financially unsophisticated, historically underserved, poor minority homeowners who are ripe for exploitation. It is no surprise to learn, therefore, that a recent study published in the American Sociological Review found that the level of black-white segregation was the single strongest predictor of the number and rate of foreclosures across U.S. metropolitan area more powerful than the overall level of subprime lending, the degree of overbuilding, the extent of home price inflation, the relative creditworthiness of borrowers, the degree of coverage under the Community Reinvestment Act, or the extent of local government regulation. (Squires 2010)

It is predicted that the United States will lose its white majority status by 2045; by 2100, there will be virtually no major city in the entire world with a white majority. Minority babies outnumbered white newborns in 2011 for the first time in U.S. history. Therefore, to ensure national unity and security, shouldn't citizens of our present time desire to ensure *all* of our nation's children's have a bright future, as secure as possible, and not allow such persistent segregation, poverty, or discrimination to continue (Peirce, 2011e).

Wilson, the Harvard professor and sociologist, noted in *The Truly Disadvantaged*, that "despite a high rate of poverty in ghetto neighborhoods throughout the first half of the twentieth century" things were quite different.

"Rates of inner-city joblessness, teenage pregnancies, out-of-wedlock births, female-headed families, welfare dependency, and serious crime were significantly lower than in later years and did not reach catastrophic proportions until the mid-1970s." In the 1940s and '50s, whites frequented inner-city taverns and nightclubs. People were not fearful of walking the streets at night, despite overwhelming poverty in these areas. There was joblessness but nowhere near the proportions of unemployment that have affected inner cities since the 1970s. There were single-parent families, but they were a small minority of black families. Even so, they tended to be incorporated into extended family networks and headed by middle-aged women who were widowed, divorced, or separated but not by unwed teenage or young adult mothers. "In short, unlike the present period, inner-city communities prior to 1960 exhibited the features of social organization— including a sense of community, positive neighborhood identification, and explicit norms and sanctions against aberrant behavior" (Wilson 1987, 3). In the 1940s, 1950s, and even the 1960s:

> Lower-class, working-class, and middle-class black families all lived more or less in the same communities (albeit in different neighborhoods), sent their children to the same schools, availed themselves of the same recreational facilities, and shopped at the same stores. Whereas today's black middle-class professionals no longer tend to live in ghetto neighborhoods and have moved increasingly into mainstream occupations outside the black community, the black middle-class professionals of the 1940s and 1950s (doctors, teachers, lawyers, social workers, ministers) lived in higher-income neighborhoods of the ghetto and serviced the black community ... their very presence provided stability to inner-city neighborhoods and reinforced and perpetuated mainstream patterns of norms and behavior. (Wilson 1987, 7)

The transformation from a goods-producing economy with union wages and benefits to a service-based economy with minimal benefits and the relocation of many manufacturing centers has had a devastating effect on new inner-city residents. Another major setback for inner-city residents is that "essentially all of the national growth in entry-level and other low-education requisite jobs have accrued in the suburbs, exurbs, and non-metropolitan areas far removed from growing concentrations of poorly educated urban minorities" (Wilson 1987, 42). Recent studies have shown that working-class men (think construction workers) have much higher rates of unemployment, and that employment instability is a major factor in the rising divorce rate and consequently out-of-wedlock births. This correlates with an insightful article by law professors June Carbone and Naomi Cahn. In it, the authors stated that we have created "a society that writes off a high percentage of men through chronic unemployment and high rates of imprisonment for minor offenses ... What we really need to do is increase our investments in children, employment stability, and healthy communities and stop pretending that family structure is simply a matter of morals or will" (Cahn 2011).

Wilson concluded in *The Truly Disadvantaged* "that the problem of joblessness should be a top-priority item in any public policy discussion focusing on enhancing the status of families," and the most important factor in the rise of black female-headed families is the extraordinary rise in black male joblessness. "We have shown here that the decline in the incidence of intact marriages among blacks is associated with the declining economic status of black men" (Wilson 1987, 104, 105). Over and over again, the research points to a lack of jobs, economic opportunity, solid benefits and decent wages, therefore any governmental policy moving forward must at least recognize these factors in urban poverty and family fragmentation. Job training for the basic trades and technology sector would go a long way in relieving poverty-related dysfunction in society.

The American economy has changed significantly over the last fifty years as manufacturing has become narrowed and specialized, while the low-skill (minimally educated) sector of the job market has become increasingly scarce. In other words, it is increasingly difficult for a high school graduate or dropout to find decent work and a living wage. The underlying problem is that there are structural failures in the economy, and we cannot simply blame the victims. "The job market that is 'natural' to the rest of us cannot help those who do not use it because of lack of skills, education, or physical or mental shortfalls. We must get people to where they can take responsibility for themselves" (P. Edelman 2001, 202). The bottom line is that joblessness triggers a whole lot of problems. Wilson wrote in *When Work Disappears* (1997) that "a neighborhood in which people are poor and working is entirely different from a neighborhood in which people are poor and jobless."

Housing and Schools

In 2011 Marion Wright Edelman said, "We are experiencing a quiet but systematic rise in school segregation across the country."

"It is common sense that the quality of public schools and the quality of cities are impacted by one another but rarely, if ever, are educational and urban policies connected," said Bruce Katz of the Brookings Institution. According to a 2002 Bipartisan Millennial Housing Commission report, housing represents the single largest expense for most families, one-fifth of the nation's economy, and by far the main source of wealth for most families who own their own home. It has been calculated as the key to asset building for the millions of renter families who have little or no wealth. The federal income tax deduction for home mortgage interest and for local property tax payments represents a transfer of more than $126 billion a year to homeowners, most of whom are in the middle- and upper-income tax brackets; that is about five times the total spent on all housing programs for low- and moderate-income earners. "Subsidized" housing is the generic term for housing units, whether in the private market or under government or nonprofit management, in which financial subsidies go to either the developer, the landlord, the tenant, or the owner. Therefore, technically speaking, every homeowner who claims the mortgage interest and property tax deduction on his or her income tax return is living in subsidized housing (Briggs 2005, 323-324), not to mention the federal mortgage guarantees that keep interest rates low.

The relationship among housing, schools, neighborhoods, and future success is clear. "The socioeconomic status of the kids in the classroom is much more important than expenditures per pupil, class size, teacher experience, instructional materials, or competition from charter or private schools that are the typical focus of school reformers" (Rusk 2003, 132).

As sociologist James Coleman wrote in his landmark book *Equality of*

Educational Opportunity (1966), "The educational resources provided by a child's fellow students are more important for his achievement than are the resources provided by the school board." Furthermore, Coleman found that "the social composition of the student body is more highly related to achievement, independent of the students' own social background, than is any school factor."

The Century Foundation and scores of other studies have found that the socioeconomic status of pupils and classmates largely determines academic outcomes, that poor children learn best surrounded by middle-class classmates, and that middle-class pupils do just fine whether they have 5 percent to 25 percent low-income classmates (Rusk 2003, 132).

Summarizing an enormous body of research, a writer for the Century Foundation had the following observation:

> What makes a school good or bad is not so much the physical plant and facilities as the people involved in it—the students, the parents, the teachers. The portrait of the nation's high poverty schools is not just a racist or classist stereotype: high-poverty schools are often subject to negative peer influences; parents who are generally less active, exert less clout in school affairs, and garner fewer financial resources for the school; and teachers who tend to be less qualified, to have lower expectations, and to teach a watered down curriculum. Giving all students access to schools with a core of middle class students and parents will significantly raise the overall quality of schooling in America." (Kahlenberg 2003)

As a result, "while income is clearly linked to academic performance, a poor child is likely to fare better just by virtue of being in a more economically diverse environment. In one study, low-income students in heavily middle-class schools did better academically than middle-class students in high-poverty schools. In another study, low-income fourth grade students who attended more affluent schools had math test scores almost two years ahead of their low-income peers stuck in high-poverty schools" (Lerner 2011).

In 2011, Joe Nocera wrote in *The New York Times,* "Going back to the famous Coleman report in the 1960s, social scientists have contended—and unquestionably proved—that student socioeconomic backgrounds vastly outweigh what goes on in the school as factors in determining how much they learn. Richard Rothstein of the Economic Policy Institute lists dozens of reasons why this is so, from the more frequent illness and stress poor students suffer, to the fact that they don't hear large vocabularies that middle-class children hear at home." Therefore, Nocera wrote: "What needs to be acknowledged, however, is that school reform won't fix everything. Though some poor students will succeed, others will fail. Demonizing teachers for the failures of poor students, and pretending that reforming the schools is all that is needed, as the reformers tend to do, is both misguided and counterproductive."

Educational historian and author of the *Death and Life of the Great American School System* Diane Ravitch wrote that "as long as our society continues to tolerate high levels of child poverty and intense racial segregation, we will continue to have low performing students and 'failing' schools." The problem and solution are obvious. Ravitch wrote, "It's facile to blame schools and teachers, but more realistic to recognize that poverty is a reflection of economic conditions. Schools cannot create jobs, provide homes for the homeless, or change the economy."

According to Briggs (2005, 7), "whether measured by median family income, poverty rate, unemployment, or other indicators, the gap between cities and suburbs widened dramatically in the post-World War II period ... School failure is, if anything more closely tied to segregation by race and class than it was thirty years ago, because millions of families with the best housing choices have exited diverse central cities for more homogenous suburban school districts." The lack of attention to persistently high segregation is dangerous because it ignores the huge contribution that segregated living makes to inequality in education, employment, health, and other areas (Briggs 2005, 13). According to a 2011 *Times Union* (N.Y.) editorial, in more middle-class and affluent districts, particularly in suburbs, the graduation rate is often above 90 percent, compared with large cities and poorer districts where less than half the students graduate in four years.

"America's real urban problem is racial and economic segregation that has created an underclass in many of America's major urban areas" (Rusk 2003, 1). "As a result, today African-American and Latino students across the country attend more segregated schools than at any point in the last 20 years. At the same time, poverty in those schools has become more concentrated: Increasing numbers of students of color now go to schools that have a majority of low-income attendees. Children at these schools, research shows, tend to fare worse academically. In some recent, high profile cases, poor women have been charged with felonies for lying about their address to get their children into better, out of district schools" (Lerner 2011).

Bucking historical trends, some minorities moved out of inner cities and some whites moved in over a ten-year period beginning in 2000, according to 2010 Census data. Though that is positive news, it must be remembered that suburbs continued to grow much faster than repopulated cities and that segregation has not visibly changed much at all, particularly in the Northeast and Midwest.

At the same time, traditional development patterns of the last sixty years (large lots, spread-out housing, and car-reliant growth on the undeveloped fringes of metropolitan areas) have begun to frustrate even middle- and upper-income families who can afford to live at a safe distance from many of the problems of cities and older, at-risk suburbs. The long commutes; loss of surrounding open space; and wasteful, car-reliant lifestyle are wearing thin on many.

The author of *The Geography of Opportunity* wrote:

> The nation's current strategy for handling race and class differences at the local level is, paradoxically, what we might call containment-plus-sprawl. It is a strategy that disperses and subsidizes new development while concentrating social and economic advantage. This system permits, and in fiscal and other terms actually encourages, some communities to function as exclusive and exclusionary clubs. Consistent with these patterns, white Americans, who have the widest housing choices, report increasing tolerance of racial and ethnic diversity in principle but little enthusiasm for policies aimed at reducing racial inequality. Meanwhile, segregated jurisdictions obscure the possibilities of forging a common interest in politics, without which basic reforms to the dominant investment and development model are all but impossible. (Briggs 2005, 311)

As the percentage of blacks and Hispanics in the population has increased, their high school graduation rate was 21 points behind that of whites, or just 57 percent, according to a 2011 *Education Week* report. "Only one-third of Americans have any college or postsecondary credentials, and the bottom two-thirds of Americans are more likely to drop out of schools and be incarcerated," the report said. Having a high-quality education system for all students regardless of the ZIP codes in which they live is increasingly the major determinant of a nation's economic fate (Jackson 2011). Richard Bader, chairman of the N.Y. State Bar Association's Law, Youth and Citizenship Committee wrote: "Our democracy can only be a self-sustaining model if our citizenry is engaged and informed, and that requires civic education. In order to preserve democracy and its ideals, youth first need to have an appreciation of it" (Bader 2011).

Inequality

The Declaration of Independence clearly states, "All men are created equal, that they are endowed by their Creator with certain inalienable Rights." One of the most famous and influential Supreme Court justices, Louis Brandeis, once said, "We can have democracy in this country, or we can have great wealth concentrated in the hands of a few, but we can't have both."

We all know that many things contribute to inequality: taxing policy, incentives, employment availability, segregation, government investments, even personal initiative, in certain instances. But when viewed historically and in the context of the rest of the industrialized world, the level of inequality in the United States is startling. In 1915, the richest 1 percent of Americans possessed about 15 percent of the nation's income. This was the era of the Rockefellers, Vanderbilts, and Carnegies, which spawned the creation of the modern income tax system as a way to prevent wealth disparities from turning America into a European-style aristocracy. The socialist movement was at its historic peak. Today, the richest 1 percent account for 24 percent of the nation's income. "According to the U.S. Central Intelligence Agency (CIA), income distribution is more unequal than in Guyana, Nicaragua, and Venezuela and roughly on par with Uruguay, Argentina, and Ecuador. Income inequality is declining in Latin America even as it continues to increase in the United States. Economically speaking, the richest nation on earth is starting to resemble a banana republic" (Noah 2010).

An analysis of IRS income data by economists Emmanuel Saez and Thomas Piketty found that in 2008 the richest 14,000 U.S. families possessed more than 22 percent of America's entire national wealth. The bottom 90 percent of the population controlled 4 percent, while the top 72 wage earners in the United States made as much as the 19 million lowest wage earners. That was the largest gap since right before the Great Depression (Franken 2010). The top earners of the country (the 1 percent) took in 93 percent of all income growth in 2010. Income for most workers has barely risen since the early 1980s, while that of the top 1 percent of wage earners almost tripled in the same amount of time.

Since the 1980s, workers have increased their productivity but did not share proportionately in the rewards of their labor. Those went largely to the top income earners. In many corporations, the CEO earns more every day than the average worker gets paid in a year (Moyers 2010).

The Economic Policy Institute issued a report in 2011 titled *Hardships in America: The Real Story of Working Families*. The report found an "astounding 29 percent of American families living in what could be more reasonably defined as poverty, meaning that they earned less than a bare-bones budget covering housing, child care, health care, food, transportation, and taxes—though not, it should be noted, any entertainment, meals out, cable TV, Internet service, vacations, or holiday gifts" (Ehrenreich 2011).

Even Alan Greenspan, the former Federal Reserve chairman and Ayn Rand acolyte, said in 2010, "This is not the type of thing which a democratic society—capitalist democratic society—can really accept without addressing." His successor at the Fed, Ben Bernanke, also expressed concern (Noah 2010). "Moreover, the United Nations Commission of Experts on Reforms of the International Monetary and Financial System, investigating the causes of the Great Recession, and the International Monetary Fund have both warned that inequality leads to economic instability" (Stiglitz 2012).

Manufactured inequality. Galbraith, the influential twentieth-century economist and presidential adviser, once said, "What is called sound finance is very often what mirrors the needs of the respectably affluent."

Inequality is not natural, any more than is getting a co-signer for a car loan and acquiring credit over time to purchase a business. The system created and nurtured in the United States has enabled untold wealth creation but was also enabled by laws, regulations, customs, and mores. In *Inequality by Design*, the six authors dismantle the notion that success is based primarily on intelligence and natural talent. They write that "the social environment is more important in helping determine which American becomes poor than is 'native intelligence.'" Furthermore, they demonstrate "that although some inequality results from market forces, much of it—and even many aspects of market inequality itself—results from purposeful, and alterable, policy" (Fischer 1996, 10). The authors point out:

> Decades of social science research refute the claim that inequality is natural and increasing inequality is fated. Individual intelligence does not satisfactorily explain who ends up in which class; nor does it explain why people in different classes have such disparate standards of living. Instead, what better explains inequality is this: First, an individual's social milieu—family, neighborhood, school, community—provides or withholds the means for attaining higher class positions in American society, in part by providing people with marketable skills. Much of what those milieus have to offer is, in turn, shaped by social policy. For example, the quality of health care that families provide and the quality of education that schools impart are strongly affected by government action. Second, social policy significantly influences the rewards individuals receive for having attained their positions in society. Circumstances— such as how much money professional or manual workers earn, how much tax they pay, whether their child care or housing is subsidized—determine professionals' versus manual workers' standards of living. In turn, these circumstances are completely or partly determined by government. We do not have to suffer such inequalities to sustain or expand our national standard of living. Thus, inequality is not the natural and inevitable consequence of intelligence operating in a free market; in substantial measure it is and will always be the socially constructed and changeable consequence of Americans' political choices." (Fischer 1996, 6-7)

The authors of *Inequality by Design* teach us that context matters tremendously when assessing an individual's possibilities. Who ends up where in life is significantly influenced by the environment he has been born into. For example, the "advantages and disadvantages that people inherit from their parents, the resources that their friends can share with them, the quantity and quality of their schooling, and even the historical era into which they are born boost some up and hold others down ... Young men who graduated from high school in the booming 1950s had greater opportunities than the ones who graduated during the Depression" (Fischer 1996, 8). Yet, in 2012, "the proportion of men of prime working age with only a high school education who say they are 'out of the labor force' has quadrupled since 1968, to 12 percent" (Kristof 2012b).

Societies, through their politics and policies, build their ladders. For example: "Laws provide the ground rules for the marketplace—rules covering incorporation, patents, wages, working conditions, unionization, security transactions, taxes, and so on. Some laws widen differences in income and earnings among people in the market; others narrow differences. Also, many government programs affect inequality more directly through, for example, tax deductions, food stamps, social security, Medicare, and corporate subsidies" (Fischer 1996, 9). In fact, a mid-twentieth century example, with obvious spillover effects to today, of blatant discrimination in the workplace is found in the Wagner Act, which made it easier for private-sector employees to unionize but did not make racial discrimination an unfair labor practice. "With all-white textile mills, strictly gendered office spaces, lily-white construction sites, and segregated hiring practices at steel mills, the occupational world was defined by gender and race. The postwar golden age, as the political scientist Ira Katznelson put it, was an age in which 'affirmative action was white'" (Cowie 2010, 238). It wasn't until the 1964 Civil Rights Act that much of these practices began to slow down. But "the new occupational opportunities for women and minorities arrived just as the call for broad economic justice was in decline" (Cowie 2010, 239). Changing attitudes in the 1970s fomented a new era of public discourse, from solidarity and battles for the common good to resignation and acquiescence. A female San Franciscan volunteer who supported the United Farm Workers for years during the 1970s summed it up: "Maybe

Vietnam, the civil rights thing, Watergate and all the rest of it wore me out. I worry more now about the price of a head of lettuce than the issue of who picked it" (Cowie 2010, 250).

So many voices tell us that inequality is the result of individuals' "natural" talents in a "natural" market. Nature defeats any sentimental efforts by society to reduce inequality, they say; therefore, such efforts should be dropped as futile and wasteful. Appeals to nature are common and comforting. As Kenneth Bock wrote in his study of social philosophy, "We have been quick to seek explanations of our problems and failures in what we are instead of what we do. We seem wedded to the belief that our situation is a consequence of our nature rather than our historical acts" (Bock 1994, 9).

Social environment "is more, not less, important than test scores in explaining poverty, likelihood of incarceration, and likelihood of having a child out of wedlock." It has been long understood that a person's economic fortunes are hostage to his or her gender, parental assets, schooling, marital status, community's economy, stage in the business cycle, and so on; intelligence is just one item on such a list (Fischer 1996, 18-19). None of this diminishes the value of hard work, perseverance, or commitment. Policy-makers and pundits sometimes fail to look at the full picture and not fall back on the easy assertion that it is simply "nature" in the free market system or "intelligence" that determines success. Ironically, the policies that have created more inequality since the 1970s such as tax breaks and advantages for the wealthy and corporations and diminished salaries and benefits for workers are "not necessary for economic growth; indeed, inequality may well retard economic growth" (Fischer 1996, 19).

A *New York Times* article put it this way:

> Men who are now in their 30s—the prime age for raising families—earn less money than members of their fathers' generation did at the same age. The median income for men in their 30s in 1974, using today's inflation-adjusted dollars, was about $40,000. Now it's approximately $35,000. If you adjust for inflation, from 1980—when Ronald Reagan was elected President—to the midpoint of the current decade, the average income for the vast majority of Americans actually declined. The peak income year for most individual American taxpayers, believe it or not, was way back

in 1973. Standards of living for most American families were maintained or improved over the decades since then because women went into the workplace in droves. (Herbert 2010b)

Emmanuel Saez, an economist at the University of California at Berkeley who is one of the world's leading experts in inequality, notes that for most of American history, income distribution was significantly more equal than today. And other capitalist countries do not suffer disparities as great as ours. "There has been an increase in inequality in most industrialized countries, but not as extreme as in the U.S., Professor Saez said ... The result is nations without a social fabric or sense of national unity. Huge concentrations of wealth corrode the soul of any nation" (Kristof, 2010a).

Looking at inequality from a structural perspective, Timothy Noah of *Slate* magazine in 2010 completed an intensive investigation into its causes. In it, he asserted that certain policies, or lack thereof, contributed to our current situation. He concluded that the decline of labor accounts for about 20 percent of America's inequality; trade with China and elsewhere, 10 percent; Wall Street and corporate boards, 30 percent; various failures in the U.S. educational system, 30 percent; immigration, 5 percent; and tax policy, 5 percent.

It is important to notice that all the sectors mentioned by Noah are affected by government policy. These are choices made by voters, though perhaps not consciously or intentionally. Consider that immigration is regulated, at least in theory, by the federal government, as are tax policy and trade. The increase and then decline of unionized labor is in large part the doing of the federal government. Government rules concerning finance and executive compensation help determine the quantity of cash that the rich take home, and education is affected by government at the local, state, and federal levels.

A *New York Times* columnist put it perfectly in his article titled "Fast Track to Inequality":

The clearest explanation yet of the forces that converged over the past three decades or so to undermine the economic well-being of ordinary Americans is contained in the new book, *Winner-Take-All Politics: How Washington Made the Rich Richer — and Turned Its Back on the Middle Class*. The authors, political scientists Jacob

Hacker of Yale and Paul Pierson of the University of California, Berkeley, argue persuasively that the economic struggles of the middle and working classes in the U.S. since the late-1970s were not primarily the result of globalization and technological changes but rather a long series of policy changes in government that overwhelmingly favored the very rich. (Herbert 2010a)

From tax laws to deregulation to corporate governance to safety net issues, government action was deliberately shaped to allow those who were already very wealthy to amass an ever-increasing share of the nation's economic benefits. Two thousand and nine in particular was a great year for those at the top, while almost everyone else lost. According to Herbert, Hacker and Pierson noted in their book that investors and executives at the nation's 38 largest companies earned a total of $140 billion—a record.

The authors described an "organizational revolution" that took place beginning in the 1980s in which big business "mobilized on an enormous scale to become much more active in Washington, cultivating politicians in both parties and fighting fiercely to achieve shared political goals. This occurred at the same time that organized labor, the most effective force fighting on behalf of the middle class and other working Americans, was caught in a devastating spiral of decline." Later in the article, Herbert quoted Hacker as saying: "We're not arguing that globalization and technological change don't matter. But they aren't by any means a sufficient explanation for this massive change in the distribution of wealth and income in the U.S. Much more important are the ways in which government has shaped the economy over this period through deregulation, through changes in industrial relations policies affecting labor unions, through corporate governance policies that have allowed CEOs to basically set their own pay, and so on."

Diversity. Benjamin Franklin once remarked that German immigrants arriving in large numbers in Philadelphia "will never adopt our language or customs, any more than they can acquire our complexion" (Briggs 2005, 310). Fast forward to the beginning of the twenty-first century: For the first time in America's history, non-Hispanic whites constitute a minority of the total population in the United States' hundred largest cities.

"During the 1990s, four of five new additions to the population—and two of three to the labor force—were people of color ... One third of all population growth in the 1990s resulted from immigration—80 percent of it from Asia, Africa, Latin America, or the Caribbean" (Briggs 2005, 2). When most developed countries are seeing population stagnation or reduction, America is growing rapidly. Other developed countries, therefore, can afford massive budget shortfalls as there are fewer replacement workers and taxpayers, along with potentially shrinking economies. The U.S. population growth should be recognized as the advantage that it is. If new immigrants do not have a place at the table, America is handing its children a weaker economy and nation.

Corporate welfare. Founding father Thomas Jefferson famously wrote, "I sincerely believe, that banking establishments are more dangerous than standing armies" and "I hope that we shall crush in its birth the aristocracy of our monied corporations, which dare already to challenge our government to a trial of strength, and bid defiance to the laws of our country."

As discussed previously, public policy in America can and does promote inequality through tax breaks and subsidies for corporations. For example, farm subsidies support the prices of basic commodities, pay farmers not to plant some of their acreage, or subsidize the price of farm products exported abroad. The programs, designed originally to help low- and moderate- income family farmers, now make large-scale farmers and agribusinesses the big winners.

"Just ten percent of America's largest and richest farms collect almost three-fourths of federal farm subsidies. These are cash payments that often promote harmful environmental practices," such as when huge amounts of water, energy, industrial chemicals, herbicides, insecticides, and fertilizers increase pollution in the land, water, and atmosphere. Moreover, "from 1995-2009 the largest and wealthiest top 10 percent of farm program recipients received 74 percent of all farm subsidies with an average total payment over 15 years of $445,127 per recipient—hardly a safety net for small struggling farmers. The bottom 80 percent of farmers received an average total payment of just $8,682 per recipient ... Washington paid out a quarter of a trillion dollars in federal farm subsidies between 1995 and 2009" (Sciammacco 2011). Farm subsidies cost taxpayers up to $35 billion annually and tie farmers in a knot of unproductive regulations (Edwards 2007).

Additional subsidies go to energy producers and other natural resource firms. In *Inequality by Design,* the authors wrote that "federally owned hydroelectric plants sell electricity to utilities at below-market rates, the Forest Service builds roads into national forests for the timber industry, and the federal government finances research for the nuclear and fossil fuels industries." In 1995, the Cato Institute estimated that at least 125 separate programs are providing subsidies to particular industries and firms, and as stated in *Inequality by Design,* many "current federal subsidies to industry are mostly historical legacies of no-longer-pressing problems (like the subsidies to miners and cattle ranchers meant to encourage settling the West) or are responses to lobbying by powerful interest groups." In addition, as pointed out in the book, the federal government "indirectly subsidizes many industries by providing free regulatory services that are crucial to doing business." The Federal Aviation Administration provides a reliable system of air traffic control to airlines as a free service to subsidize their operations and thus airline passengers. That is not an aberration, as one author pointed out:

> Coast Guard rescue and enforcement activities subsidize commercial boat companies and pleasure boat operators. The Securities and Exchange Commission's fees charged to financial firms do not cover the full costs of registering and monitoring securities transactions. Businesses using inland waterways do not pay what it costs the federal government to maintain and operate them. Industry subsidies also operate indirectly through special exemptions and deductions written into tax codes. The best known is the oil depletion allowance, which allows oil and natural gas companies to deduct a percentage of their gross income for tax purposes. One might argue that these expenditures are good for the economy as a whole and ultimately good for everyone. That may well be so, but they do redistribute wealth upward. In the end, they most benefit the shareholders of the corporations that are subsidized. (Fischer 1996, 145-146)

In the midst of the Republican presidential primary season in January 2011, E.J. Dionne Jr. wrote in the *Washington Post* that "capitalists of (Mitt) Romney's sort never want to acknowledge how much their ability to make money depends on what government does. How does it structure the laws related to property, taxation, and debt? What rules does it write on how companies can be acquired and how power within firms is apportioned among shareholders, employees, managers, and other stakeholders? These are not natural laws. They are the work of politicians and the lobbyists who influence them."

Taxes. From World War II until 1970, the United States employed a steeply progressive tax system. In fact, "millionaires in 1960 had an official federal tax rate of more than 85 percent, although many loopholes made that only a nominal rate" (Philips 1994).

According to Fischer, "federal tax and spending cuts had two indirect, but unequal, results. First, cuts in federal spending shifted burdens to state and local governments, whose taxes and user fees increased sharply. The percentage of average families' income going for state and local taxes increased from 9 to 10 percent, and the relative burden on poorer families increased even more." There were other effects as well:

> The most striking impact of changes in federal tax policy was to increase the pretax incomes of the very wealthy. In the early 1980s, the maximum tax rates on income from investments (capital gains and unearned income) dropped sharply. This increased the net value of stocks, bonds, and other financial assets, sparking a boom in the prices of such assets and the income their owners received. This in large measure explains why the richest 1 percent saw a 90 percent growth in their incomes in the 1980s. Millionaires did not multiply overnight because there was a sudden increase in individual talent. Political choices in the 1980s, in large part choices about tax policy, reshaped inequality in America. (Fischer 1996, 147-148)

Stiglitz, the economist, wrote in 2011 in *Vanity Fair* that "one big part of the reason we have so much inequality is that the top 1 percent want it that way. The most obvious example involves tax policy. Lowering tax rates on capital gains, which is how the rich receive a large portion of their income, has given the wealthiest Americans close to a free ride." He added: "It should not make jaws drop that a tax bill cannot emerge from Congress unless big tax cuts are put in place for the wealthy. Given the power of the top 1 percent, this is the way you would expect the system to work."

Stiglitz had another perspective when he wrote: "Of all the costs imposed on our society by the top 1 percent, perhaps the greatest is this: the erosion of our sense of identity, in which fair play, equality of opportunity, and a sense of community are so important. America has long prided itself on being a fair society, where everyone has an equal chance of getting ahead, but the statistics suggest otherwise: the chances of a poor citizen, or even a middle-class citizen, making it to the top in America are smaller than in many countries of Europe."

No one likes paying taxes. Things, however, may not be as bad as the rhetoric you hear on an almost-daily basis. Bruce Bartlett, senior policy analyst under President Ronald Reagan, said in 2011 that the federal tax rate was the lowest it had been in sixty years. According to a 2011 report by the Citizens for Tax Justice, among Organization for Economic Cooperation and Development (OECD) countries, an organization of thirty-three developed nations, only two countries have lower taxes as a share of GDP than the United States: Chile and Mexico. Of the twenty-five OECD nations with taxes higher than the U.S., twenty-two have taxes that are at least 25 percent higher and fifteen have taxes at least 50 percent higher. Furthermore, the U.S. collects less corporate taxes as a share of GDP than all but one of the twenty-six OECD countries for which data are available.

"A stark example of the fundamental unfairness that is now so widespread was in *The New York Times* in March of 2011 under the headline: 'G.E.'s Strategies Let It Avoid Taxes Altogether.' Despite profits of $14.2 billion—$5.1 billion from its operations in the United States—General Electric did not have to pay any U.S. taxes last year" (Kocieniewski 2011). This was despite the fact that corporate profits in America hit an all-time high at the end of 2010. Jane White, author of *America, Welcome to the Poorhouse,* wrote in The Huffington Post that "corporations reported an annualized $1.68 trillion in profit in the fourth quarter, exceeding the previous record of $1.65 trillion in the third quarter of 2006." Furthermore, "between tax breaks, tax cuts and the fact that hedge fund managers can pay capital gains tax instead of income tax, we've created a corporate welfare state. The corporate share of the nation's receipts has shrunk from

30 percent of all federal revenue in the mid-1950s to 6.6 percent in 2009" (White 2011). A 2011 report by the Greenlining Institute said that U.S. corporations as a whole avoided $60 billion in taxes the previous year. The report mentioned that eight of the top 12 companies effectively paid no federal income taxes from 2008 through 2010.

Nearly two-thirds of U.S. companies and 68 percent of foreign corporations do not pay federal income taxes, according to a 2008 congressional report. "The Government Accountability Office (GAO) examined samples of corporate tax returns filed between 1998 and 2005. In that time period, an annual average of 1.3 million U.S. companies and 39,000 foreign companies doing business in the United States paid no income taxes—despite having a combined $2.5 trillion in revenue" (Goldman 2008).

In 2011, Vermont senator Bernie Sanders compiled a list of some of the 10 worst corporate income tax avoiders. Exxon Mobil made $19 billion in profits in 2009. It not only paid no federal income taxes, it actually received a $156 million rebate from the IRS, according to its SEC filings. Bank of America received a $1.9 billion tax refund from the IRS in 2010, although it made $4.4 billion in profits and received a bailout from the Federal Reserve and the Treasury Department of nearly $1 trillion. From 2005 to 2010, while General Electric made $26 billion in profits in the United States, it received a $4.1 billion refund from the IRS. Chevron received a $19 million refund from the IRS in 2010 after it made $10 billion in profits in 2009. Boeing, which received a $30 billion contract from the Pentagon to build 179 airborne tankers, got a $124 million refund from the IRS in 2010; Valero Energy, the twenty-fifth--largest company in America with $68 billion in sales in 2010, received a $157 million tax refund check from the IRS and, from 2007 to 2010, a $134 million tax break from the oil and gas manufacturing tax deduction.

Goldman Sachs in 2008 only paid 1.1 percent of its income in taxes even though it earned a profit of $2.3 billion and received almost $800 billion from the Federal Reserve and U.S. Treasury Department. In 2010, Citigroup made more than $4 billion in profits but paid no federal income taxes. It received a $2.5 trillion bailout from the Federal Reserve and U.S. Treasury. ConocoPhillips, the fifth-largest oil company in the United States, made $16 billion in profits from 2007 through 2009 but received $451 million in tax breaks through the oil and gas manufacturing deduction. From 2005 to 2010, Carnival Cruise Lines made more than $11 billion in profits, but its federal income tax rate during those years was just 1.1 percent.

Woodrow Wilson once said that "big business is not dangerous because it is big, but because its bigness is an unwholesome inflation created by privileges and exemptions which it ought not to enjoy."

As a result of the above, economist Jeffrey Sachs of Columbia University wrote in 2011 that "both the U.S. and U.K. are battling deficits of about 10 percent of gross domestic product. The situation in the U.S. is far graver. Total government (federal, state, local) revenues as a share of GDP in the U.S. are now 32 percent, roughly 9 percentage points below the UK and 15-20 percentage points below countries such as Denmark, Finland, Norway, and Sweden, which all have much lower budget deficits (or a surplus in the case of Norway) and highly effective public services." Those countries have better educational outcomes and employment numbers, higher trade balances, a lower poverty rate, and smaller budget deficits than the U.S.

History has shown that the inequality we are currently experiencing has not been this severe since right before the Great Depression. After that "the top income tax rate rose to 63 percent during the first Roosevelt administration, and 79 percent in the second. By the mid-fifties, as the United States faced the expenses of the Cold War, it had risen to 91 percent" (Krugman 2007, 47). The forty years following the crash saw sharply increasing levels of income equality, growth, security, and prosperity, combined with massive public investment.

As Tim Dickinson wrote in *Rolling Stone* in November 2011: "The frenzied handouts to the rich during the Bush era coincided with the weakest economic expansion since World War II—and the only one in modern American history in which the wages of working families actually fell and poverty increased. And what little expansion there was under Bush culminated in the worst fiscal crisis since the Great Depression" (Dickinson 2011).

Unions. According to economists Richard Freeman of Harvard and David Card of Princeton, 20 percent of the growth in wage differentials among male workers in the United States in the 1980s can be explained by the pronounced drop in the percentage of unionized workers. "Between 1970 and 1990 the proportion of the labor force that was unionized dropped more than 45 percent to only 11 percent of the private sector, virtually the lowest unionization rate in the industrialized world ... By the early 1990s the percentage unionized in the private sector in Canada was almost three times larger than in the Unites States. Partly because of these differences in unionization rates, wage inequality grew much less in Canada than in the United States in the 1980s ... Interestingly, Western Europe's economic growth outpaced ours between 1970 and 1990."

Market forces alone cannot explain the increase in inequality since the 1970s. If so, one would expect other advanced industrial countries to have experienced similar increases. "They participate in the same world markets, use similar technologies, and have similar types of industries and occupations. Yet these other countries experienced neither the same large increases in wage inequality nor the drops in the real earnings of the less skilled" (Fischer 1996, 148-149).

Turning even more talking points on their head is that researchers have found only a weak relationship between executive compensation and productivity. Similarly, there is no evidence that teachers unions are holding back our schools. Finland, which is currently doing significantly better than the U.S. in test scores, has teachers who are almost totally unionized. "The [American] states with the best student performance on standardized tests tend to be the ones with the strongest teachers unions" (Collins 2010). David Macaray, author and former union representative, wrote in The Huffington Post in August 2011 that "virtually every study ever conducted by reputable educational professionals has shown that the defects plaguing our school system are not the fault of the teachers."

"Both unionization rules and wage-setting practices are the result of policy choices. And these policy choices have profound effects on the amount of inequality we see in American society today. Recent statistics show that before 1974 American workers' increases in productivity were rewarded by increased wages. Since 1974, this has no longer been true" (Fischer 1996, 149-152). "The weekly earnings of non-supervisory workers increased 62 percent between 1947 and 1972 before stagnating indefinitely thereafter" (Cowie 2010, 28). This has had a profound effect on people's ability to support families. "For men without college degrees, 1972-3 marked—in economic terms—the best year of their lives, and earnings adjusted for inflation have gone downhill over the forty years since then," wrote Thomas Edsall of *The New York Times*. "Only men with college degrees, and especially those with post graduate degrees, did better in 2008 than they had in 1973."

"Nationally, the National Low Income Housing Coalition calculates that a household needs to earn $37,960 in 2012 to afford a two-bedroom unit at the national average fair market rate of $949 a month. By comparison, someone earning the current federal minimum wage, working 40 hours a week, earns only $15,080 a year" (Khimm 2012). Polls reveal that most Americans think that people who work full time should not live in poverty. *Slate* writer Noah, author of *The Great Divergence*, wrote, "Draw one line on a graph charting the decline in union membership, then superimpose a second line charting the decline in middle-class income share and you will find that the two lines are nearly identical." Noah also pointed out that the majority (75 percent) of increased corporate profits between 2000 and 2007 were the result of "reductions in wages and benefits." JP Morgan's Michael Cemblast, global head of investment strategy, wrote that "U.S. labor compensation is now at a 50-year low relative to both company sales and U.S. GDP."

Labor economist Richard B. Freeman pointed out that the hourly earnings of workers dropped by 8 percent from 1973 to 2005 while productivity shot up 55 percent or more (Geoghegan 2011).

Chicago labor lawyer Thomas Geoghegan argued in his 1991 book *Which Side are You On?: Trying to be For Labor When It's Flat on Its Back* that enacting the Taft-Hartley Act in 1947 sealed labor's demise. He wrote:

> First it ended organizing on the grand, 1930s scale. It outlawed mass picketing, secondary strikes of neutral employers, sit-downs: in short, everything Congress of Industrial Organizations founder John L. Lewis did in the 1930s ... The second effect of Taft-Hartley was subtler and slower working. It was to hold up any new organizing at all, even on a quiet, low-key scale. For example, Taft-Hartley ended "card check" ... Taft-Hartley required hearings, campaign periods, secret ballot elections, and sometimes more hearings, before a union could be officially recognized. It also allowed and even encouraged employers to

threaten workers who want to organize. Employers could hold "captive meetings," bring workers into the office and chew them out for thinking about the union. And Taft-Hartley led to the 'union-busting' that started in the 1960s and continues today. It started when a new "profession" of labor consultants began to convince employers that they could violate the pro-labor 1935 Wagner Act, fire workers at will, fire them deliberately for exercising their legal rights, and *nothing would happen*. The Wagner Act had never had any real sanctions .... So why hadn't employers been violating the Wagner Act all along? Well, at first, in the 1930s and 1940s, they tried, and they got riots in the streets: mass picketing, secondary strikes, etc. But after Taft-Hartley, unions couldn't retaliate like this, or they would end up with penalties, fines, and jail sentences. (Noah 2010)

More recently, Geoghegan's 2010 book *Were You Born On the Wrong Continent?* made the point that unions in other countries have thrived and helped ensure much less income inequality. He wrote: "It's no accident that the social democracies, Sweden, France, Germany, which kept on paying high wages, now have more industry than the U.S. or the U.K." (Noah 2010). Presciently, as we've seen since his book has come out, Germany is now experiencing a recovery much faster than the U.S. In the countries of the European Union, the earnings of about 70 percent of employees are covered by collective agreements. Furthermore, high-wage Germany nearly ties with China as the leading exporter in the world, well ahead of the United States. At the same time, the average number of paid vacation days in the U.S. is 13, versus Germany's 35. New mothers in the U.S. get three months of unpaid job-protected leave but only if they work for a company of 50 or more employees, while Germany mandates four months' paid leave and will pay parents 67 percent of their salary to stay home for up to 14 months to care for a newborn. In *Were You Born on the Wrong Continent?* Geoghegan wrote, "It's not just that the Germans can outcompete us, but they seem to be doing it with one hand tied behind their backs."

The International Labour Organization concluded that there is little or no evidence of a correlation between executive pay and company performance and suggested that excessive salaries likely reflect the dominant bargaining position of executives. Undoubtedly, there is plenty to criticize and correct regarding unions, but the right to organize is fundamental and has benefited millions of working American families over the last century.

Leo Hindery Jr., chairman of the New America Foundation, a non-profit, nonpartisan public policy institute, wrote in 2011 of the changing landscape:

> Throughout my long business career as a Fortune 500 company CEO and otherwise, I have held myself to the maxim that when American workers compete on level playing fields, they and the companies they work for thrive—and the nation prospers, as it did for a full century before unbridled and unfair globalization began to run amok. Now, however, workers everywhere are competing against a combination of illegal foreign subsidies, currency manipulation and shameful environmental practices that swamp any measure of true and fair comparative advantage. No worker should ever have to work without organizing protections, but especially now. And anyone who denies this denies the iron fists of management across the industrial bargaining table ... Today, with real unemployment at 18 percent, which is more than twice the misleading official rate, the U.S. needs more, not fewer, union members, because unions represent the best path back to fair dealing. Without union voices, workers have little or no say in their future.

Running in place. Jefferson Cowie wrote in *Staying Alive*, "Absent a meaningful framework in civic life, fear and anger can quickly take the place of the pride and honor of work" (Cowie 2010, 362).

"It is absurd to conceive liberty as that of the business entrepreneur, and ignore the immense regimentation to which workers are subjected," argued John Dewey in 1935. "Full freedom of the human spirit and of individuality can be achieved only as there is effective opportunity to share in the cultural resources of civilization." For Dewey, one of America's greatest philosophers, any political system that failed to make "full cultural freedom" available through "genuine industrial freedom as a way of life" was little more than "degenerate and delusive" (Cowie 2010, 368).

For millions of Americans, they are simply running in place, just staying afloat economically. Living paycheck to paycheck is a way of life for them. Barbara Ehrenreich, in her book *Nickel and Dimed*, vividly captures the near impossibility of juggling dead-end jobs and high-cost, often unfit housing.

Eddie Sadlowski, the famous steel worker and union leader whom *Rolling Stone* in the mid-1970s once called an "old-fashioned hero of the working class," feared an economically disarmed working class that is fast becoming a reality. "First we stopped noticing members of the working class, wrote one critic, and now we're convinced they don't exist" (Cowie 2010, 367).

By the early 2000s, families were spending twice as much (adjusted for inflation) on mortgages as they did a generation previously. They also had to pay twice as much to hang on to their health insurance. That caused problems for many, as one author showed:

> To cope, millions of families put a second parent into the workforce. But higher housing and medical costs combined with new expenses for child care, the costs of a second car to get to work and higher taxes combined to squeeze families even harder. Even with two incomes, they tightened their belts. Families today spend less than they did a generation ago on food, clothing, furniture, appliances, and other flexible purchases—but it hasn't been enough to save them. Today's families have spent all their income, have spent all their savings, and have gone into debt to pay for college, to cover serious medical problems, and just to stay afloat a little while longer ... America without a strong middle class? Unthinkable, but the once-solid foundation is shaking. (Warren 2009)

In 2010 one in eight Americans was on food stamps. At the end of 2011, one in five Americans was unemployed or underemployed, one in nine families could not make the minimum payment on their credit cards, and one in eight mortgages was in default or foreclosure.

Yet, this is our current situation. Wilkinson and Pickett, authors of *The Spirit Level*, clearly showed that countries with bigger income differences tend to have much lower social mobility. Of the eight western industrialized countries for which data is available, the United States has the lowest social mobility rate—a far cry from the American Dream. It is a fact that social mobility is lower in more unequal countries.

Chapter 4
Security

"Where justice is denied, where property is enforced,
where ignorance prevails and where any one class is made
to feel that society is in an organized conspiracy to oppress, rob
and degrade them, neither persons nor property will be safe."

—Frederick Douglass

MOTHER TERESA ONCE SAID, "If we have no peace, it is because we have forgotten that we belong to each other." Security may seem like a strange topic to include in a discussion about growth and prosperity. But as I will attempt to show, growth and prosperity cannot occur without it. Security, in this context, refers to the safety and well-being of one's life, home, family, and neighborhood. It also refers to the outside threats as a result of America's consumer-driven lifestyle. Global warming, climate change, and terrorism that threaten Americans' way of life are examples of outside threats. Finally, we cannot ignore the country's severe infrastructure deficiencies, for example, failing levees, bridges, airports, and water and sewer lines.

"A National Strategic Narrative" offered us a present-day non-partisan blueprint for understanding and reacting to the changes of a twenty-first century world. The 2011 article was written by U.S. Navy Capt. Wayne Porter and U.S. Marine Col. Mark "Puck" Mykleby, two special assistants to Chairman of the Joint Chiefs of Staff Mike Mullen. (The pair wrote the piece under the pseudonym "Mr. Y," a play on the 1947 article "The Sources of Soviet Conduct" written by "Mr. X"—George Kennan—for *Foreign Affairs*).

The "Mr. Y" narrative emphasized that America must move from national security to national prosperity and security. Specifically, the authors said, "our security lies as much or more in our prosperity as in our military capabilities .... It follows logically that prosperity without security is unsustainable. Security is a state of mind, as much as it is a physical aspect of our environment. For Americans, security is very closely related to freedom, because security represents freedom from anxiety and external threat, freedom from disease and poverty, freedom from tyranny and oppression, freedom of expression but also freedom from hurtful ideologies, prejudice and violations of human rights .... We must recognize that security means more than defense." Part of that, they wrote, entails pressing past "a strategy of containment to a strategy of sustainment (sustainability)."

"Evidence shows that communities and societies with high degrees of inequality tend to be troubled and torn." Homicides are more common in more unequal countries. Evidence shows that as inequality increases, so does violent crime (Fischer 1996, 212, 135). Another fascinating discussion in *The Spirit Level* brought up the effects of pride, shame, and status in unequal societies. "One of the most common causes of violence, and one which plays a large part in explaining why violence is more common in more unequal societies, is that it is often triggered by loss of face and humiliation when people feel looked down on and disrespected" (Pickett 2009, 40). When people have nothing else, these feelings are exacerbated.

Although the U.S. experienced an unexplained anomaly in 2011 concerning stagnant crime statistics, despite increasing inequality, the fact remains that America is still much more crime ridden than other industrialized countries. Even more interesting is the decline in the face of very recent reductions in incarceration rates. As the percentage of people behind bars has decreased, the assumption was that crime would increase. Crime experts are baffled at these anomalies. Yet, despite the overall good news, where there are pockets of poverty, crime has increased, as evidenced in the murder rates in Detroit, Newark, and Baltimore.

Veteran criminologist James Allen Fox of Northeastern University wrote: "Although homicides were down sharply in more affluent areas and among those 25 and over, the sound of gunfire was all too common in some poor neighborhoods. It's not rosy everywhere." It is no coincidence that the Institute for Economics and Peace's 2012 U.S. Peace Index showed that Louisiana was the least peaceful state in America for the twentieth year running. The least peaceful metropolitan area was Detroit-Livonia-Dearborn in Michigan. Conversely, Maine was America's most peaceful state for the eleventh year running. Maine also had the least cost to taxpayers as a result of the least violence. Consistent with this book's thesis, the index noted that the more peaceful metro areas were found to have lower poverty, inequality, and unemployment rates. Michael Shank, U.S. vice president at the Institute for Economics and Peace, wrote that "the total cost of violence in the U.S.—including lost productivity from violence—was conservatively calculated to be over $460 billion." But, "according to the index, "if all the states in the U.S. had the same level of peacefulness as the most peaceful state of Maine, $274 billion worth of extra economic activity could be generated." Lastly, the index noted that "what is absolutely clear is that peaceful states perform better across a range of economic, health, education and community factors. They have higher high school graduation rates, lower poverty, better access to basic services, higher labor force participation rates, higher life expectancy and less single-parented families. Even social capital—like volunteerism, civic engagement, trust, and group membership—is higher in more peaceful states. Therein lies the lesson" (Shank 2012).

According to a 1991 study by Helen Ladd and John Yinger that analyzed demographic profiles, economic base, and fiscal health, for every 1 percent increase in the poverty rate of a city, the cost of police services per resident increased 5.5 percent. A similar fate could be in store for many older suburbs where poverty is increasing.

Fyodor Dostoyevsky wrote in *The House of the Dead* that "the degree of civilization in a society can be judged by entering its prisons." The harshness of the U.S. prison system at federal, state, and county levels has led to frequent condemnations by Amnesty International, Human Rights Watch, and the United Nations Committee Against Torture. The development of the American "supermax" prison, designed to create a permanent state of social isolation, has been condemned by the United Nations committee on torture.

American prison populations have been increasing steadily since the early 1970s. As a result, "no country on earth imprisons more people per capita than the United States. We imprison a larger proportion of its population than Russia or Belarus. Our incarceration rate is eight times that of France" (Cole 2011).

According to the 2011 "World Prison Population List" published by the International Centre for Prison Studies at Kings College in London, Canada has 117 people per 100,000 incarcerated; France, Belgium, and Germany have 96, 97, and 85, respectively; while the U.S. has a whopping

754. "From 1925 to 1975, the country's [U.S.] incarceration rate was stable at roughly 100 prisoners per 100,000 people. Since then it's hardly stopped multiplying ... In Britain, by contrast, the rate is just 148 of every 100,000 people behind bars, in Australia 126, in Japan 63. This amounts to 2.3 million people behind bars at a public cost of up to $50,000 a cell slot a year" (Peirce, 2010a).

"California now spends more money on prisons than on higher education. It spends about $216,000 per year on each juvenile detainee, and just $8,000 on each child in the troubled Oakland public school system" (Kristof 2010b). "Former California Governor Arnold Schwarzenegger pointed out that in 1980, 10 percent of his state's budget went to higher education and 3 percent to prisons; in 2010, almost 11 percent went to prisons and only 7.5 percent to higher education" (Carter 2011). "New York state spends $210,000 a year for each youth held in juvenile prison—and 75 percent are re-arrested within three years of release" (Bornstein 2011).

This contrasts significantly with what has been happening in other rich countries. In the 1990s, according to the United Nations Programme Network Institutes Technical Assistance Workshop, the prison population was stable in Sweden and declined in Finland; it rose by only 8 percent in Denmark and 9 percent in Japan. Prison rates have been falling in Germany since at least 2003, according to the "World Prison Population List."

In *Preventing Violence*, prison psychiatrist James Gilligan wrote that the "most effective way to turn a non-violent person into a violent one is to send him to prison." He wrote, "The criminal justice and penal systems have been operating under a huge mistake, namely, the belief that punishment will deter, prevent or inhibit violence, when in fact it is the most powerful stimulant of violence that we have yet discovered."

Therefore, as Wilkinson and Pickett pointed out in *The Spirit Level*, because prison is not effective at either deterrence or rehabilitation, then a society must be willing to maintain a high rate (and high cost) of imprisonment for reasons unrelated to effectiveness.

A 2010 report issued by the Pew Charitable Trusts, *Collateral Costs: Incarceration's Effect on Economic Mobility*, demonstrated that America has the highest incarceration rate in the world, with a 300 percent increase since 1980. It has more inmates than the top thirty-five European countries combined. The study indicated that 1 in 87 working-age white men is in prison or jail, compared with 1 in 36 Hispanic men and 1 in 12 African-American men. More young (20-34) African-American men without a high school diploma or GED are currently behind bars (37 percent) than employed (26 percent). Perhaps most disturbing is the 2.7 million American children who have a parent behind bars, a huge increase from 1985 when 1 in 125 kids had an incarcerated parent, compared with 1 in 28 today. In addition, the report said, "two-thirds of these children's parents were incarcerated for non-violent offenses" (Sanders 2010). Meanwhile, "Harvard sociologist Bruce Western wrote that our society's attempt to increase public safety through an ever-increasing reliance on imprisonment may instead be having the opposite effect by undermining families and cleaving poor black communities from the mainstream of American life" (Froomkin 2012).

Adam Gopnik wrote in *The New Yorker* in January 2012: "There are more black men in the grip of the criminal-justice system—in prison, probation, or on parole—than there were in slavery [in 1850]. Over all, there are now more people under 'correctional supervision' in America—more than six million—than were in the Gulag Archipelago under Stalin at its height."

In recent years, America has expanded its penal institutions at an unprecedented rate while contracting its welfare programs. What response could policy-makers desire? In his 1998 book *Crime and Punishment in America*, sociologist Elliott Currie pointed out that, since 1984, California built only one new college but twenty new prisons.

Inequality seems to make countries socially dysfunctional across a wide range of outcomes. According to the Southern Poverty Law Center, a prominent civil rights organization, the number of domestic hate and extremist groups in the United States grew to record levels in 2011. This is the eleventh consecutive annual increase and the highest number (1,018) since tracking began in the 1980s, almost double the number from 2000 (602). Analysts of these groups are increasingly concerned due to "widespread political, economic and social distress," said Brian Levin, director of the Center for the Study of Hate and Extremism at California State University.

Former U.S. Secretary of State Colin Powell and his wife are the founders of America's Promise Alliance, which strives to lift children out of poverty. One of the group's goals is to cut the dropout rate in half. The plan is to provide better schools and more community intervention in the lives of at-risk kids. Powell framed it as not just a moral obligation but a matter of national security. America's Promise enlists businesses, nonprofits, and faith groups to get involved with at-risk kids. It also urges communities to look at factors that improve the odds for success, such as universal early childhood education. To ignore the bifurcation, or level of unequal opportunity in American society today, is in conservative columnist David Brooks words, "national suicide."

Mortality

President John F Kennedy, in a special message to Congress on February 20, 1961, said: "Our progress as a nation can be no swifter than our progress in education. The human mind is our fundamental resource."

When kids are not safe, they cannot learn. According to a 1997 Centers for Disease Control report: "American children are more at risk from firearms than the children of any other industrialized nation. In one year, firearms killed no children in Japan, 19 in Great Britain, 57 in Germany, 109 in France, 153 in Canada, and 5,285 in the United States." In the USA, a child is killed by a gun every three hours, according to the Children's Defense Fund. And, according to the 2009 book *Community Health Nursing*, each year more children and teens die in the U.S. from gunfire than from cancer, pneumonia, influenza, asthma, and HIV/AIDS combined. Between 1979 and 2001, gunfire killed ninety thousand children and teens in America, according to data from the Children's Defense Fund and the National Center for Health Statistics. The rate of firearm deaths among those under age fifteen is almost twelve times higher in the United States than in twenty-five other industrialized countries combined, said the Centers for Disease Control and Prevention. *New York Times* columnist Mark Bittman wrote in August 2012: "Since 9/11, thirty-three Americans have been killed by 'terrorists'; roughly 150,000 Americans have been killed by non-terrorists, that is, your run-of-the-mill murderers ... In the U.S., there are nearly three (2.98) gun murders per 100,000 people. In Britain, by contrast, there were 18 gun homicides in 2009 (a rate of nearly zero—actually 0.03—per 100,000)."

"Within any society, while it is generally young men who are violent, most young men are not. Just as it is the discouraged and disadvantaged among young women who become teenage mothers, it is poor young men from disadvantaged neighborhoods who are most likely to be both victims and perpetrators of violence" (Pickett 2009, 132). Gary Slutkin, a Chicago-based physician and founder of CeaseFire, an anti-violence and anti-gang operation, argued that "violence is an infectious disease," a "condition 'transmitted' from one person to another socially, through peer to peer neighborhood social pressures, just as insidiously as contagious bacteria" (Peirce, 2009a).

Wilson, the Harvard sociologist whose pioneering work boldly confronted ghetto life while exploring economic explanations for persistent poverty, defined culture as the way "individuals in a community develop an understanding of how the world works and make decisions based on that understanding." For some young black men, Wilson wrote, the world works like this: "If you don't develop a tough demeanor, you won't survive. If you have access to weapons, you get them, and if you get into a fight, you have to use them" (Cohen 2010).

Going beyond American gun violence, we should also recognize the drastic increase in military suicide rates due to stretched-to-the-limit troops on multiple deployments. The toll it is taking on them and their families is enormous and can largely be attributed to extended oil wars and our oil and automobile addiction. We justifiably went to war to eliminate the terrorists who committed the atrocities of 9/11, killing almost three thousand Americans in one day, but Stiglitz, the economist, has estimated that the final cost to the U.S. of prosecuting the Iraq war will be $3 trillion. Combine that with the more than six thousand American military casualties prosecuting both the Iraq and Afghanistan wars at the end of 2011. These casualties almost seem to be accepted as a condition of modern life, and the numbers are still mounting as of this writing. Meanwhile, today's military is largely made up of poor and middle-class kids, in sharp contrast to a generation ago. In 1956, four hundred of seven hundred fifty men who graduated from Princeton went on to serve in the armed forces. In 2011, six members of the graduating class joined the military.

Compare those statistics with the average forty thousand traffic fatalities every year due to our sprawled-out lifestyle. Suburban residents were three times more likely to be killed or injured by traffic accidents than city residents, according to a 1996 study written by Alan Durning, founder of the Sightline Institute, a Seattle-based environmentally oriented nonprofit organization. Author and planner Jeff Speck pointed out that if the entire U.S. shared New York City's traffic death rate, we would save more than twenty-five thousand lives per year.

Durning noted that "traffic accidents kill more Northwesterners each year than gunshot wounds or drug abuse do; almost 2,000 people in the region died—and 168,000 were injured—in car wrecks in 1993 alone . . . The young are especially endangered. Traffic accidents are the leading cause of death among Americans aged 10 to 24, and 5- to 15-year-olds are the age group most likely to be run over by motor vehicles while bicycling." This tragic and common news is due in no small part to the development patterns that we as a society currently live by. Yet, prior to 1930, the death of a child due to an automobile accident drew enormous attention and, in most cases, the driver was held criminally responsible and charged with "technical manslaughter." Mayors used to dedicate monuments to the victims of traffic crimes, accompanied by marching bands and children dressed in white. Peter Norton, an assistant professor at the University of Virginia and author of *Fighting Traffic: The Dawn of the Motor Age in the American City,* wrote that "there was a lot of anger in the early years, a lot of resentment against cars for endangering streets." Norton related how the automobile lobby ultimately changed laws and regulations to relax penalties for crimes and adopt traffic statutes to supplant common law. "The statutes were designed to restrict pedestrian use of the street and give primacy to the car. The current configuration of the American street, and the rules that govern it, are not the result of some inevitable organic process," wrote Sarah Goodyear in "The Atlantic Cities," in 2012.

Combine those statistics with the forty-five thousand deaths per year, on average, from lack of health insurance. A poor economy and no jobs have traditionally meant no insurance.

Concerning national security, a Department of Defense report said that "nearly one-fourth of the students who try to join the U.S. Army fail its entrance exam, painting a grim picture of an education system that produces graduates who can't answer basic math, science, and reading questions ... The military must recruit about 15 percent of our nation's youth, but only one-third are eligible. More high school graduates are going to college than in earlier decades, and about one-fourth are obese, making them medically ineligible. In 1980, by comparison, just 5 percent of youth were obese" (Turner 2010).

At the same time, in science achievement tests in 2003, American students ranked twentieth out of forty surveyed countries. In a survey by the Organization for Economic Cooperation and Development, America ranked ninth in the world on the Adult Literacy Scale and twelfth in student reading ability. In much of Europe, Canada, Japan, and Russia, enrollment levels of three and four-year-olds in pre-school are running at about 75 percent; in the U.S., it is little more than 50 percent, according to the 2008 U.N. Human Development Report. The report also ranked the U.S. forty-second in terms of life expectancy and thirty-fourth in terms of infants surviving to age one. The U.S. infant mortality rate is on a par with some Third World countries and that of Croatia, Cuba, Estonia, and Poland. The report stated that if the U.S. could match top-ranked Sweden, about twenty thousand more American babies a year would live to their first birthday.

Energy and Climate Change

"The Security Council expresses its concern that possible adverse effects of climate change may, in the long run, aggravate certain existing threats to international peace and security." That was the assessment of the United Nations in a 2011 announcement.

The U.S. National Academies of Science, national scientific academies from around the world, and 97 percent of the world's climate scientists agree that climate change and global warming is a fact. The U.S. military has deemed climate change a national security threat. Global climate change "presents a serious national security threat which could impact Americans at home, impact U.S. military operations, and heighten global tensions," according to a 2007 study released by a blue-ribbon panel of retired admirals and generals from the Army, Navy, Air Force, and Marines. Retired U.S. Army General Gordon Sullivan and former Army chief of staff said: "People are saying they want to be perfectly convinced about climate science projections, but speaking as a soldier, we never have 100 percent certainty. If you wait until you have 100 percent certainty, something bad is going to happen on the battlefield." Some of these threatened regions can become breeding grounds for extremism and terrorism. The military, therefore, is analyzing effects and strategies on how to deal with mass migrations, coastal flooding, droughts, and water shortages. Millions of people stand to experience great upheaval in the coming years if global climate change goes unchecked. Wars over land, water, and food can erupt at any time. Desperate people will take desperate actions. Assessing how this affects America is essential to its long-term national security. A federally funded research and development center's report highlighted several formal findings including:

- Projected climate change poses a serious threat to America's national security.
- Climate change acts as a threat multiplier for instability in some of the most volatile regions of the world.
- Projected climate change will add to tensions even in stable regions of the world.
- Climate change, national security, and energy dependence are a related set of global challenges.

The report also made several specific recommendations:

- The national security consequences of climate change should be fully integrated into national security and national defense strategies.
- The U.S. should commit to a stronger national and international role to help stabilize climate changes at levels that will avoid significant disruption to global security and stability.
- The U.S. should commit to global partnerships that help less-developed nations build the capacity and resiliency to better manage the deleterious effects of climate.
- The Department of Defense should enhance its operational capability by accelerating the adoption of improved business processes and innovative technologies that result in improved U.S. combat power through energy efficiency.
- The DOD should assess how rising sea levels, extreme weather

events, and other possible changes in climate over the next thirty to forty years will affect worldwide U.S. military installations (CNA 2007).

Few know that the federal government subsidizes much of the industries that contribute to climate change. According to a Congressional Research Service memo to Representative Diana DeGette, D-Colo., in May 2007, the research group estimated that U.S. energy subsidies alone were between thirty-seven billion and sixty-four billion dollars in 2003 and were increased by two to three billion dollars annually by the provisions of the Energy Policy Act of 2005.

Examining per-person energy consumption and sustainability, physicist Geoffrey West made an interesting observation. "A human being at rest runs on 90 watts," he wrote. "That's how much power you need just to lie down. And if you're a hunter-gatherer and you live in the Amazon, you'll need about 250 watts. That's how much energy it takes to run about and find food. When you add up all our calories and then you add up the energy needed to run the computer and the air conditioner, you get an incredibly large number, somewhere around 11,000 watts." What other kind of animal requires 11,000 watts to live? Well, the largest mammal on earth, the blue whale, does not need that much. "Our lifestyle is unsustainable," West added. "We can't have seven billion blue whales on this planet. It's not even clear that we can afford to have 300 million blue whales" (Lehrer 2010).

In an essay in the November/December 2010 issue of *Foreign Affairs*, U.S. Secretary of State Hillary Clinton wrote in preparation for the *Quadrennial Diplomacy and Development Review:* "Strengthening middle classes around the world will be key to creating just and sustainable international order that lies at the heart of the United States' national security strategy ... Poverty and repression do not automatically engender terrorism, but countries that are impoverished, corrupt, lawless ... are more prone to becoming havens for terrorists and other criminals."

Zbigniew Brzezinski, President Jimmy Carter's national security adviser, wrote in his 2012 book *Strategic Vision: American and the Crisis of Global Power* that "the world is now interactive and interdependent. It is also, for the first time, a world in which the problems of human survival have begun to overshadow more traditional international conflicts. Unfortunately, the major powers have yet to undertake globally cooperative responses to the new and increasingly grave challenges to human well-being—environmental, climactic, socioeconomic, nutritional, or demographic."

As Speth noted in *The Bridge at the Edge of the World* (page 25), "climate change is not only an environmental and economic issue; it is also a profoundly moral and human issue with major implications for social justice and international peace and security."

Transportation and Infrastructure

Jane Jacobs, a pioneering author and urban observer, wrote in 1954, "The erosion of cities by automobiles proceeds as a kind of nibbling. Small nibbles at first but eventually hefty bites. A street is widened here, another is straightened there, a wide avenue is converted to one-way flow and more land goes into parking. No one step in this process is in itself crucial but cumulatively the effect is enormous."

The United States came out of World War II the richest and most powerful country in the world, its infrastructure and homeland almost completely unscathed. With the home front safe, America went on an unprecedented and unfettered expansion of infrastructure that targeted roads, bridges, schools, hospitals, airports, railways, ports, dams, water lines and air control systems. While the rest of the world was rebuilding and regrouping, the United States had the opportunity to simply improve and expand.

Experts say that the infrastructure largely created in the 1940s and 1950s that contributed, enabled, and enhanced America's unprecedented wealth creation must now be upgraded, reinforced, and expanded, similar to what Europe and Japan faced after World War II. According to Felix Rohatyn, in his 2009 book *Bold Endeavors*, "three-quarters of the country's public school buildings are outdated and inadequate. More than a quarter of the nation's bridges are obsolete or deficient."

A 2005 report issued by the American Society of Civil Engineers (ASCE) documented and predicted a dangerous future. It stated that 27 percent of the nation's 590,750 bridges, for example, are "structurally deficient or functionally obsolete." It also said that an estimated $268 billion will be required to restore schools to "good" condition, and that in New York City, officials estimated they would need $1.7 billion for deferred maintenance on eight hundred decaying school buildings.

In 2009, the ASCE gave the nation's roads a D-minus, down from a D in 2005. It wrote that "rehabilitating a road that had deteriorated is substantially more expensive than keeping that road in good condition." According to the American Association of State Highway and Transportation Officials, every dollar spent to keep a road in good condition avoids six to fourteen dollars needed later to rebuild the same road once it has deteriorated significantly. In the past several years, gas tax revenue has failed to adequately fund the nation's transportation demands, and states can expect to receive fewer federal dollars in the future (Smart Growth America and Taxpayers for Common Sense 2011). Along the same lines, a December 2011 analysis by the Institute on Taxation and Economic Policy, a nonprofit, nonpartisan research organization, showed that because state gas taxes are not adjusted for inflation and are a fixed rate collecting the same amount per gallon year after year, "gas taxes are a less significant part of families' household budgets than they have been in eighty years." This deterioration of funding and road and transit maintenance results in what the ASCE estimated is a $130 billion drain on the economy in the form of vehicle repair costs and travel time delays caused by deficiencies in America's transportation systems. The report noted that "if every state updated its gas tax rate to match the level of purchasing power it had the last time it was raised, state gas tax revenues would be roughly $10 billion higher per year." From 2008 to 2010, Congress transferred $34.5 billion from general fund revenues to make up for the funding shortfall. Meanwhile only two countries have lower gas taxes than the U.S., Kuwait and Saudi Arabia.

The ASCE estimated in 2009 that it would take $11 billion *annually* to replace aging drinking water facilities. Half the locks on more than 12,000 miles of inland waterways are functionally obsolete. A 2011 report by the Urban Land Institute said that America needs to invest $2 trillion to rebuild roads, bridges, water lines, sewage systems, and dams that are reaching the end of their planned life cycles. According to the U.S. Conference of Mayors in 2011, "every dollar invested in water and sewer improvements [has] the potential to increase the long-term gross domestic product by more than six dollars." The ASCE also said that America's declining surface transportation infrastructure will cut more than $3 trillion from the GDP over the next decade.

To put that into context, "over the next decade airline passenger travel is anticipated to increase by about one third. Freight tonnage will grow by nearly one half" (Rohatyn 2009, 2). The sixteen hours of delay the average motorist experienced in 1982 became forty-seven hours in 2003. Traffic congestion is costing us, cumulatively, 3.7 billion hours of travel delay, wasting more than two billion gallons of fuel each year.

"Greater demand multiplied by increased deterioration is an equation that can only produce woeful results for the nation. Aviation delays will cost the U.S. economy an estimated $30 billion by 2015. Traffic congestion will waste untold hours, further pollute the air, and burn nearly $100 billion each year in wasted fuel. More consequentially, each year an estimated 13,000 deaths can be attributed to poor highway maintenance" (Rohatyn 2009, 2). The National Highway Traffic Safety Administration said that since 2005, fatalities have dropped 25 percent, from a total of 43,510. The same estimates also project that the fatality rate will be the lowest recorded since 1949. The decrease can perhaps be in part contributed to the lagging economy, but enforcement, regulation, and safety requirements are enormous factors; in other words, certain laws are working.

"The aging of our nation's infrastructure has lessened our productivity, undermined our ability to compete in the global economy, shaken our perceptions about our own safety and health, and damaged the quality of American life" (Rohatyn 2009, 2, 3). In 2012, a report was issued by the Alliance for American Manufacturing titled *Preparing for 21st Century Risks*. In it, co-authors Tom Ridge, former first assistant to the president for homeland security, and Robert B. Stephan, former assistant secretary of homeland security for infrastructure protection, noted the danger of America's increasing dependence on foreign-made materials and supplies. They concluded that America's way of life "is dependent upon a vibrant economy, the existence of which is based upon a skilled work force, innovation and a world-class critical infrastructure. Much of this critical infrastructure is vulnerable to attack, catastrophic weather events, and obsolescence and deterioration. Immediate national security, preparedness and economic needs require an equally strong domestic manufacturing base which, for many reasons, has eroded over the years" (Gerard 2012).

By 2043, it is estimated that there will be one hundred million to one hundred forty million more of us. With the roadways around our metropolitan regions already clogged, how will we ever stay mobile? It is estimated that California will need an additional $37 billion per year just to maintain its existing highway system.

It doesn't seem as if there are many options. If we "stay the course," we can keep driving as we have. Yet, in 1980, 64.4 percent of us drove to work alone; in 2000 it was 75.7 percent, according to the Transportation Research Board's "Commuting in America" survey by Alan Pisarski. Carpooling dipped from 19.7 percent to 12.2 percent over the same period. Transit use went from 6.2 percent to 4.6 percent. And walking dropped from 5.6 percent to 2.9 percent, as workplace locations exploded (along with our waistlines).

In the twenty-first century, given the heavy usage of personal and commercial vehicles our development patterns require, thirty-seven square miles will need to be paved over and fourteen hundred miles of interstate-grade highway built for every one million new people.

"A household with access to transit spends 9 percent of its income on transportation, compared with 25 percent for the car-dependent" (Katz 2010).

In a 2006 report titled "Edging Toward Equity," Mary Gonzalez wrote: "Several years ago, the Gamaliel Foundation uncovered the fact that more than $600 billion had been earmarked for transportation in the greater Chicago area. The city of Chicago was to receive only 15 percent of the money, despite the fact that it encompasses 40 percent of the population. Similarly, professor Myron Orfield of the University of Minnesota described how in developing the wealthy suburb of Minnetonka, more than $360 million in public funds were required, but only $30 million came from the people who purchased the homes. The rest was a government subsidy to people of wealth."

In a 2003 report, the Lincoln Institute said that the public sector in the Northeast could save forty billion dollars over twenty-five years with more compact development—that is, building communities that are closer together.

A 2011 report by the Leadership Conference on Civil and Human Rights argued that inadequate mass transit creates barriers to employment.

It reported that sixty percent of suitable jobs for those in welfare-to-work programs are not accessible by public transportation. It also cited a Brookings Institution study that found 45 percent of jobs in the nation's ninety-eight largest metro areas are located ten miles or more beyond the urban core (Kambitsis 2011). This dynamic could not be more hostile to sustainability. "Each new decade produces a new, farther flung community that replaces a closer in community from which it draws residents and resources, without offering any assistance in managing the fallout. Each iteration of this trend hobbles transit, weakens urban school systems and entrenches segregation," wrote Angie Schmitt in 2012 for Streetsblog, an online daily news source that discusses sustainable transportation and livable communities.

At the same time, inadequate public transit and sprawl decrease access opportunities for work. "For example, even with commutes in excess of one hour, welfare recipients in Boston can access only 14 percent of the entry-level jobs in the fast-growth areas in the metropolitan area. In the Atlanta metropolitan area, according to HUD, less than half of the entry-level jobs are located within a quarter mile of a public transit system" (Briggs 2005, xii).

The federal government spends approximately six times as much on highways as on mass transit. At the same time, transportation currently accounts for the second-largest household expense for most families and sometimes the largest for low-income Americans. The way gas prices are rising, transportation costs will only grow for auto-dependent people. If regions cannot reduce this cost for residents through better transit, better land use development or both, residents will have less disposable income and therefore less money to spread around the local economy.

Part Two

Solutions

"Our future may be beyond our vision, but it is not beyond our control."
—Robert F. Kennedy

THE YEAR TWO THOUSAND AND NINE was the two hundredth anniversary of the stirring Gallatin Plan of 1809. Many planners consider it the most far-reaching, broad-based plan the country had ever seen. Yet, most people have never heard of it.

The Gallatin Plan laid out the blueprint of American investment for the next few decades. Conceived by Albert Gallatin, one of the most influential Treasury secretaries in American history, the plan "laid out a system of ports, roads, and canals to encourage interior settlement and facilitate commerce. The entire projected expense for all the construction work proposed by Gallatin was $20 million." This was an astronomical sum at the time. Gallatin, therefore, suggested spending two million dollars a year for ten years, and also selling stock in the various turnpikes and canals to finance their eventual upkeep and improvements ... A statue of Gallatin stands in front of the U.S. Treasury building in Washington, D.C (McNamara 2011).

Following up on the one hundred-year anniversary of the Gallatin Plan, in 1908, Theodore Roosevelt convened a conference of governors at the White House to launch a series of conservation plans drafted by the Inland Waterways Commission to target underperforming regions of the South and West with irrigation, river restoration, and dam projects. In the 1930s, President Franklin Delano Roosevelt charged the National Resources Planning Board and the Bureau of Public Roads with developing a plan for a national network of "superhighways" that provided the template for the Interstate Highway System, later funded by Congress with the passage of the Interstate and Defense Highways Act in 1956. This interstate system had a lasting effect on the development of the nation, fueling the economy, suburbanization, and the growth of metropolitan regions (Fishman 2007).

"Most of us would agree that the national government should be concerned with protecting disappearing species, the integrity of rivers that cross state lines, our coastlines, our forests, and regions of special significance for their scenic, ecological, or historic values" (Babbitt 2005, 6).

In fact, the federal government does have a viable tradition of engagement in land use. As outlined by Bruce Babbitt in *Cities in the Wilderness,* the Federal Endangered Species Act directly affects regional and land-use planning, particularly open-space planning for biologically unique and significant areas. Cooperation at local, state, and federal levels, along with private industry, has led to mutually beneficial projects that have had positive economic and environmental effects on regions, states, and the country, as a whole. It is a significant moment when a project will result in enduring success for generations to come.

According to Babbitt (2005, 8), federal farm policy "has influenced the use of the land since the beginning of the Republic, nearly always directed toward expanding production through the draining, clearing, and planting of more land." With the globalization of the agricultural economy and the World Trade Organization as the arbiter of agricultural policies that subsidize prices and encourage overproduction, the United States will be required to dismantle production subsidies, which reach as high as fifteen billion dollars or more per year. Babbitt called this situation a great opportunity to restore America's forested riverbank areas, "where floodplains, biodiversity and watersheds are vitally important for reducing environmental impacts associated with natural disasters."

Cities in the Wilderness outlines successful efforts undertaken by federal agencies, or at their behest, that have led to widely successful projects both economically and environmentally that have provided an enduring legacy for generations to come. The author wrote:

> The federal government has always been involved in land use planning, going clear back to George Washington's proposals to improve navigation on the Potomac River. And as the nation moved west, Congress sent army engineers to survey and stake out transcontinental railroad routes, which the federal government then subsidized with generous land grants. To this day the Army

Corps of Engineers serves as an engineering and construction company, dedicated to opening lands for development by planning and building flood-control projects throughout the nation. And in arid regions where there is not enough water, another agency, the Bureau of Reclamation, dams the rivers to divert the waters to subsidize more growth and development. And there is the land use planning embodied in the interstate highway program under which the federal government has funded and directed national development with a network of more than forty thousand miles of highways. (Babbitt 2005, 60-61)

The government still influences land use by its funding of airports, highways, reservoirs and water projects, federal farm subsidies, and protective tariffs. As Babbitt stated in an interview with *Terrain.org: a Journal of the Built and Natural Environment* in the spring of 2006: "Sprawl is erasing the distinction between the built environment and the natural environment. And both the quality of urban life and the integrity of our natural ecosystems are declining." In the same interview, Babbitt highlighted the fact that a Republican, Richard Nixon, was the first and so far only president to advocate national land-use planning legislation.

Land-use planning has thus been a federal function since the nation's founding. Republican President Teddy Roosevelt was the leader in wilderness preservation. According to Douglas Brinkley's book, *Wilderness Warrior: Theodore Roosevelt and the Crusade for America*, during his presidency, Roosevelt created enough federal bird reservations, national game preserves, national forests, national parks, and national monuments to have saved 234 million acres of American wilderness from being despoiled, 50 percent of the size of the Louisiana Purchase.

The phrase on the back of American coins reads, *"E pluribus unum"*— "from many, one." Given the inspirational history of American ingenuity, hard work, and solidarity in propelling its citizens into the future, it is unfortunate that trust in our government may be lost. Poll after poll suggests a lack of trust in our national leaders. There are, however, numerous examples of U.S. leaders taking bold measures and propelling the nation toward exceedingly high rates of economic growth.

It is important to acknowledge that the United States government has an extraordinary history of solving challenging problems while using its power to create private wealth and regional and national prosperity. In fact, the United States could never have become the unprecedented superpower of the world without such actions. From ending slavery or child labor and the 70-hour work week to championing women's right to vote, trade union rights, the progressive income tax, unemployment compensation, Social Security, and the many regulatory protections for consumers, workers, and the environment, the U.S. government's actions were the ladder of opportunity for millions of poverty-stricken Americans and immigrants of all ethnicities. In particular, these policies and programs created a stable middle class and a very wealthy upper class. As noted earlier, poverty was significantly reduced as a result of federal action in the form of food stamps, the Earned Income Tax Credit, and indexing Social Security to inflation. Approximately forty million people would be added to the poverty statistics if we ended these programs.

With 12.7 million Americans unemployed as of July 2012, and millions more stuck in part-time jobs because they couldn't find full-time work, perhaps we can be inspired by these additional examples of positive government action:

1. The Louisiana Purchase. This vast area (828,000 square miles) was purchased by the federal government for approximately $27 million in 1803. To put it in perspective, the federal government collected only $10 million in taxes the previous year. The process, negotiations, and follow-up spurred many serious and significant debates. The result, however, was that war with France was averted, the Mississippi River was open for travel and trade, and the land area of the country was doubled. One hundred and sixty-acre tracts were then carved out of the territory and sold by the government for $1.64 per acre. Eventually, people were given title to land simply by living and farming on it. In the long term, this helped enable the United States to become more egalitarian and prosperous.

2. The Erie Canal. Following a number of detailed requests and proposals made to the federal government, the state of New York decided to undertake the canal's construction in 1817. Though the plan was first discussed in 1724, construction was not begun until nearly a century later after many

studies, debates, denials, controversies, political shortsightedness, and wars. This publicly financed project single-handedly created the "Empire State" and ensured its legacy. The canal led to New York's ascension as the nation's chief port and created unprecedented growth throughout the Northeast. Interestingly, after thorough debate and analysis, it was decided that the canal should not be financed or run by the private sector. The Canal Commission wrote: "Too great a national interest is at stake. It must not become the subject of a job, or a fund for speculation ... Such large expenditures can be more economically made under public authority, than by the care and vigilance of any company" (Rohatyn 2009, 33). The project cost seven million dollars, a truly vast sum at that time. As a result, however, the country's gross national product nearly doubled, and New York City became a world commercial and cultural capital.

3. The transcontinental railroad. Abraham Lincoln knew that the future of the nation's commerce lay in moving goods and people east and west. Despite the Civil War, Lincoln was able to pass legislation to make this happen. The benefit to the nation was enormous. The federal government lent sixty-four million dollars to construct two competing railroads—one traveling east and one west. By 1869, the government had earned a profit of more than $103 million on its loans. Cities and towns sprouted up along the length of the system and furthered the growth and prosperity of the nation.

4. Land-grant colleges. The idea that the lost opportunity of a college education was not only a loss to individuals but also to the country was the impetus that spurred this project. The Morrill Act of 1862 was inspired by the concept that the "enemy of American success is not failure but the lack of opportunity" (Rohatyn 2009, 76). In America, opportunity was a paramount concern of many, as one writer explained:

> Even before the birth of the republic, there was a growing mood in the colonies that in the New World education should not be a privilege available only to the elite. In Europe, education had been open only to the ruling classes. It was one more way those with advantages institutionalized and passed on their power and prosperity. Life in America, the colonists hoped, would be different. In the New World, what once were privileges would be

deemed an inalienable right. Starting in 1743, Benjamin Franklin began publishing essays maintaining that freedom and equality were intrinsically intertwined with education. A free society, he wrote, must be an educated society. In his Proposals Relating to the Education of Youth in Pennsylvania, published in 1750, Franklin, the instinctive democrat, urged that schooling be provided to all children in the colonies, not merely the sons and daughters of the rich. (Rohatyn 2009, 76, 77)

The established elites were still uncomfortable with this radical idea. They called it monstrous, iniquitous, "an unconstitutional robbing of the Treasury." Nevertheless, the wartime Congress understood Morrill's logic: that land grants would not be an expenditure but an investment. Morrill's vision of an America where an activist and democratic government took the responsibility to provide the opportunity for a college diploma to a broad segment of the population became a reality. Today, America is a nation whose strength and wealth are built on opportunity, knowledge, innovation, and excellence, something that would never have been possible without Morrill's unflagging tenacity and fair-minded vision (Rohatyn 2009, 83-86).

5. The Homestead Act. In 1852, America was a gigantic place. After the Louisiana Purchase, the annexation of Texas, the establishment of the Oregon Territory, and the Mexican secession of its northern lands, the country had a lot of space to stretch out into. Nearly the entire population still lived along the East Coast. The country determined that, "if only wealthy elites were allowed to purchase the new lands, if vast tracts became personal fiefdoms, if opportunities for the poor and the working class were eliminated in the West, then the founding constitutional ideals of equality and opportunity would be undermined. America could in time be transformed into a restrictive nation where one's status at birth largely predetermined one's fate" (Rohatyn 2009, 89). After a ten-year fight that included, debate, confrontation, stalling, and mischief by wealthy congressional landowners, President Lincoln signed the Homestead Act into law in 1862. As a result, between 1850 and 1920, the number of farms quadrupled, waves of new immigrants flocked to America to find opportunity, and a total of three hundred million acres of federal land was transferred to private individuals.

Notwithstanding the political corruption that ensued or the extraordinary injustices heaped on Native Americans, wealth creation for mainly white settlers mushroomed.

6. The Rural Electrification Administration. The electric bill for Franklin Roosevelt's modest vacation home in rural Georgia was four times the bill for his upstate New York mansion. This was in 1924, nine years before he would become president and three years after he had contracted polio. The shock of seeing the electric bill caused him to do a little research. Roosevelt was "a believer in the fundamental human right of all Americans regardless of accidents of birth or geography to have the opportunity to fulfill their personal ambitions." Roosevelt found evidence that major electrical companies had been discriminating against farmers and other rural customers. The utilities were ignoring the needs of the rural people, condemning them to "arduous lives without the commonplace benefits that electricity brought to most twentieth-century homes and businesses" (Rohatyn 2009, 134).

Electricity transformed America. Menial and time-consuming tasks were reduced to simple chores. Businesses grew at an unprecedented rate with electric power. But the utility companies became powerful monopolies guided simply by the profit motive. They saw no benefit of extending power to sparsely populated rural areas. Therefore, "by the thirties, only about 10 percent of all farms had been electrified ... while the cities were bustling with the benefits" (Rohatyn 2009, 136). Without electricity, on average, a farmer spent ten hours per week carrying water. Plowing, planting, and harvesting were done with human and animal power (Rohatyn 2009, 137).

In 1936, a year after it was created, the federal Rural Electrification Administration (REA) was authorized to spend $420 million over ten years to finance and bring power to rural homes. At the time, more than a third of all American families had incomes of less than $1,000 per year. The REA was one of the largest capital investment projects of the New Deal. Rural homesteads could now enjoy the benefits city dwellers had taken for granted. As a result, "the intense privation and grueling drudgery of farm life disappeared. Thousands of new jobs took root in a countryside where appliances and plumbing were soon commonplace .... An electrified America was a stronger, better educated, more prosperous, and more democratic republic" (Rohatyn 2009, 151).

7. The Reconstruction Finance Corporation. President Herbert Hoover established the RFC during the Depression to lend federal capital to failing private businesses. Running for president and noting his desire to see poverty eliminated, Hoover declared in 1928, "We in America are nearer to the final triumph over poverty than ever before in the history of any land" (Rohatyn 2009, 156). Then in 1929, the stock market crashed. Unemployment skyrocketed, homelessness became epidemic, and destitution became a serious problem. Despite Hoover's traditional minimal government *laissez faire* attitude, he moved to request two billion dollars in federal funds be provided as loans to private businesses. To put this sum in perspective, the entire federal budget for his predecessor, Calvin Coolidge, was three billion dollars. Today, as then, we hear the same arguments used: state socialism, a millionaires' dole, reward for speculation, and so forth (Rohatyn 2009, 158). By 1932, however, the RFC had distributed two billion dollars in loans; as it turned out, this was not enough. Franklin Roosevelt was swept into the presidency with an enormous victory in the 1932 election, and after taking office, he immediately emphasized that America needed to address its problems with the urgency of a country going to war. By 1935, after Roosevelt took decisive action and made unprecedented moves, the money markets had finally stabilized. The RFC then continued to assist the nation. It granted $1.5 billion to the Federal Emergency Relief Administration, and provided funding to the Public Works Administration, the REA, the Resettlement Administration, and the Federal Home Loan Bank. The Commodity Credit Corporation received $1.6 billion for aid to farmers. The RFC also helped finance the Electric Home and Farm Authority and the Export-Import Bank, created to promote trade with the Soviet Union.

Legislation was written in 1935 to extend the RFC and add new powers. One item was the establishment of a mortgage bank that would capitalize the mortgage market and finance new construction. The administration could now buy railroad securities to stabilize deteriorating railroads. By 1936, however, the president, concerned with deficits, drastically cut spending and the RFC's purchases. The country slid back into recession in

1937-1938. Therefore, in April 1938, the president re-energized the RFC and once again expanded it. By early 1940, the economy was stabilizing.

By the end of World War II, the RFC had disbursed thirty-seven billion dollars. This helped win the war, permanently stabilized the economy, and set the stage for the colossal postwar boom. Knowing the enormous benefits these programs bestowed caused the daring leader of the RFC to state in 1939, "It is important for government and its representatives to realize the essential nature of business enterprise in this country, just as it is for businessmen to get it through their heads that government is in business to stay" (Rohatyn 2009, 176-177).

8. The G.I. Bill. Passed in the midst of the greatest war ever seen, the G.I. Bill was "a landmark law whose benefits to the nation can be measured in the quantifiable revenues that accompany new jobs, new construction of homes, and new tax proceeds. But no less significant, it was also legislation that in many incalculable ways changed the fabric and spirit of American life. The G.I. Bill made the country better educated, more egalitarian, and more optimistic, a land where the prospect of opportunity lifted and energized the citizenry" (Rohatyn 2009, 180). Nevertheless, the legislation still had its detractors. Some thought it would be a disincentive for returning GIs to not look for work. Others weren't sure of sending hardened veterans to colleges and universities, normally the respite for the well-off and privileged. The effect of it, however, enabled millions of Americans to become homeowners and helped create what has been called "the greatest generation." The mortgage rate was set at 4 percent and the VA guaranteed up to 50 percent of an entire loan. Farms and businesses were also eligible. Homes were purchased with no money down. The economy and home construction boomed, and the suburbs grew. Historian Stephen Ambrose said "the G.I. Bill was the best piece of legislation ever passed by the U.S. Congress, it made modern America." It helped create a booming middle class—from one in ten Americans before the war to one in three Americans a decade after. A 1988 congressional study found that every dollar spent on education under the bill returned seven dollars through increased productivity, consumer spending, and tax revenue.

9. The Interstate Highway System. Passed under Republican President Dwight Eisenhower in 1956, the interstate highway system was projected

to cost fifty billion dollars at a time when the entire federal budget was seventy-one billion dollars. It was the largest public works project in American history at that time. Construction continued for forty years, rather than the thirteen expected. Despite the now-established negatives associated with exponential highway growth—such as destruction of urban neighborhoods, traffic congestion, sprawl, air pollution, and increased dependence on foreign oil—the benefits in economic prosperity to the country as a whole are clear. New industries sprang up alongside the new thoroughfares, including fast-food chains, gas stations, hotels and motels, as well as auto repair shops and the associated financing and insurance companies. As a result of the roads and the increase in driving, a powerful coalition of car-highway advocates was created, including cement, asphalt, and steel producers; petroleum companies; road contractors; banks; and hotel operators. "By the mid-twentieth century, one in every six Americans, however tangentially, would earn his or her living from the automobile and associated industries" (Rohatyn 2009, 207). Acknowledging these benefits are essential in understanding the negatives we now associate with this system. The building boom it created energized the economy and helped build the middle class and way of life most Americans today take for granted. "American history shows that economic growth, the creation of wealth, employment, and opportunity, are all built on the platform of investment" (Rohatyn 2009, 222).

As evidenced by the aforementioned examples, many governmental programs and policies helped usher in unprecedented national prosperity. Millions of Americans went from destitution to prosperity as a result of these programs.

Twentieth century middle-class wealth creation and suburban growth have been enabled by 1) low-cost home mortgages, 2) the secondary mortgage market, 3) pro-homeowner tax policies, 4) federal transportation policy, 5) sewage plant expansion, and 6) unions.

1. Low-cost home mortgages. Today, housing represents nearly two-thirds of all middle-class wealth. The FHA insured low-interest mortgage loans made by banks as well as savings and loan associations. During its early decades, racial discrimination was policy, as only "racially homogenous" neighborhoods were insured. This was referred to as "redlining," in which

certain areas, populated by minorities, would be off-limits for mortgage loans. The practice continued unofficially for a large part of the twentieth century. Low-cost mortgage loans from the VA financed homeownership for fourteen million veterans and did not require a down payment. People who were not otherwise interested in moving out to the suburbs because they like the amenities and closeness of cities were given an offer they couldn't refuse. "Imagine, a six-room house with a yard of its own which could be 'carried'—amortization, taxes, insurance—for a monthly payment lower than the rent on our one-room apartment" (Schliveck 1965).

The federal government has been involved in the mortgage market since the 1930s, and its history has not always been fair, but today, "a market without government support would almost certainly involve the demise (for most of middle-class America) of that populist favorite, the low-cost 30-year fixed-rate mortgage. For a homeowner, a mortgage with a 30-year fixed rate (especially one that he can pay off early without a penalty) is a wonderful thing. For lenders and investors, however, it is a financial Frankenstein's monster—an unnatural product filled with the potential for losses. Absorbing some of the risk of those losses is a large part of what the government does in the housing market (Fannie and Freddie and FHA)" (McLean 2011). William Gross, co-founder and managing director of the investment firm Pimco, said that mortgages without a government guarantee would cost at least several percentage points more. If that's correct, thirty-year mortgages would be much more expensive, and the pool of potential homebuyers much smaller (McLean 2011).

2. The secondary mortgage market. To meet the pent-up housing demand in the South and West, a whole network of systems, agencies, and regulation was created to allow more funding for mortgage lending. These included Fannie Mae, Freddie Mac, and Ginnie Mae, or the Government National Mortgage Association. This allowed an avalanche of new funding for further expansion of homeownership and middle-class growth. "The financial impact of federally chartered mortgage pools was even greater than the FHA and VA backing of private lenders" (Rusk 1999, 88). In 1995, these programs, along with the Farmers Home Administration, accounted for "more than $1.8 trillion in the federally organized mortgage pools, the great bulk of it invested in suburban single-family homes." Conversely, direct subsidies for

low-income households totaled less than twenty-six billion dollars. Therefore, "the federal government provides approximately forty times more support for suburban-oriented, middle-income homeownership than it does for largely city based, lower income rental housing" (Rusk 1999, 89).

3. Pro-homeowner tax policies. Since the creation of the income tax, taxpayers have been able to deduct home mortgage interest against their tax liability; no such tax offsets exist for apartment renters. The annual value of the mortgage interest deduction and local property tax payments and capital gains exclusion is estimated to be more than $126 billion in tax breaks. Treating this "tax expenditure," as economists refer to it, as if it were a budget appropriation has turned the mortgage interest deduction into the federal government's sixth-largest expenditure after Social Security payments, national defense, Medicare, interest paid on the national debt, and Medicaid assistance. Interestingly, Canada and Australia have achieved America's high level of homeownership without such tax subsidies. In addition, "Congress exempted home sellers from any capital gains tax liability if they bought a home of equal or greater price. The effect was to encourage homebuyers to step up constantly in price, and often step out of central cities and older suburbs as well" (Rusk 1999, 89-90).

Home ownership represents an integral part of the American Dream but, historically, also the largest component of most Americans' wealth. Clearly, the government subsidized, encouraged, and enabled this growth. The manipulation of the mortgage market by private investment schemes led to the crash of 2008 and destroyed trillions in equity but, overall, homeownership has been an enormous contributor to middle-class wealth and security.

4. Federal transportation policy. "From 1956 to the mid-1990s, when the 54,714-mile interstate highway system was nearing completion, the federal government spent a total of $652 billion (in 1996 dollars)" (Rusk 1999, 91). However, despite the program's original emphasis on long-distance interstate roads, more than half of the funds had gone into building 22,134 miles of new highways within metropolitan areas. "This fostered a vast decentralization of the country's urban centers. By contrast, under the Urban Mass Transit Act of 1964, federal aid to public bus and subway systems, which tend to promote greater centralization, totaled only $85

billion (in 1996 dollars). Federal transportation policy, in effect, channeled almost seven times more money into suburban sprawl than into helping maintain more compact urban centers" (Rusk 1999, 91). As stated earlier, by the mid-twentieth century, one in every six American workers earned a living building, selling, repairing, insuring, driving, or servicing vehicles and highways.

5. Sewage plant expansion. The Clean Water Act of 1972 enabled the country to clean up many lakes and streams. But approximately one-third of that funding has gone to support new and expansive suburban growth, not to remedy old problems.

6. Unions. As discussed earlier, unions were a stabilizing force for unchecked corporate abuse during a great portion of the twentieth century. Acknowledging their influence is essential in understanding the era of a large, comfortable middle class during the twentieth century. As their influence and numbers have waned, so have the incomes, benefits, and stability they contributed to the American middle class. It is no coincidence that the last time union membership was this low was the year before the Great Depression. Unions allowed millions of American factory workers, mechanics, drivers, and tradesmen to enjoy an income sufficient for one parent to work while the other stayed home with the kids. There is no question that a certain level of financial comfort was experienced for millions of families, in large part, because of unions.

Many industrialized countries maintain a significant union force today in contrast to the United States. Look no further than Canada, which has weathered the economic storm that began in 2008 quite well. The country's unionized workforce is approximately 30 percent compared to the United States, at fewer than 12 percent. The Scandinavian countries and Germany have weathered the global recession very well with a large union force. Interestingly, one hundred percent of Finland teachers are unionized, yet they still have the best scores on student achievement tests. Perhaps in the future, American policy-makers could consider these facts when trying to limit unions.

Chapter 6
Regional Policies

*Competitiveness between two communities gets us nowhere.
We've been asleep at the switch too long."*

—Michael Crow, Arizona University president

IN A MESSAGE TO CONGRESS on housing and community development on March 9, 1961, President John F. Kennedy, showing incredible insight for the time period, wrote:

> The city and its suburbs are interdependent parts of a single community, bound together by a web of transportation and other public facilities and by common economic interests. Bold programs in individual jurisdictions are no longer enough. Increasingly, community development must be a cooperative venture through the common goals of the metropolitan region as a whole.
> This requires the establishment of an effective and comprehensive planning process in each metropolitan area embracing all major activities, both public and private, which shape the community. Such a process must be democratic—for only when the citizens of a community have participated in selecting the goals which will shape their environment can they be expected to support the actions necessary to accomplish these goals. (Finley 2008, p. 161)

It is about time we truly embrace his message and create coordinated regional policies. In a November 2011 article in *USA Today*, reporter Haya El Nasser wrote that "the long-struggling U.S. economy has made once-competing municipalities more receptive" to working with each other against other regions of the nation and the world rather than against each other. She added, "They're reaching across county lines and even state borders and aligning themselves as one economic bloc."

125

Bruce Katz, vice president at the Brookings Institution and founding director of the institute's Brookings Metropolitan Policy Program, wrote in *Brookings* in April 1999 that there are three main reasons we need to address the problems of the cities and suburbs as a region: 1) the recognition that metropolitan areas constitute the real competitive units in the new economy, 2) the growing awareness that complex issues such as air quality and traffic congestion cross political boundaries and are immune to localized fixes, and 3) the coexistence of persistent joblessness in the central cities and labor shortages in the suburbs (Briggs 2005, x). More recently, in 2011, Katz wrote, "With many national and supranational levels of government dangerously adrift, the onus is on cities and metros to act like the engines of national prosperity they are and lead the economy-shaping, talent-preparing, place-making, and environmental-stewarding that this disruptive period demands."

In *Curing Urbanitis,* William Finley wrote: "Because the forces creating sprawl are so powerful and generally beyond the control of local governments, no one local entity except a form of regional government can halt it .... The only feasible path for metropolitan leaders, faced with these demographic challenges, is to start thinking regionally on all issues, beyond transportation and water supply, including housing, education, social services, language training, religious tolerance and, especially, urban growth boundaries" (Finley 2008, 54-55). Furthermore, he wrote that "regional issues are not design assignments; they are political, societal, and economic" (Finley 2008, 86).

In the future, regions will need to leverage their strengths in order to compete in the global economy. Americans are not only in competition with other towns, cities, and states but with other countries that are largely backing private industry. This isn't the same world of the 1950s and 1960s, when growth and prosperity were practically guaranteed. New, innovative solutions are needed now. For that reason, a holistic, regionwide strategy must be nurtured. To do that, it is essential to leverage a region's resources, such as hospitals, biotechnology firms, universities, the arts community, agriculture interests, and manufacturing companies. Whatever the strengths of a region, the leaders of those industries, companies, and governments must be conversing and strategizing together. It ought to be possible to create an agency to represent all concerns. In fact, it is imperative. Perhaps a merger or committee made up of members of the regional economic development center, planning agency, transportation committee, university leaders, environmental protection groups, arts and cultural organizations, workforce development officials, and youth empowerment nonprofits could be created. They could coordinate the promotion of regional assets and schedule strategic improvements.

Solutions will require broad support, integrating economic competitiveness, fiscal security, and social and environmental justice. Other stakeholders could include employers, unions, public school officials and advocates, faith institutions, and traditional (for-profit) and affordable-housing developers. The key, however, is for an agency to have "teeth," so to speak, with regulating and enforcement power.

The emphasis, according to Briggs (2005, 339), should be on expanding choices and improving access to opportunity. He wrote: "There was nothing natural or inevitable about the current shape of things—the uneven geography of opportunity, the sprawl in housing and jobs, the sharp segregation by race and class. Nor are the alternatives to these patterns predetermined. But communities do have choices, and we should get on with the work of understanding and pursuing them." After all, billions of local, state, and federal dollars are underwriting sprawl.

Responses to our crises must arise at the regional level. With only a few exceptions, state and federal direction have not been effective enough to date. William Shutkin, a global leader in sustainability and social entrepreneurship and author of the award-winning book *The Land That Could Be*, discussed "civic environmentalism" in which members of a particular geographic area or political community work together to create a future that is environmentally healthy and economically vibrant at the local and regional levels. He wrote, "Civic environmentalism entails a set of core concepts that embraces civic action and community planning in the part of a diverse group of stakeholders aimed at promoting both environmental protection and democratic renewal: participatory process, community and regional planning, environmental education, industrial ecology, environmental justice and place" (Shutkin 2000, 128).

Authors and scholars Richard Nathan and Gerald Benjamin, in

Regionalism and Realism, A Study of Governments in New York Metropolitan Area, identified four values of metropolitan realism in the United States: equity, efficiency, competitiveness, and community pride. The authors explained that redistributive metropolitanism, or regionalism, stresses greater equity between races and social classes; functional regionalism emphasizes governmental efficiency; and economic regionalism focuses on improving a region's competitiveness. They wrote that, moving forward, policy-makers must take these competing values into account when trying to establish effective regional approaches to issues such as sprawl, transportation, and even waste management.

Consolidation of local governments may not be a politically viable move, but we must at least establish and foster a spirit of cooperation. Sharing services among municipalities is a strategy increasing in frequency as more communities face new budget shortfalls and greater inconsistencies in revenues. Experience has shown that in the long term, efficiencies would be gained for communities through shared services and agreements, whether it's through police and fire departments, emergency medical services, garbage removal, or infrastructure maintenance and services.

Building the Case

"The first lesson of the global economy," wrote Theodore Hershberg, professor at the University of Pennsylvania and director of the Center for Greater Philadelphia, "is that regions—not cities nor the suburban counties that surround them—will be the units of economic competition ... Economic survival requires that cities and suburbs work together to develop human resources, lower the cost of services, and maximize returns from investment capital. To compete effectively, regions have to be cohesive ... In a nation with precious few examples of regional government, this means that cities and suburbs have to find ways to work together for their mutual benefit." William Barnes and Larry Ledebur of Cleveland State University argue that the United States does not have a single national economy but rather a group of regional economies linked in a common market (Nathan 2001, 47).

In *Who's Your City?* (2008), Richard Florida wrote: "The place we choose to live affects every aspect of our being ... People are not equally happy everywhere, and some places do a better job of providing a high quality of life than others."

Regions have unique identities. In his book, Florida wrote that city and regional leadership "must be aware of the powerful role played by psychology. Places really do have different personalities. Those personalities stem from their economic structure and inform and constrain their futures. It's a lot easier to go out and attract a new company, or even build a new stadium, than it is to alter the psychological makeup of a region. Regional leaders must become more aware of how their region's collective personality shapes the kinds of economic activities that it can do and the kinds of people it can attract, satisfy, and retain" (Florida, 2008, 213).

Today's winners become tomorrow's losers. As witnessed across the country and in many recent reports, suburban poverty has grown at unprecedented rates. It is not just an inner-city problem anymore. We cannot continue leaving our problems behind and moving farther away from the central city.

Development such as in Ohio, where residents consumed land at almost five times the rate of population growth—a ratio similar to upstate New York, Pennsylvania, and Michigan—is not sustainable. Even in upstate New York, the total amount of urbanized land grew by 30 percent between 1982 and 1997 while its population grew by only 2.6 percent. Pennsylvania's urbanized footprint grew 47 percent between 1982 and 1997 while its population increased just 2.5 percent.

We have to end the notion that one man's sprawl is another's tax base. Sprawl clearly affects all negatively; it may be someone else's tax base, but it also means depleted land, natural resources, contaminated air and water, and increased dependence on fossil fuels.

A 2008 study by the Federal Reserve Bank of Cleveland showed that overall economic growth is slower in regions with high poverty, segregation, and wide income disparities (Pastor 2010).

In 1992, Senator Bill Bradley, D-N.J., said cities "are poorer, sicker, less educated, and more violent than at any time in my lifetime ... and that the future of urban America will take one of three paths: abandonment, encirclement, or conversion" (Rusk 1999, 19). Are we any better off than when he made that speech?

Rusk, author of *Inside Game Outside Game*, summarized the situation succinctly:

> Urban sprawl and racial segregation feed upon and reinforce each other. The greater the sprawl, the more far-flung the dispersion of middle-class households. The greater the dispersion of middle-class households, the greater the abandonment of older neighborhoods in central cities and older suburbs. The greater the abandonment of older neighborhoods, the greater the concentration of poor minorities in those areas. The greater the concentration of poor minorities, the greater the increase in crime and violence, drug and alcohol addiction, family disintegration, unemployment and welfare dependency, school failure, and neighborhood deterioration. The greater the social meltdown of the "inner city" (which now connotes a set of social conditions more than location), the greater the incentives for those remaining residents who can choose where to live—middle-class households—to join the suburban diaspora .... And so, the cycle of peripheral growth and core abandonment accelerates in many metropolitan areas across the country. (Rusk 1999, 66)

The pattern cannot continue indefinitely. As we've sprawled out, so has our government, with our associated representation widely dispersed. In the 1950s, there were 168 metropolitan areas. "Sixty percent of the nation's metropolitan residents had been governed by 193 city councils or commissions and by 193 mayors or city managers. By 1990, almost 70 percent of the population of the same 168 regions fell under the governance of approximately 9,600 suburban cities, towns, villages, townships, and counties" (Rusk 1999, 67).

By 2001, the New York metropolitan region had 2,179 governments in an area that includes New Jersey, Connecticut, and thirty-one counties. New Jersey had the highest number of local governments per square mile in the nation. Local government density in New Jersey was 8.5 times the national average (Nathan 2001, 17). "Given the way local government is financed in America, economic competitiveness drives localities away from—not toward—collaboration, and as a general rule, social equity is best advanced as a byproduct of regional reform, not as its focal purpose" (Nathan 2001, 32). Equity must be part of a larger picture of economic competitiveness that should include environmental sustainability and security. Ultimately, regional reform is integral to the dual objectives of growth and prosperity because, as is the cyclical nature of things, the inner-ring suburbs become the next area of blight and poverty. Those suburbs, however, don't have the historic collection of cultural attractions, parks, museums, and enclaves of well-functioning cities. Can we keep moving farther and farther out?

The 2012 Planning Advisory Service report by Joseph Schilling and Alan Mallach titled *Cities in Transition* said that "growth oriented planning hasn't just failed post-industrial shrinking cities; it isn't working for many inner-ring suburbs like Euclid, Ohio, or Orange, New Jersey, either. These aging suburbs have inherited many of the problems associated with their central cities; however, they frequently lack assets like regional employment centers or cultural institutions that remain bright spots for many traditional urban centers. The key theme of *Cities in Transition* is that planners working in these cities need to embrace a new paradigm based on sustainability instead of growth" (Morley 2012).

Further evidence that cities and suburbs are interdependent include two findings: 1) that the higher the ratio of city to suburb per capita income, the higher the metropolitan employment and income growth and the greater the increase in housing values, and 2) that improvements in central city capital stock also increase suburban housing values, suggesting, as Paul Gottlieb put it in *The Effects of Poverty on Metropolitan Area Economic Performance*, "that suburban residents may have an incentive to increase contributions toward city infrastructure" (Briggs 2005, x). Metropolitan regions compete for jobs in the global economy against city-states that don't have the local, parochial interests our fragmented governance structure creates.

Wilson, the professor and sociologist, wrote in *The Geography of Opportunity* that a metropolitan region is at a severe disadvantage if it lacks a healthy urban core. In this era of low information costs, high mobility, and intense global competition, firms choose among regions when determining where to locate. A major factor in this decision is the health of the central city. According to HUD, even firms that choose to locate in suburban areas will select among surrounding vibrant central cities (Briggs 2005, x).

After all, many of the elements essential for a first-class region are found in the central cities, such as top-flight hospitals, universities, and research centers; county courts and offices; and state government.

In addition, we should recognize that there are two kinds of suburbs: older-ring and newer, outer. Generally, as Rusk wrote, "the older, inner suburbs adjacent to the city feature a crumbling tax base, a growing concentration of poor children in the public schools, an eroding job market, population decline, crime, disinvestment, and deserted commercial districts." These residents are as much victims of the uneven geography of housing opportunity as are the residents of the inner city. We see that the deterioration of the central city does not simply stagnate or end there.

Conversely, the newer, or outer, suburbs are gaining economically. At the same time, according to HUD, they are also "straining under sprawling growth that creates traffic congestion, experiencing overcrowded schools, loss of open spaces, and other sprawl-related problems combined with a lack of affordable housing. In many cases they are choking on development, and the local governments cannot provide the services that residents need or demand" (Briggs 2005, xi).

Top Three Fixes

There are three regional-scale solutions that have been shown to provide some relief to the issues described in the first part of this book. Many planners agree that these solutions—regional land-use planning, fair-share housing, and revenue sharing—seem to be the most practical and realistic. Once enabled through state legislatures, these solutions help to improve regional coordination.

Concerning regional land-use planning, while local governments may employ a variety of planning and zoning techniques to address concerns presented by the prospect of large-scale commercial or industrial development, they fail to take into account and effectively manage the interconnectivity and effects of such development on all neighboring municipalities. "Because economic activity (and its environmental and social impacts) does not recognize jurisdictional boundaries, regional planning is a better way to accurately achieve the economic and environmental health of a region, while also providing for the needs of individual localities. By working together, municipalities can articulate and achieve common goals that include effective strategies for, among other things, protecting common resources, coordinating public infrastructure, sharing [the] tax-base, and planning for commerce and industry" (Salkin 2004-2005). The effect of Oregon's statewide land-use law on Portland has been phenomenal. "After two decades of implementing an anti-sprawl urban growth boundary, the Portland area is clearly marching to a different drummer than most of urban America—and reaping enormous benefits from a booming economy and high quality of urban life," said Rusk (1999, 12).

Regional land-use planning can help preserve one's quality of life as well, whether it is in a downtown core or suburb. If people don't want their community growing commercially in a sprawl-creating strip mall fashion, regional land-use planning can help spread the development to grow more thoughtfully and equitably, perhaps concentrating development in other more appropriate areas. Regional land-use planning can help to protect environmentally sensitive lands and water bodies, and historic and cultural resources, while helping to build fairness into future development. Especially in fast-growing metropolitan areas, regional land-use planning can reduce auto dependence, increase mobility, improve air quality, and create more affordable communities. Local input is maintained, but the shortcomings of fragmented governmental authority are overcome.

Concerning fair-share housing, essential factors for a thriving region are inclusionary zoning and housing policies. Integrating low-income households into middle-class communities in order to diminish racial and economic segregation and concentrated poverty are essential. Everything old is new again. Although it started sooner, generally up until around the 1960s, the typical pattern of American life was one in which people of various income levels lived within a short walk of each other. This benefited entire communities. "In the regional economy, housing is the linchpin to quality of life: access to high-quality schools, jobs, services, and recreation. Increasing the supply of affordable housing is essential to improving housing opportunity ... To reach equity goals, affordable units must be spread across the region" (Briggs 2005, 290-291). Because if we truly believe what we say, that "we pride ourselves in equality of opportunity and justice" (not necessarily of outcomes because that is up to an individual's work ethic), then "one's home address should not be a determinant of one's life chances. The services, amenities, and opportunities that are essential for healthy, livable communities should be accessible to all neighborhoods .... Metropolitan areas that pay attention to *both* regional growth and central city poverty are more likely to thrive" (Briggs 2005, 290-291).

For example, the Minnesota Legislature passed the Land Use Planning Act of 1976, which required communities to make plans for meeting their share of regional housing needs. The Twin Cities fair-share program became one of the highest-performing regional programs in the nation. Prior to changes in national policy, local leadership, and demographics, the share of subsidized units in the cities of Minneapolis and Saint Paul fell from 82 percent to 59 percent. As Myron Orfield noted in *Urban Sprawl: Causes, Consequences and Policy Responses*, the support of these programs was based on a "hard-headed calculation of the costs of inequity and the destructive competition for development among municipalities in the region" (Briggs 2005, 250-252). Over time, however, after some regulations and policies were dismantled and others simply ignored, extremely high concentrations of minorities—and subsequent poverty—returned to the central cities. Notably, this also led to a decline in the older suburban areas. Orfield, in his 2002 book *American Metropolitics: The New Suburban Reality*, noted that "in the 1990s, 41 percent of the Twin Cities regional population lived in at-risk suburban communities. Yet, together with the central cities, these areas had 65 percent of the region's population but 83 percent of the poor" (Briggs 2005, 252). Given what has been learned from this example, a region needs an advocate or active community board to monitor progress and prevent a reversal of gains.

The landmark New Jersey Supreme Court case in 1975 (Mount Laurel I) said that "exclusionary zoning violated the general welfare provision of the state constitution by failing to address regional housing needs. The Court indicated that local governments throughout the state had an affirmative obligation to include low and moderate income housing in their development plans" (Briggs 2005, 321). Building affordable units that do not contribute to sprawl would be a win-win for everyone.

In Massachusetts, state statute "Chapter 40B," enacted in 1969, was an early attempt to undermine exclusionary housing practices. According to Spencer Cowan in his study, *Antisnob Land Use Laws and Suburban Exclusion*, it is potentially one of state's most effective policy tools for ensuring that affordable housing is spread fairly across all communities. Chapter 40B is "meant to encourage the production of affordable housing in all communities throughout the commonwealth. The law addresses the shortage of affordable housing statewide by reducing unnecessary barriers created by local approval processes, local zoning, and other restrictions." Strengthening 40B could lead to the creation of mixed-income communities that could help alleviate problems of concentrated poverty. These examples could be built on or replicated elsewhere (Briggs 2005, 299).

Developers could be required to build a certain percentage of units suitable for low- and moderate-income families, along with expedited approval for low- and moderate-income housing projects. In addition, a reduction in development fees for affordable housing could be implemented. Montgomery County, Md., passed the Moderately Priced Housing (MPH) Law in 1974. A provision of the MPH Law requires that between 12.5 percent and 15 percent of the houses in new subdivisions of twenty or more units be moderately priced. This has been a highly successful program in reducing income and racial segregation in comparison to many other parts of the country.

Furthermore, it should be recognized that the federal government defines affordable housing as that which does not cost more than 30 percent of household income, regardless of dollar amount. Yet, "on average, a parent working full time must earn almost $15 an hour, about three times the federal minimum wage, in order to afford a 'modest' two-bedroom home or apartment, by federal standards. This minimum 'housing wage' is much higher in many of the nation's most vibrant metropolitan economies" (Briggs 2005, 324). This means that there is an affordability crisis occurring in many of our metropolitan regions due to both stagnant wages and increasing housing costs over the past thirty years. Federal and state government could increase grants, loan guarantees, and tax credits to nonprofits, businesses, and state and local governments to create, encourage, and implement affordable housing.

Lastly, in the definitive study on trends in concentrated poverty, *Poverty and Place: Ghettos, Barrios, and the American City* (1997), Paul A. Jargowsky found that ghetto poverty was a function of both racial segregation and metropolitan economic growth. He wrote:

> Ghetto poverty is not primarily the product of ghetto culture that discourages upward mobility, but the product of metropolitan labor markets and residential settlement patterns .... Vigorous enforcement of antidiscrimination in housing, scattered site public housing, and zoning requirements that encourage mixed income developments can all play a role in reducing the segregation of blacks and the black poor ... This has both an immediate effect—reducing ghetto poverty—and a direct, long-term effect—the increased earning potential of children who attend better schools, grow up in safer, more stimulating environments, and see better role models of success in mainstream economy. (Rusk 2003, 56, 57)

Concerning revenue sharing, regional tax-base sharing would go a long way toward solving regional inequities. Ideally, it would be done in combination with regional land use, transportation planning, and growth management strategies. "By using tax-base sharing, all participating municipalities in the region agree to share tax proceeds from new development, thereby eliminating inter-jurisdictional competition and encouraging cooperation on regional economic goals" (Salkin 2004-2005).

Tax-base sharing among municipalities also has proved to be an effective way to manage the inequality created when local communities compete with one another for big-box or large-scale commercial or industrial revenue sources, thereby eliminating the race-to-the-bottom mentality that includes ever-higher governmental subsidies to businesses and the negative effects of community parochialism. "Local governments in a metropolitan area may choose to form contracts with one another in order to offset the regional burdens created by local land use decisions, and to ensure that everyone shares in the benefits derived from new development projects ... Maine has enacted legislation that authorizes the creation of tax sharing districts among local communities. The law states that municipalities entering into such agreements are free to adopt their own allocation formulas, and to make agreements with other, non-adjacent municipalities" (Salkin 2004-2005). In New Jersey, a tax-base-sharing approach was enacted by the legislature for the Hackensack-Meadowlands area. The Dayton, Ohio, area's ED/GE plan—the nation's most significant voluntary, multijurisdictional revenue-sharing program—is a huge success story. Yet, the state-mandated tax-base-sharing program in the Minneapolis-St. Paul area has had more than a hundred times the fiscal impact of the Dayton area's plan.

Though these three strategies are not all-encompassing or a panacea, they do offer the possibility of incremental change, something that is clearly needed for the United States to continue to be competitive in the twenty-first century. Opportunities must be available to all for nationwide prosperity. Facilitating increased opportunity, reducing sprawl, and boosting economic competitiveness will only benefit future generations.

Examples

The basic assumption, said the E3 Network, a national group of more than two hundred economists, is that "a clean and safe environment is a birthright of every person. It is not a commodity to be distributed on the basis of purchasing power, nor a privilege to be distributed on the basis of political power. This is inseparable from promoting social justice. Without a fair distribution of wealth and power, neither the free market nor government regulation will guarantee environmental quality and human well-being."

In 1994, Virginia officials noticed that they were losing out to North Carolina on significant growth opportunities due to the latter state's liberal annexation policies. In response, the mayors, city managers, and chamber of commerce presidents of fifteen major Virginia cities got together and formed an urban partnership. Top executives from many of the state's major corporations were also included, partly as a result of it losing out to North Carolina for a new National Football League franchise, the Carolina Panthers. (Virginia's governments were too fragmented and didn't, or couldn't, get their act together). The urban partnership concluded that "business leaders emphasized that all parts of a region need to be healthy for the region to be competitive in a global economy." Anthony Downs of the Brookings Institution emphasized that "it is up to suburban leaders to change attitudes about mutual interdependence and mutual membership in a single metropolitan community." Representative Norman Sisisky observed that "our destinies are linked together whether we like it or not." Business leadership makes the difference (Rusk 1999, 295).

Innovative initiatives already have taken place. For example, triple bottom line accounting—also referred to as the three pillars: people, planet, profit—has been used successfully in certain communities and socially conscious businesses. The method, coined by international authority on corporate responsibility and sustainable development John Elkington, captures an expanded spectrum of values and criteria for measuring organizational (and societal) success: economic, ecological, and social equity. Since 2009, TBL accounting has been used on a regional scale in Cleveland, Ohio, as part of a ten-year initiative to create a sustainable economy. The city has come a long way since 1969, when the Cuyahoga River caught fire. That experience led to a new mandate and a new coalition in city hall and resulted in significant public-private partnerships to guide downtown and neighborhood development. Major progress was made in both places, but it wasn't a complete success because a crucial ingredient, equity, was left out. As Nathan (2001, p. 50) pointed out in *Regionalism and Realism*, racial division, struggling schools, political fragmentation, and large income and education disparities still exist. Perhaps this new accounting effort will be the solution area leaders have been seeking.

Grand Rapids, Mich., and the surrounding region created the nation's first "Community Sustainability Partnership." Triple bottom line accounting was used there as well. At the end of 2011, the region used fourteen major indicators related to both the quality of life and environmental factors to determine progress made toward sustainability.

While it is not easy to replicate exact models, many areas of the country have taken certain measures to mitigate sprawl and its effects. Each of those regions initiated what was most feasible given the diverse stakeholders, unique circumstances, bureaucracies, and challenges. Doing nothing was no longer considered an option. Realistic, concrete, and holistic solutions must be implemented in the new millennium as we move forward in other parts of the country.

Chattanooga, Tenn., took matters into its own hands as a result of devastating environmental problems. The city reputedly had the worst air quality in the U.S. in 1969, so officials took decisive action to become competitive again. Public-private partnerships, formed in the 1970s, helped make Chattanooga the "poster child for the livable city," as David Crockett, a fifth-generation descendant of the frontiersman and councilman, named it. Major progress was made to bring stakeholders together and generate hundreds of millions of dollars in investments. But, until equity is made a cornerstone of regional improvement, racial division, struggling schools, political fragmentation, and large income and education disparities may continue.

Angered by countless farms being turned into subdivisions, farmers in Portland, Oregon, spurred creation of the state's growth management laws in the 1970s. Today, metro Portland has the only elected regional government in the country. It covers four counties, the city of Portland, and twenty-three other municipalities. Portland is the nation's model for regional land-use planning and growth management. According to the Portland Metro website: "It is a product of visionary leadership in the 1970s that set the stage for the quality of life we enjoy today in Oregon. That quality of life, in turn, accords the region and Oregon a unique advantage to compete in the global economy."

In Canada, the former regional government of Toronto, called Metro Toronto, was seen as integral to the city's reputation as one of the most livable cities in North America and the world. From 1954 to 1997, Metro Toronto was responsible for the metropolitan area's growth, which included transportation and land-use planning; all major infrastructure systems (water, sewer, highways, transit, regional parks); local public school financing; and a regionwide police department. Where subsidized housing would be located, for example, was never a matter for local governments to decide. Social housing was always controlled by Metro Toronto or even by the provincial government of Ontario. "As a result, social housing is widely dispersed and concentration of Toronto's poorest residents is averted" (Rusk 1999, 149). The ills of city life that many Americans tolerate today are refuted by Toronto. Since 1997, however, when the political winds changed, Metro Toronto's influence has been minimized. New suburban communities have sprouted up outside the influence of Metro Toronto, a pattern that is indistinguishable from American suburbs. As a result, no one can predict what will happen there in another fifty years.

In New York, the state paid $1.4 billion in tax credits and infrastructure support to one company to expand operations in a wealthy upstate suburb. It is the largest public-private investment in New York state history and is expected to draw much further investment. In 2010, construction started in Saratoga County on what GlobalFoundries said would become the first independent semiconductor manufacturing plant in the U.S., at a cost of $4.6 billion. The plant, located at the Luther Forest Technology Campus, is intended to be a state-of-the-art facility that ultimately is predicted to create at least fourteen hundred high-tech jobs and spur an additional five thousand jobs in the local economy.

Fierce competition against regions long established in computer chip fabrication across the globe culminated in the agreement. The process took many years of dedication and unparalleled commitment. As of mid-2012, however, a multijurisdictional, regional analysis of the economic, ecological, and social equity effects of the plant had not been completed. With growth now certain, current residents should be aware of its true impacts on the region. Optimistically, an expenditure of such an extraordinary sum would benefit all residents of the region while not excessively contributing to sprawl, inner-city decline, or a further loss of farming or quality of life for current and future residents. Rather, it should reverse some of these trends. There is no question that the project puts a relatively small upstate area (in terms of population) with great scenic beauty on the global map for future attention and development, which can be a positive thing. But moving forward, the project should, at the very least, not exacerbate certain undesirable conditions. A cautionary tale can be seen in Austin, Texas, which experienced explosive growth in the 1980s and 1990s, when more than a dozen chip-fabrication plants were built. Greater Austin's population essentially tripled. But local advocates for low-income families claim that poverty indicators actually worsened in Austin following the high-tech boom. New York can learn from Austin's mistakes and make sure equity considerations are paramount.

In addition to the GlobalFoundries project, much can be learned from New York state's strategy to create the College of Nanoscale Science and

Engineering (CNSE) at the University at Albany. It is the first college in the world dedicated to research, development, education, and deployment in the emerging disciplines of nanoscience, nanoengineering, nanobioscience, and nanoeconomics. As of this writing and according to the college website, the Albany nanotech complex is more than a twelve billion-dollar megaplex that has attracted more than two hundred fifty global corporate partners and is the most advanced research complex at any university in the world. It is ranked as the world's number one college for nanotechnology. To that effect, New York state has contributed about one billion dollars to it.

In 2007, *Small Times* magazine, a nanotechnology trade publication, wrote that CNSE "is widely recognized as a global resource for research, development, workforce education, and economic outreach in nanotechnology and its applications."

The nanoscale college began as a combined vision of government, academia, and industry. The common goal was to propel New York to a leadership position in technology and economic development. Working together, the partners leveled the playing field in competing with other countries where government-subsidized industrial clusters are common.

Semiconductor device manufacturing spread from Texas and California in the 1960s to the rest of the world, including Europe, Israel, Japan, Taiwan, Korea, Singapore, and China. Today, it is a global business. Communities such as Hillsboro, Oregon, outside Portland; and Chandler, Arizona, outside Phoenix (where Intel Corp., AMD's main rival, is located), have welcomed multiple-chip fabrication plants and experienced substantial growth. These are investments that changed the landscape and character of communities for generations. Recognizing and fully accounting for that change is essential for regional leaders. The Luther Forest and nanoscale college examples (when it includes the three E's: environment, equity, and economy) can be repeated as an economic development strategy across the country. Only then can states and regions more effectively compete against foreign countries that are luring industry with the full force of their national governments.

"I am the master of my fate. I am the captain of my soul."
—William Ernest Henley

As shown, federal and state government can play an enormous role in encouraging and rewarding regional planning and collaboration. Yet, they have not nearly done as much as they should. It is time to take a holistic approach to metropolitan development. With a coordinated effort land can be saved, cultural resources preserved, and sustainable practices integrated. For example, many Metropolitan Planning Organizations (MPOs) are focused solely on transportation as mandated by law. Yet, the Albany, N.Y., Capital District Transportation Committee has taken very innovative steps. Its Linkage Program is an integrated land use and transportation planning program recognized nationally as a best practice in livability planning. The program provides technical assistance for joint regional-local planning initiatives that link transportation and land use. It's one step in the right direction that could be replicated elsewhere. Other regional data management agencies could combine efforts with workforce development professionals and human service providers.

Similarly, HUD could pay more attention to the larger metropolitan issues and expand and enhance the Office of Sustainable Housing and Communities' Sustainable Communities Initiative. After all, Congress created HUD in 1965 "to provide assistance for housing and for the development of the Nation's communities ... that will have a major effect on urban community and suburban development." HUD's annual funding has been whittled away to a total of $53 billion that is distributed through the fifty states to hundreds of communities. In 1969, Congress created the Environmental Protection Agency (EPA) to "encourage productive and enjoyable harmony between man and his environment ..." Further, the law stated, "The Congress ... recognizes the profound impact of man's activities on the ... natural environment, particularly the profound influences of population growth, high-density urbanization, industrial expansion ... and recognizes further the critical importance of restoring and maintaining environmental quality to the overall welfare and development of man ..." In recent years, EPA's multibillion-dollar budget has been devoted mainly to clean air, global climate change, clean water, land preservation, healthy communities, and environmental stewardship. "Its work is somewhat ignored, although often valued because it prevents the worst, tries to remedy disasters, and sets standards on pollution. Its plate is too full to expect it to deal directly with problems of the growth of cities" (Finley 2008, 95-96).

Continued and further coordination among HUD, the U.S. Department of Transportation, and the EPA is essential to encourage more consistent and complementary policy-making.

Another proposal with enormous potential is the creation of a national infrastructure bank similar to the World Bank or European Investment Bank. A $60 billion investment could be used to insure bonds of state and local governments to provide subsidies and issue bonds to finance itself. According to Felix Rohatyn, an American investment banker known for his role in preventing the bankruptcy of New York City in the 1970s, this institution could easily provide $250 billion of new capital for construction and maintenance projects and would result in the creation of millions of new jobs. As of 2011, the federal government spent $73 billion annually on infrastructure projects, yet no system is in place to strategically guide it. Projects would be proposed, and applications submitted to the national infrastructure bank for review and consideration. If the national benefits are compelling, a project could be strategically approved.

President Franklin Roosevelt said, "There are many ways of going forward, but only one way of standing still." Time is running out. Perhaps it is out for many of our environmental challenges. Nevertheless, we can no longer simply discuss the problems we face. Action is needed now. If the government can't or won't act on our behalf, we can and must. As Rabbi Abraham Heschel aptly put it: "We are not all equally guilty but we are all equally responsible" for building a decent and just America (Edelman 1992, 55). While the country waits for national action, infrastructure is deteriorating, and businesses and citizens are losing their edge. We are becoming less competitive in the global economy while exacerbating environmental damage. It is for these reasons that the next phase of ingenuity and solidarity must be created and nurtured at the local and regional level. Moving forward means we each must say: "I can help; I can contribute; I can advocate; I can work hard; I can believe."

Potential Policies and Programs

The prophet Mohammed once said, "A person's true wealth is the good he or she does in the world." While state and federal action are ideal due to their potential resources and capacity, certain measures can be addressed at the local, regional, and even individual level. Several of the most essential strategies are:

- Promoting the role of higher education.
- Encouraging a more efficient land-use and transportation strategy.
- Coordinating support for local farms, businesses, and nonprofits.
- Promoting energy-efficient construction and green jobs.
- Fostering youth programs.

The role of higher education cannot be emphasized enough. Countless cultural, intellectual, and social benefits accrue when universities and colleges are fully integrated into the surrounding community. Promoting a region as a center for higher education—essentially, by asserting the role of higher education in the economic, cultural, and social life of the area—benefits all residents. Regions with a cluster of colleges and universities already have a large advantage over those without them. One successful off-campus program features people working in the local communities to stimulate civil rights movements that advocate for social, economic, and even environmental justice. Another program offers a city arts movement that engages community members. And a "Go To College" program encourages elementary school pupils to visit and connect with a university's students and faculty.

Some universities have instituted community and regional environmental sustainability workshops in which students participate in science, public policy, and community action events and publications. In one metro urban studies course, a class immerses itself into a pressing local issue and investigates, advocates, and participates in the proceedings. Another innovative program included "writing for social change" in which students write opinion, editorials, or grant proposals for local community charities.

Higher education's leadership is critical in helping businesses become sustainable; to have strong, thriving, and secure communities; and to provide economic opportunities for the broadest number of people. Higher education fills a crucial role in producing an educated and engaged citizenry and the knowledge needed for a thriving and civil society. The challenges associated with creating vibrant, secure communities and strong economies while preserving our life-support system can be addressed because of the strength of our higher education institutions.

Some successful examples include the Ohio Housing Research Network, Michigan State University's Urban Affairs Department, and Wayne State University's College of Labor, Urban and Metropolitan Affairs, which conducts training programs for business leaders and public officials and administrators. Portland State University's Institute of Metropolitan Studies is engaged in analyses of developments in its region. Virginia Commonwealth University's Center for Urban Studies provides staff support to Virginia's Urban Partnership; Ohio Urban Universities Program links research efforts among the state's major urban universities; the Higher Education Consortium for Urban Affairs of St. Paul, Minn., has innovative programs as previously mentioned (such as civil rights, city arts, writing for social change, and so forth). These programs and initiatives could be expanded, nurtured, and duplicated elsewhere. There are hundreds of areas across the country where similar programs could be duplicated.

Another strategy, encouraging more efficient land use and transportation, includes embracing smart growth (compact, mixed-use forms of development), appropriate transit-oriented development (TOD), and New Urbanism. The latter is defined as an urban design movement that promotes walkable neighborhoods that contain a range of housing and job types. New Urbanism and transit-oriented development are buzz words that, essentially, translate to more compact, less automobile-dependent growth to reduce sprawl and environmental deterioration. There are numerous books, articles, and reports that describe in detail how to implement these concepts. As the saying goes, "They are not producing more land." We need to preserve the land we have and incorporate healthy, sustainable practices. Otherwise, as the "tragedy of the commons" demonstrates, overuse and exploitation will diminish the integrity of the land and its capacity to ensure survival. In pursuit of our individual desires, sometimes we create a socially undesirable outcome. For example, "when a natural resource—such as a fishery or underground aquifer—is made available to all, individuals will tend to exploit the resource far beyond the optimal level. This problem arises because the incentives of individuals diverge from the common good" (Speth 2008, 92).

A 2010 study published by a coalition of industry and government stakeholders in Ontario, Canada, said that avoiding urban sprawl could reduce pollution and boost the economy. The study warned that the "business as usual scenario could wind up costing billions of dollars and lock the country into a path that ensures higher energy consumption and pollution." The coalition group that spearheaded the study, Quality Urban Energy System of Tomorrow (QUEST), said that Canadians could save money and create jobs by coordinating sustainable strategies in 120 cities and communities that make up 95 percent of the population. That starts with land use. The resulting savings in energy consumption alone could result in up to $29 billion in savings for the economy over forty years (DeSouza 2010). In addition, as Housing and Urban Development Secretary Shaun Donovan said in 2011, "the costs of commuting and time lost in congestion are five times higher than 25 years ago."

From "Growing Wealthier: Smart Growth, Climate Change and Prosperity" by the Center for Clean Air Policy, we have seen evidence of how the application of smart growth principles can improve the bottom line for businesses, households, and governments by increasing property values, cutting fuel and infrastructure costs, creating jobs, enhancing public health, and strengthening communities. In Dallas, Texas, in the first year after a light rail system began operating in its downtown, the city's retail economy grew by 33 percent. In Portland, an investment of $103 million in streetcars attracted $3.5 billion in private investment. In Denver, Colo., households within a half mile of a light rail line rose in value by 18 percent between 2006 and 2008, while other Denver homes lost an average of 7.5 percent in value.

Smart growth benefits are also evidenced by the following examples:

- Properties with a high "Walk Score" (walkable, mixed use neighborhoods) value appreciated nearly 2 percent more annually than properties with low Walk Scores (as defined by a large-scale, public-access walkability index that assigns a numerical walkability score).
- One billion dollars in stimulus money spent on transit creates approximately twice the amount of jobs as one billion dollars spent on highways.
- A Transportation Research Board study concluded that shifting 15 percent of new growth into more developed areas by 2025 could save the nation $105 billion in road infrastructure costs.

Furthermore, a 2010 University of New Hampshire study showed that walkable neighborhoods make people happier. The study, titled "Examining Walkability and Social Capital as Indicators of Quality of Life at the Municipal and Neighborhood Scales," said that "those living in more walkable neighborhoods trusted their neighbors more; participated in community projects, clubs and volunteering more; and described television as their major form of entertainment less than survey participants living in less walkable neighborhoods."

"A study by researchers of 280 U.S. counties rated by how sprawled-out their development is showed that the ten counties highest in 'smart growth' ... had less than a quarter the per capita traffic fatality rates than the ten with the most scattered and single use growth patterns" (Peirce 2011c).

There is pent-up demand for transit-oriented development. According to a Reconnecting America study from 2008, almost a quarter of all renters and buyers will want TOD housing in 2030. Los Angeles is expected to have a 544 percent increase in demand for TOD housing, or approximately 1.4 million households, by 2030. The pattern is nationwide. But if an area's zoning laws are antiquated, TOD might be illegal (Simril 2010).

"The U.S. is in the midst of a demographic shift that is changing the nation's housing preferences and development patterns. The two largest demographic segments—millennials, who are entering the workforce, and baby boomers, who are leaving it—are most interested in walkable neighborhoods that offer a variety of housing choices, convenient transportation options, shopping, restaurants, parks, and cultural amenities" (Environmental Protection Agency 2010).

Surveys by real estate adviser Robert Charles Lesser & Co reveal that up to 88 percent of Generation Y (those born between 1979 and 1996 who number about 80 million) prefer to live in an urban setting. One-third are willing to pay for walkability.

The National Association of Realtors reported that 56 percent of respondents to its 2011 survey want smart-growth neighborhoods over neighborhoods that require more driving between home, work, and recreation. According to the survey, 77 percent of respondents said they would look for neighborhoods with abundant sidewalks and other pedestrian-friendly features.

The coming demographic shift figures to be enormous. "Households with children will drop from 45 percent in 1970 to 27 percent in 2030. Households without children will rise sharply, and the market will be dominated by aging baby boomers. Three million people turn 65 each year" (Lincoln Institute for Land Policy 2011). The Urban Land Institute's Jonathan Miller, author of a report titled "Emerging Trends in Real Estate" in 2011, advised people to "avoid commodity, half-finished subdivisions in the suburban outer edge and McMansions; they are so yesterday."

A 2011 study by the Jonathan Rose Companies titled *Transit Outperforms Green Buildings* said that "transit-oriented development is the key to cutting energy consumption—even more so than Energy Star construction or green cars, according to a peer reviewed study supported by the EPA .... No factor has a bigger impact than going from conventional suburban to transit oriented design."

A 2008 Urban Land Institute Study titled *Growing Cooler: The Evidence on Urban Development and Climate Change* said that TOD can reduce vehicle miles traveled by anywhere from 20 to 40 percent per capita, relative to sprawl.

Researchers at Rutgers University have estimated that compact development such as reusing vacant urban space and investing in our existing cities, small towns, and villages could save the U.S. about $4 billion each year in public service funds. They estimated that Americans will spend about $190 billion on extending sewer and water lines to single-family homes between 2000 and 2025. Over the same period, they project the U.S. could save $110 billion in road building costs under a managed-growth plan.

"Good transit, good urban planning, livable communities—those are the kinds of things that matter most to tech people and tech companies when it comes to attracting companies and making them stay here," said Sandelman Software Works founder Michael Richardson, who has been involved in Ottawa's technology sector since 1988. Public transportation, therefore, must be re-emphasized at all levels. Advocates within the region can come together to join partnerships and coalitions. Typically, transit agencies are quasi-governmental in nature, but transit advocates can be found at the grassroots and local levels. Sound and strategic investing for increased transit use is critical because, as was noted earlier, the current mismatch in funding for highway rather than transit has helped to create our current level of sprawl.

Similarly, we must always include equity and fairness considerations in all regional and local decision-making by ensuring that gentrification does not harm current residents and that displacement of people is not forced.

A third strategy, coordinating support for locally based business and nonprofits, would go a long way toward creating regional benefits. "For the fourth year in a row a national survey of independent businesses has found that those in communities with an active 'buy local' campaign have experienced markedly stronger revenue growth compared to those located in areas without such a campaign" (Mitchell 2011). Small local businesses, which provide uniqueness and community character, are the largest employer nationally. Nonprofit organizations receive an average of 250 percent more support from smaller business owners than they do from large businesses; therefore, profits stay local. Regions stand to benefit if residents support these local groups.

One study in particular—*The Economic Impact of Locally Owned Businesses vs. Chains: A Case Study in Midcoast Maine*—is frequently quoted by "buy local" campaigns around the country. Conducted in 2003 by the Institute for

Local Self-Reliance, the Midcoast report suggested that for every $100 spent on local businesses, about $45 stays local. Compare that with $100 spent at a big-box store or out-of-state-based franchise. The study claimed that only $14 stays local, while the rest is shipped off to a corporate home office. Residents who support locally based businesses and nonprofits thus shield themselves from the increasingly volatile nature of the global markets.

Other media sources state that locally owned independent businesses return approximately 80 percent of each dollar spent back to the community. This assists the community through a "multiplier effect": one dollar spent at a locally owned business will return five times that amount within the community through employees' wages and purchases of materials and supplies at other independent businesses.

Chain restaurant and retail businesses, though they may provide essential services, may not be as involved in the region as locally owned companies. How many times a day or week do we visit a corporate gas station, restaurant, drugstore, clothing store, coffee shop, or bookstore? A pertinent question would be: Do these businesses contribute to the community in which they are located at the same level as the "mom and pop" stores and services do? As an ancient African proverb states, "It takes a village to raise a child." Each community or region has historically been able to tap into its local businesses for some sort of financial assistance. We all have a role to play, both individually and corporately, and if it is only the local mom and pop stores or restaurants sponsoring teams, holding fund drives, and donating equipment or food or funds, it shouldn't be too much to ask nonparticipating businesses to do what they can. A thriving democracy is dependent on quality citizen and corporate involvement. We all have a stake in the outcome of our communities and regions.

Furthermore, supporting local farms and farmers markets is essential for regional prosperity. As Jonathan Swift wrote in *Gulliver's Travels*, "Whoever can make two ears of corn, or two blades of grass, to grow upon a spot of ground where only one grew before, would deserve better of mankind, and do more essential service to his country, than the whole race of politicians put together."

To save farms, cities must be safe, secure, attractive, and thriving—thereby discouraging sprawl. Supporting locally grown and produced goods and services goes a long way toward reducing transportation costs, among other things. Rather than having produce and supplies shipped across oceans and continents, we can buy locally and reduce greenhouse gases and all associated waste.

Furthermore, Jeff Pfizer, leader of the local food movement in Chattanooga, Tenn., said that less than one tenth of 1 percent of the region's food spending goes to area farms. "Raising the figure to 5 percent would represent $100 million in economic development," he said. Pfizer further noted that supporting the local food movement links city and country, protects farmland and watersheds from new subdivisions, and responds to the threat to national security posed by long supply lines (Peirce, 2011b).

Communities benefit tremendously when they embrace rural regionalism, mainly farming country. The Sierra Business Council in eastern California, the Loess Hills Alliance in Iowa, the Highland Communities Initiative in western Massachusetts, and the Western Kansas Rural Economic Development Alliance are great examples of partnerships created from the ground up. Concerning the Kansas example, Max Lu wrote in *Planning* magazine in 2010 how "friendly competition" was created among member communities, and that "people now realize that they are all in it together. Incorporated in 1995 as a 501(c)(6), they now have quarterly meetings, a website, reports issued, staff provided and training [available] to member communities. Since the 1990s about two dozen large dairies have moved to the areas from states such as California, Minnesota, New Mexico, Pennsylvania, and Washington."

Fixing agricultural subsidies is essential to a healthier society. "Nearly 90 percent of the (U.S.) corn crop is used for either ethanol or animal feed" (Bittman 2011b). Furthermore, agricultural subsidies have brought us high-fructose corn syrup, factory farming, fast food, and monoculture. The fortunes of Pepsi, Dunkin' Donuts, KFC, and others have blossomed because of cheap corn and soy. "Over the years, prices of fresh produce have risen, while those of meat, poultry, sweets, fats and oils, and especially soda, have fallen" (Bittman, 2011a).

"Agritourism is the second-leading source of income revenue for farmers in New York state behind milk," said state Senator Steve Englebright of Setauket, L.I.

Few realize that a vegan diet is not only enormously healthful but benefits the world in terms of less pollution, emissions, and environmental degradation. According to a 2006 Food and Agriculture Organization of the United Nations report, the livestock industry is one of the largest contributors to environmental degradation worldwide, and modern practices of raising animals for food contribute on a "massive scale" to deforestation, air and water pollution, land degradation, loss of topsoil, climate change, the overuse of resources including oil and water, and loss of biodiversity. The report concluded that "the livestock sector emerges as one of the top two or three most significant contributors to the most serious environmental problems, at every scale from local to global." Cornell scientists claimed that the U.S. could feed eight hundred million people with grain that livestock eat. The result is that producing animal-based food is typically much less efficient than the direct harvesting of grains, vegetables, legumes, seeds, and fruits for human consumption.

Dennis Avery, director of the Centre for Global Food Issues, said, "The world must create five billion vegans in the next several decades, or triple its total farm output without using more land."

A simple, direct, and immediate way to advance the above-mentioned agricultural and farming goals is to support existing nonprofits that focus on land preservation, conservation, farmland, and watershed protection. This would complement the smart growth efforts and local farming movement while reducing the negative effects of sprawl. These nonprofits act where government cannot or has become too complacent. Land trusts can work with land owners to provide easements and protections for farmland that is otherwise under development pressure while protecting water quality and conservation efforts across a region. Agricultural stewardship nonprofits are other vital avenues that can be used to protect farms and communities.

The fourth strategy is two-fold: promoting energy-efficient construction and the green jobs movement. The two goals complement and reinforce each other. The International Energy Agency released a publication in 2009 that estimated that existing buildings are responsible for more than 40 percent of the world's total primary energy consumption and 24 percent of global carbon dioxide emissions.

A 2007 study by Davis Langdon, a global construction consultant, showed that over a twenty-year span, some green buildings have yielded $53 to $71 per square foot back on investment. One of the best ways to implement change is to incorporate LEED (Leadership in Environmental and Energy Design) certification. That can be voluntarily implemented in the private sector or encouraged at the governmental level. As defined by the U.S. Green Building Council, LEED is "a third-party certification program and the nationally accepted benchmark for the design, construction and operation of high-performance green buildings. LEED gives building owners and operators the tools they need to have an immediate and measurable impact on their buildings' performance. LEED promotes a whole-building approach to sustainability by recognizing performance in five key areas of human and environmental health: sustainable site development, water savings, energy efficiency, materials selection and indoor environmental quality."

At the very minimum, certain energy savings and efficiencies must be encouraged at all costs. The borough of West Chester in Pennsylvania became the first municipality in the country to enact a local ordinance requiring private commercial businesses be designed to earn the Energy Star certification as defined by a joint program of the EPA and the U.S. Department of Energy. The city of Alpharetta, Georgia, twenty-five miles north of Atlanta, created a Green Communities Ordinance, granting expedited permitting, plan review, and building site inspections for all privately owned new construction projects that will earn LEED or Energy Star certification.

A green design example includes the Garland, Texas, tree canopy program (tree planting to reduce stormwater runoff). It is credited with diffusing nineteen million cubic feet of runoff per storm, an amount of water that ordinarily would require $38 million in retention infrastructure (Center for Clean Air Policy 2011).

"New York City plans to build green infrastructure to cut down discharges into its combined sewer system—a project expected to save about $1.5 billion in treatment and infrastructure costs over 20 years. Replacing streets in Seattle with permeable pavement and other green infrastucture has cut paving costs nearly in half," wrote Nate Berg in "The Atlantic Cities" in 2012. "Through energy savings, air and water filtering and carbon storage, the urban trees of Tennessee account for more than $638 million in benefits," according to a 2012 report by the U.S. Forest Service.

The average homeowner would save almost $90 a year just by switching to energy-saving lightbulbs. The 2007 law signed by President George W. Bush that would gradually phase out old-fashioned incandescent lightbulbs in favor of new energy-efficient ones would eliminate the need for 33 large power plants, according to one estimate (McMahon 2011).

Supporting the Green Jobs Movement directly advances LEED/energy-efficient construction goals. Former presidential adviser Van Jones discussed this in his book *The Green Collar Economy*. Similarly, Green Jobs For All is a national organization working to build an inclusive green economy strong enough to lift people out of poverty through job training and opportunity. The realities of global warming and peak oil ensure the world will generate millions of clean energy jobs in the coming decade.

The fifth strategy, and probably the most promising of all the previously mentioned solutions for lasting community improvement, is fostering youth programs, an umbrella term that includes inner-city and rural village-focused youth development, mentoring, job training, and after-school programs. Although the effects are not as immediately quantifiable, no one can argue that improving the life opportunities of inner-city youth will contribute enormously to the overall quality of the neighborhood, region, and nation. "There is no finer investment for any country than putting milk into babies," said Winston Churchill. Frederick Douglass once noted, "It is easier to build strong children than to repair broken men." Kathleen Kennedy Townsend, daughter of Robert Kennedy, once asked, "How can they (students) learn American history and the meaning of democracy without understanding in the most personal and direct manner the spirit of community service, justice, civic participation and freedom?" A report from the Campaign for Education Equity noted that the combined income and tax losses for one group of 18-year-olds that drop out are $192 billion, approximately 1.6 percent of the U.S. GDP.

According to the *Be A Mentor* not-for-profit in Hayward, Calif.:

Children struggle without positive adult influence. Lacking nurturing, guidance, support and opportunity from a young age, they begin to experience and perceive the world as a place without opportunity or hope. If they had dreams as young children, the circumstances of their lives often crush their dreams and leave them, as teenagers, lost, hurt and angry. Young people who have been neglected and abused, live in neighborhoods and communities where every day their hopes get crushed by circumstance, and look at the world as an unfriendly and even hostile or violent adversary generally resign themselves to a lifetime of poverty, escapism by drugs and alcohol, unemployment and underemployment, gang participation and incarceration.

The National Strategic Narrative released by the Woodrow Wilson Center for International Scholars noted that, "Without a doubt, our greatest resource is America's young people, who will shape and execute the vision needed to take this nation forward into an uncertain future" (Mr. Y 2011).

In 1997, General Colin Powell started America's Promise, a youth mentoring nonprofit dedicated to helping children at risk. According to the group's website:

We are an alliance born of the recognition that when too many children are at risk, we are a nation at risk. With less than one-third of America's young people receiving the essential resources they need for success, we're witnessing today an increased risk of substance abuse, crime and school drop outs. We can't afford this loss of human potential and reversing this tide must be a national priority. Everything we do as an Alliance is built around the framework of ensuring that more young people experience more of the Promises: Caring Adults, Safe Places, A Healthy Start, Effective Education, and Opportunities to Help Others. Children who receive at least four of the Five Promises are more likely to avoid violence, contribute to their communities, achieve high grades in school, and mitigate gaps across racial and economic boundaries.

"A growing number of evaluations suggest that volunteer mentoring relationships can positively influence a range of outcomes, including improvements in peer and parental relationships, academic achievement, and self-concept, as well as lower recidivism rates among juvenile delinquents, and reductions in substance abuse" (Rhodes 2001).

The *Be a Mentor* nonprofit notes that "research and surveys indicate that most young people, regardless of their attitude, want positive interaction with adults in their lives, and when they have it, they are more likely to stay in school, attend classes, be less disruptive when attending class, get better grades and go to college. Rather than becoming financial, emotional and political drains on their community, at-risk youth with mentors become productive, contributing members of it."

Big Brothers Big Sisters pioneered youth mentoring in 1904. An independent national study surveyed their programs and methods spanning a five-year period and found that children involved in Big Brothers Big Sisters mentoring programs were more likely to graduate and stay out of trouble when compared to their peers without mentors. They also found that they improved their school grades and relationships with others.

Furthermore, a 2000 report from the U.S. Department of Justice, Office of Justice Programs, Bureau of Justice Assistance titled "Investing Wisely in Crime Prevention: International Experiences" stated that "it is estimated that encouraging social development of children and families decreases crime and yields returns up to $7.16 for every $1 spent. In order to decrease crime by 10 percent, 228 additional tax dollars per family would need to be spent on incarceration compared to just a $32 increase to help at-risk children complete school."

Lastly, Geoffrey Canada's experiment with the Harlem Children's Zone Promise Academy to improve the lives of inner-city kids who otherwise have an almost negligible chance of success in life is truly amazing. President Obama, who began supporting and replicating the program across the country in 2010, said: "The philosophy behind the project is simple—if poverty is a disease that infects an entire community in the form of unemployment and violence, failing schools and broken homes, then we can't just treat those symptoms in isolation. We have to heal that entire community. And we have to focus on what actually works ... And it is working ... And if we know it works, there's no reason this program should stop at the end of those blocks in Harlem." Areas that missed out on funding must start their own programs, perhaps building off existing ones. The children's zone Baby College and the immersive, intensive educational programs for everyone from infants up to adults are producing miraculous results, reversing intergenerational poverty once and for all. Numerous independent studies by economists, sociologists, psychologists, and neuroscientists all support and reinforce what Canada has created. As Paul Tough wrote (p. 282) in his 2008 seminal analysis of Canada's work, "To change the trajectory of a poor child in an inner city neighborhood, this research shows, you need to: intervene early in the child's life; continue to intervene throughout adolescence; give him extra time in school and extra support outside of school; involve his parents if possible but be prepared to compensate for their absence; focus on improving his cognitive skills but also nurture his noncognitive, social, and emotional skills." Strive Partnership in Cincinnati is a similarly successful program. And in Somerville, Mass., YouthBuild is another successful example. YouthBuild encompasses 273 programs scattered across the country that offer education, counseling, job training, community service, leadership development, and job placement services. More than half of the unemployed or undereducated young who enter the program turn their lives around. These successful efforts must be replicated nationwide on a massive scale.

The Center for Cities and Schools at the University of California at Berkeley put out a report in June 2011 titled *Opportunity Rich Schools and Sustainable Communities: Seven Steps to Align High Quality Education with Innovations in City and Metropolitan Planning and Development*. The authors emphasized that "the fate of young people who live in opportunity-starved communities is directly linked to the 'shared fate' of their communities, regions, and the nation."

As a result, they wrote, community development requires a holistic look at educational and youth opportunities to ensure a region's success. Among the steps the authors recommended are: engaging school leaders, families, and young people in planning and development; establishing a shared vision and metrics linking high-quality education to economic prosperity at community and regional levels; supporting the whole life of learners through services and amenities; aligning bricks-and-mortar investments for regional prosperity; maximizing public transportation and pedestrian options; and institutionalizing what works to secure gains and ongoing innovation. In the end, as the report emphasized, the challenges are not insurmountable and must be confronted. "Not doing so inhibits the innovations necessary for city and regional planning to ameliorate the deep racial and economic inequalities across metro regions that limit individual potential and threaten community prosperity."

Other Strategies

Besides those five core solutions, other important strategies include 1) creating mechanisms for helping neighborhoods build social capital, 2) promoting the arts and culture, 3) fostering metropolitan business plans, 4) expanding the chamber of commerce model, and 5) improving coalitions and partnerships.

Building social capital in neighborhoods can be a tremendous investment, and creating mechanisms to do so is critical. In April 2011, Federal Reserve Chairman Ben Bernanke called for more lending to people and small businesses in lower-income neighborhoods, saying they were disproportionately hurt by the recession. Community loan funds are key to creating social capital. These loan funds and the administrators typically collaborate with a wide range of donors and lenders, and with business, nonprofit, and government partners. Together, they provide the financing and support for people of low and moderate incomes. Another form of capital is a community benefit agreement (CBA) from developers for projects adjacent to lower-income areas. If a project receives certain tax credits or other special benefits, perhaps certain public improvements or amenities to improve neglected communities could be included in the deal, "a rising tide lifts all boats" strategy. The Partnership for Working Families has a suggestion for a successful CBA. The group posits that a project-specific, negotiated agreement between a developer and a broad community coalition that outlines the expected contributions to the community and ensures support is essential. As the Dukakis Center for Urban and Regional Policy noted, if a developer is getting tax deferments or breaks or credits, it may be possible to negotiate the CBA for living wages, local hiring and training programs, affordable housing, environmental remediation, or funds for community programs.

A strategy of promoting the arts and culture, including emphasis on an area's history, has been shown to boost regional growth and prosperity. "Not only do our arts and culture preserve and promote deeper aspects of who we are as people, they too represent cornerstones of our economic well-being" wrote Russell Bishop in a 2010 article in The Huffington Post. A 2010 report by The European House-Ambrosetti, a professional consulting group, that looked at the United Kingdom, Europe, U.S., and Japan and ninety-five key economic performance indicators found that every $100 invested in the arts and culture produces a further $2.49 in GDP growth, and that for every three jobs created in the arts and culture, another two jobs are created in the private sector.

The role arts and culture could play in urban development, including revitalizing our communities and neighborhoods, is enormous. Because many elementary and high schools are cutting arts programs to save money, colleges and universities could perhaps fill the void. The Social Impact of the Arts Project, a research center at the University of Pennsylvania's School of Social Policy and Practice that is supported in part by the Rockefeller Foundation, studied local communities, particularly those in Baltimore and Philadelphia. "The center found that the arts had extraordinarily beneficial effects in those cities, including greater civic engagement; more social cohesion; improved child welfare, specifically in reducing delinquency and truancy; higher incomes; higher local property tax revenue; and greater economic activity" (Learsy 2010).

A third strategy, fostering metropolitan business plans, as discussed by the Brookings Institution, is a new concept that northeast Ohio, Minneapolis-Saint Paul, and Seattle are applying. Essentially, it is a consortia of regional leaders that came together to combine private-sector business planning with regional economic development. It includes four basic action items: analyzing the market position of the region; identifying strategies to capitalize on assets; specifying products, policies, and interventions; and establishing detail-oriented operational and financial plans (Muro 2011).

The Commercial Club of Chicago, an organization of 400 of the metropolitan area's most important business leaders, created the Chicago Metropolis 2020 to reverse the effects of suburban sprawl, racial segregation, and economic isolation that threatened the city's vitality. Specifically, it stated that, "when a substantial minority of the population is shut out, isolated, and without hope, the economic and social well-being of the whole region is threatened. The fate of everyone in this region is inherently connected." More than a hundred major area employers pledged that "in making decisions relating to the expansion of an existing facility or the location of a new facility in a given community, we will give substantial weight to whether a community has zoning, building, and land use policies that allow the construction of housing which is affordable to working people; and whether a community is served by reliable and accessible mass transit, especially mass transit near work sites" (Rusk 2003, 125).

Recruiting high-quality employees is a priority for businesses, and it's easier for them and others if the community is healthy and vibrant, both economically and environmentally, said a University of Michigan Center for Local, State and Urban Policy report.

In other words, to make metro areas more economically competitive, William Stafford of the Citistates Group said: "Each area (metro region) should develop an honestly frank business plan or economic strategy. That plan should recognize the economic crisis but be aspirational. That plan should include a strong focus on how to employ the less educated in the metro, creating a fair and productive economy."

A fourth strategy, expanding the chamber of commerce model, is one that more leaders should consider. Most of us are well aware of the benefits that a local chamber of commerce provides in promoting and encouraging regional businesses. Along the same lines, perhaps a region could create a chamber of commerce for the poor, the working class, and the environment, an advocacy agency that promotes, protects, and enhances the experience of its members Or, if capacity is lacking to start something new, simply creating a poverty reduction and sustainability initiative through an existing chamber of commerce could go a long way toward building partnerships and complementing and enhancing the traditional mission of chambers of commerce and existing poverty-reduction agencies.

Imagine having to support yourself and three others on $22,350 per year, the official 2011 U.S. poverty level for a four-person household. Holding poverty simulations is one way to understand what some households are up against economically. The National League of Cities wrote in 2008: "A poverty simulation is a tool that enables participants to view poverty from different angles in an experiential setting. Within a 2-3 hour time frame, poverty simulations allow participants to experience what it is like to live in a low-income family trying to survive from month to month. The simulations provide an opportunity for the public, including problem solvers in the business and civic communities, to learn why poverty is an issue that impacts everyone." Conducting a poverty simulation gives officials an opportunity to launch regionwide discussions about poverty and forge a deeper understanding of the issue in order to take anti-poverty efforts to the next level. Savannah, Ga., is a city that successfully uses poverty simulations to educate the community about poverty and to build support for anti-poverty initiatives. Kalamazoo, Mich.; Bryan, Texas; and Erie County, Penn., are some others that have successfully used this strategy.

Finally, an overall strategy of improving coalitions and partnerships is essential to any of the above programs and policies. A well-connected network of advocates and leaders is the key to moving forward. All groups and otherwise independent agencies need to interact to create quality regional growth. Urban, rural, and suburban interests should be represented at the table together, debating needs and working to come up with well-thought-out approaches to problem-solving. Otherwise, as the legendary standup comedian Jackie "Moms" Mabley once said, "If you always do what you always did, then you'll always get what you always got!"

There is strength in relationships, strength in diversity, strength in resources, and strength in numbers. Authors Feighery & Rogers in "Building and Maintaining Effective Coalitions" define "coalition" as a group of individuals representing diverse organizations or constituencies who agree to work together to achieve common goals. Diverse groups come together to work toward a common goal that they could not bring about independently. Partnerships imply businesslike arrangements whereby two or more partners agree to work toward a common goal or interest. These strategies will "unleash the collective genius," as Paul David Walker wrote, because nobody is as smart as everybody.

Funding Plans

Rumi, an ancient Muslim mystic, once wrote: "There is a candle in your heart, ready to be kindled. There is a void in your soul, ready to be filled. You feel it, don't you?"

The Book of John (3:16-18) of the Holy Bible says, "How does God's love abide in anyone who has the world's goods and sees a brother or sister in need and yet refuses to help? Little children, let us love, not in word or speech, but in truth and action."

There are a number of potential funding mechanisms that can be used to implement any one of the previously mentioned alternative strategies for regional improvement. Collectively, perhaps, it could be called a Growth, Prosperity, and Security (GPS) Fund. A local or regionally based voluntary strategic fund could be created to direct funds to inner-city youth education and empowerment programs, and to mitigate negative home and neighborhood influences. The strategic fund could also be directed toward expanding land-preservation programs provided by land trusts and nonprofits that emphasize farmland and watershed protection. Funds could purchase development rights or conservation easements in high-growth rural areas. Funds could be used to grow workforce development and job-training programs, connecting employees to jobs. This is similar to what was proposed by Martin Luther, the iconic figure of the Protestant Reformation and spiritual leader for seventy-five million Lutherans. Harvard professor, Steven Ozment wrote in *The New York Times*: "[Luther] made the care of the poor an organized, civic obligation by proposing that a common chest be put in every German town, rather than skimp along with the traditional practice of almsgiving to the needy and deserving native poor, Luther proposed that they receive grants, or loans, from the chest. Each recipient would pledge to repay the borrowed amount after a timely recovery and return to self-sufficiency, thereby taking responsibility for both his neighbors and himself. This was love of one's neighbor through shared civic responsibility, what the Lutherans still call 'faith begetting charity.'"

A well-publicized and funded regional loan and grant fund to invest in distressed areas would be a great way to encourage growth, perhaps through the GPS fund or another source. A constituency could be built if there were a coordinating agency that strategically loaned or granted funding to small startup companies in high-need areas and regularly, and publicly, reported their successes. This would further the growth and participation rates. Three potential income sources include:

1. A voluntary surcharge. This could be added to local cable or utility bills

and go directly toward these programs. The regional utility or cable company would then send this allocation out every month to the designated agency.

2. A sales tax increase of a half percent or less. This could be implemented to sustain the GPS Fund. The sales tax proposal would need to be approved by states or county governments, but an advocacy coalition could be built at the local level.

3. Donation boxes. These secure boxes, which, thanks to modern technology, now accept credit card donations, could be scattered in high-traffic areas throughout a region. They might include charity pictures, quotes, and statistics emphasizing their effect and successes. How many times a day do workers walk by a candy machine and spend a dollar or two on a snack or a drink or on lottery tickets? Just one dollar a month dropped in the donation box by half the population in a region could provide enormous benefits for thousands of people. My region alone would have almost five hundred thousand dollars a month for this fund, or six million dollars per year, a considerable amount for such an insignificant donation.

Chapter 8
Conclusion

"Plans are nothing; planning is everything"
—Dwight D. Eisenhower

DO YOU REMEMBER THE FEELINGS you had when you heard, saw, or read about the events of 9/11? We can all remember exactly where we were, what we were doing, and what the day was like. I can imagine it was similar to the feelings Americans had in December 1941 when they learned that Pearl Harbor had been attacked, or perhaps after Hurricane Katrina hit the Gulf Coast in 2005. If you were like most people, the absolute devastation you initially witnessed and felt inside was replaced by raw concern, sense of community, and brotherhood with the victims. Consider the solidarity you felt with New Yorkers and Americans after September 11 and how powerful and motivating the emotions were. This led to an immense outpouring of generosity and kindness toward the victims, families, and even to New York in general. This unity of mission and sense of purpose is common whenever a devastating natural disaster or community upheaval occurs, and it is exactly that solidarity and good judgment that must be activated today to tackle the serious, inseparable issues presented in this book.

It is my belief that the issues of environment, equity, and economy must be considered together when analyzing policies in the twenty-first century. Only with a full accounting of the effects of those policies through a true cost-benefit analysis will projects benefit the individual, investors, the community, and future generations. In the absence of an absolutely perfect, or "silver bullet," solution, the various proposals put forth in Part Two can alleviate much of the challenges discussed in Part One. The problem is that humans are not perfect. My Catholic faith reminds me of this regularly. Our human solutions, therefore, can only strive for perfection. We must not let the perfect be the enemy of the good. This threat of imperfection did not prevent us from putting a man on the Moon, or enacting the massive

Marshall Plan after World War II to rebuild Europe. Together, with the presumption of goodwill and confidence in our ability to work toward the common good, progress can be made.

James Rouse, the pioneering real estate developer, urban planner, civic activist, and philanthropist, wrote in a 1963 lecture titled "It Can Happen Here, A Talk on Metropolitan Growth":

> We can't plan effectively for the future growth of American communities unless we start at the beginning—and that beginning is people ... I believe that the ultimate test of civilization is whether or not it contributes to the growth—improvement—of mankind. Does it uplift, inspire, stimulate, and develop the best in man? An inspired and concerned society will dignify man; will find ways to develop his talents; will put the fruits of his labor and intellect to effective use; will struggle for brotherhood and for the elimination of bigotry and intolerance; will care for the indigent, the delinquent, the sick, the aged; will seek the truth and communicate it; will respect differences among men.

Rouse, who also founded Columbia, Maryland, a holistically planned community of 100,000, was a true visionary. Of that community, which was started in the early 1960s and completed in the 1990s, *Curing Urbanitis*, author Finley wrote: "It is a joy to visit and tour...there are no overhead wires, no billboards, no strip centers, no garish signs. But there are millions of street trees, miles of safe pathways, clubs and social groups to meet every human need, a community foundation, occasionally troubling teenagers, colleges, wonderfully named streets and places and, true to the early promise, over 60,000 jobs."

Similarly, former secretary of the Interior and governor of Arizona Bruce Babbitt wrote in *Cities in the Wilderness*: "Landowners, developers, farmers, planners, historic preservationists, conservationists—wherever we reside, in cities, in suburbs, or in rural areas, we must all begin to comprehend our surroundings as landscapes and watersheds. We must explore what they mean in our lives and determine how to live in and use them while conserving their essential functions, passing them intact and unimpaired to future generations ... Development should enlarge the possibilities for human progress, creativity, and quality of life, which it cannot accomplish by continually eroding the beauty and productivity of the natural world." Housing advocates and school reformers should be included with this association to focus energy on the neglected inner cities and rural areas.

About a hundred years ago, Teddy Roosevelt wrote of our natural landscapes, "We regard Attic temples and Roman triumphal arches and Gothic cathedrals as of priceless value, but we are, as a whole, still in that low state of civilization where we do not understand that it is also vandalism wantonly to destroy or to permit the destruction of what is beautiful in nature, whether it be a cliff, a forest, or a species of mammal or bird." Since the Industrial Revolution, we've witnessed a massive re-engineering of the earth's topography, including the mountains, valleys, rivers, lakes, and streams and even still pollute the air, destroy forests, and exterminate species of fish, birds, and mammals. Part One showed that the health and quality of our society and environment is in danger due to the cumulative effect of these changes. When toxic chemicals are increasingly found in our food, air, and water, and we rely on industrially produced food for sustenance, our life systems are in danger. Action, as outlined in Part Two of this book, must be taken to resolve these impacts. Ideally, a mobilization of society around the common goal of sustainability will take place. In "Our Common Future," the 1987 U.N. report, the oft-quoted statement, "Meeting the needs of present generations while not compromising the ability of future generations to meet their own needs," leaves much to be desired given the evidence cited in Part One of this book. Compromising is an understatement. In the absence of massive political mobilization to change policies, individuals, communities, and regions must do their part, as outlined in Part Two.

Cultural historian, ecotheologian, and Passionist priest Thomas Berry wrote in *The Dream of the Earth* (1998):

> Any progress of the human at the expense of the larger life community must ultimately lead to a diminishment of human life itself. A degraded habitat will produce degraded humans. An enhanced habitat supports an elevated mode of the human. This is evident not only in the economic order, but also throughout the

entire range of human affairs. The splendor of earth is in the variety of its land and its seas, its life forms and its atmospheric phenomena; these constitute in color and sound and movement that great symphonic context which has inspired our sense of the divine, given us our emotional and imaginative powers, and evoked from us those entrancing insights that have governed our more sublime moments.

Paul Gilding, the veteran Australian environmentalist and entrepreneur, wrote in his 2011 book *The Great Disruption: Why the Climate Crisis Will Bring On the End of Shopping and the Birth of a New World* that "we are heading for a crisis-driven choice. We either allow collapse to overtake us or develop a new sustainable economic model. We will choose the latter. We may be slow, but we're not stupid." Offering a deeper consideration in *The Dream of the Earth,* Berry wrote that "the time has now come, however, when we will listen or we will die. The time has come to lower our voices, to cease imposing our mechanistic patterns on the biological processes of the earth, to resist the impulse to control, to command, to force, to oppress, and to begin quite humbly to follow the guidance of the larger community on which all life depends. Our fulfillment is not in our isolated human grandeur, but in our intimacy with the larger earth community, for this is also the larger dimension of our being. Our human destiny is integral with the destiny of the earth."

Using the accounting approach outlined earlier called triple bottom line—with its commitment to people, planet and profit, or the three E's (environment, equity, and economy)—corporations and governments can meet all dimensions of our sustainability goals (meeting the needs of the present without compromising the ability of future generations to meet their own needs). This will help us to more closely evaluate scenarios and discover whether quality-of-life issues such as health, happiness, friendship, and community life are impacted or improved on. Discussions of prosperity should not simply focus on national GDP.

At the community or regional level, utilizing the strategies and solutions discussed in this book will alleviate many of the challenges we currently face. For too long, planning has been left out of the mainstream conversation. Yet it is planners who see the entire landscape, the broad policy implications, and the societal impacts. Good regional planning can have profound results. It must. Though not generally considered before, "equity considerations" must be present in planning conversations as we move forward. As Wilkinson and Pickett clearly demonstrated in *The Spirit Level*: "The truth is that the vast majority of the population is harmed by greater inequality ... Across whole populations, rates of mental illness are five times higher in the most unequal compared to the least unequal societies. Similarly, in more unequal societies, people are five times as likely to be imprisoned, six times as likely to be clinically obese, and murder rates may be many, many times higher." A 2006 study by S.V. Subramanian and I. Kawachi of the Harvard School of Public Health showed that income inequality exerts comparable effects across all population subgroups, whether people are classified by education, race or income—so much so that the authors suggested that inequality acted like a pollutant spread throughout society.

If we are not including desegregation, equitable development, and fairness in our future planning and community development, then we are leaving out an enormous opportunity for real growth and prosperity. Take, for example, the untapped human capital in our poorest and most underserved urban and rural neighborhoods. To succeed in the twenty-first century, we must redirect this source to productive use. As *Who's Your City?* author Richard Florida noted, "Our future economic success is increasingly dependent on our ability to harness the creative talents of each and every member of the workforce—regardless of sex, age race, ethnicity, or sexual orientation."

Consider the deteriorating public infrastructure already in place in our neglected inner cities and rural villages: trillions of dollars' worth of roads, sidewalks, sewers, water lines, electric transmission, historic housing, and community buildings. Now combine that with the enormous squandering of human potential, and there is no wonder there are fiscal and emotional crises everywhere. To see such waste, neglect, and disregard has got to have, at the very minimum, a detrimental effect on a region's psyche. In fact, that is exactly what occurs, according to Wilkinson and Pickett. Unequal societies have lower life expectancies, higher rates of heart disease, and poorer spiritual and psychological health than those that have more equality. Today's feelings of alienation and disenchantment have their roots in the neglected inner cities and rural areas. Now that these insecurities have spread to the middle class, perhaps the nation will take appropriate and comprehensive action.

Thomas Adams, a pioneering leader in urban planning in three countries during the first half of the twentieth century, said: "A home is not a detached unit but a part of a neighborhood, which in turn is part of a town; and the good quality of the home usually depends at least as much on its surroundings as on its design and construction. Hence, the vital importance of ground planning and control of the development of neighborhoods."

People have a responsibility, obligation, and vested interest in the quality of neighboring cities and towns. We cannot continue to sacrifice the good of the public for the benefit of the private. Community must come back into normal conversation and thought. Competition in our hyperconnected world will not allow such waste. Only an efficient and compassionate use of resources will keep America a leader in the world.

Key investments are essential to economic security. The first must be in our poverty-stricken inner cities and rural areas. Simply waiting for state or federal action is no longer an option. Regions must coordinate and take action. We need to train our young and unemployed. Self-destructive behaviors such as resignation to unemployment, self-doubt, alcohol and drug abuse, disintegrating families, and lack of engagement in children's education all help to create intergenerational poverty. Some of these issues are being addressed by small nonprofits and social service agencies, but they are largely ignored by mainstream leaders. Professionals and scientists agree that family planning, job training, drug counseling, and similar activities are essential in turning the tide. Such programs as Geoffrey Canada's successful Harlem Children's Zone, the Strive Partnership in Cincinnati, or the federal government's "Promise Neighborhoods" must be increased or replicated by local and regional organizations. After all, as Finley wrote in *Curing Urbanitis*, "The United States of America will never be whole or rightfully proud until the nation unites in holistic caring for the people left at the bottom."

As has been proved over and over again, investing in ourselves brings returns. As noted earlier, the "socialist" G.I. Bill, Interstate Highway System, railroads, canals, and public education created vast wealth and tremendous opportunities for millions. An economy built on representative, democratically instituted laws and regulations as opposed to strict laissez faire capitalism, includes protections for individuals, markets, and corporations. As the analogy goes, this is the difference between the economy working like a barroom brawl, in which there are no rules, and like a boxing match, in which regulations and standards rule the day.

Adam Smith, the economist the American Right loves to praise as the father of the free markets and capitalism, also believed that sometimes government intervention was necessary, "especially when the object is to reduce poverty." Smith passionately argued that "when regulation is in support of the workman, it is always just and equitable; but it is sometimes otherwise when in favor of the masters." He saw a clear intent on the part of employers "always and everywhere" to keep wages as low as possible. His economic policy was not solely intended for the maximization of national income. "It had social and moral objectives," wrote Alan B. Krueger, professor of economics at Princeton University. Stiglitz, the Noble Prize-winning economist observed: "History has shown that in every successful country, the government had played an important role. Yes, governments sometimes fail, but unfettered markets are a certain prescription for failure."

People may fear change, but as discussed in the Introduction, it is inevitable. The end goal is positive change for a better future. Our future is a choice, based on policies, regulations, and decisions to ignore or disregard science, compassion, or responsibility. This can actually be an optimistic view of our current condition. As noted in *Inequality by Design*, it puts us as a society in charge of our fate. Today, we are more unequal than we have been since the Great Depression. We are, in fact, more unequal than any other affluent Western nation. Deliberate and pragmatic policies could reduce and reverse our rush to a polarized society. As has been noted, reducing inequality has been accomplished before, such as improving the economic fortunes of the elderly. By the same token, we have expanded inequality as well, such as with tax expenditures that benefit many of the already advantaged.

The experience of other nations proves that there is much more that can be done to reduce inequality if we choose to. For example, in the 1950s, overall health and life expectancy in the United States was surpassed only by a few countries. Japan's citizens, on the other hand, had relatively poor health. Yet, by 1980, Japan had the highest life expectancy of all developed countries, while the U.S. continued to slip down the rankings. (In 2012, Japan's life expectancy was third highest among developed nations; the U.S. was listed at number fifty, and its poorest residents lived an average of five fewer years than the national norm.) In addition, Japanese income differences narrowed during the forty years after the Second World War. While the health of Japan's population improved rapidly, its crime rate decreased, putting it almost alone among developed countries. In the U.S., in the meantime, income differences widened from 1970 on. We should remember that near the end of World War II, when planning for post-war recovery, President Roosevelt laid out a bill of rights for Americans, similar to the first ten amendments added to the U.S. Constitution. Roosevelt's "economic bill of rights" would guarantee:

- The right to a useful and remunerative job in the industries or shops or farms or mines of the nation.
- The right to earn enough to provide adequate food, clothing, and recreation.
- The right of every farmer to raise and sell his products at a return that would provide him and his family a decent living.
- The right of every businessman, large and small, to trade in an atmosphere of freedom from unfair competition and domination by monopolies at home or abroad.
- The right of every family to a decent home.
- The right to adequate medical care and the opportunity to achieve and enjoy good health.
- The right to adequate protection from the economic fears of old age, sickness, accident, and unemployment.
- The right to a good education.

After World War II, Roosevelt's bill of rights was adopted by Japan, Germany, and Italy. For those countries, the words became a reality; for an enormous segment of the American population, however, Roosevelt's ideals have not been realized.

Few would argue with, as Wilkinson and Pickett put it, a "friendlier society, with less violence, better mental health, more involvement in community life and so on." Do we believe it is attainable? The citizens of Santa Barbara, Calif., do. In response to a devastating oil leak from the Union Oil Company's offshore drilling operation that destroyed beaches, fish, and wildlife, the citizens wrote the "Santa Barbara Declaration of Environmental Rights" and catalyzed the environmental movement of the 1970s. They wrote "We propose a revolution in conduct toward an environment which is rising in revolt against us. Granted that ideas and institutions long established are not easily changed; yet today is the first day of the rest of our life on this planet. We will begin anew." It is truly a hopeful statement in response to such devastation.

Rather than burying one's head in the sand, it is the only way to move forward. Integrating the solutions presented in Part Two to combat the issues presented in Part One is a path forward for national growth, prosperity, and security. Integrating regional planning to reduce sprawl, combat poverty, and decrease inequality is a win-win strategy. When places are pedestrian-friendly and accommodate families, the elderly, and the poor, we become a more inclusive, fair, and just society. We therefore increase mobility, equality, freedom, and opportunity. When a community is safe for kids and the elderly, we allow aging in place rather than the exodus of the wealthy and elderly that is occurring today.

As mentioned earlier, America's annual death rate easily surpasses 100,000 due to gun violence, traffic fatalities (driven, at least in part, by our sprawled-out lifestyle), suicides in our overextended military, and lack of health insurance by those—including the jobless—who cannot afford it. Deaths, in very large measure, that can be attributed to the domestic and international policies or lack thereof that the U.S. has chosen to live by. Instead of accepting this as part of the American way of life, wouldn't it be wiser to prioritize the strategies discussed in Part Two to minimize these numbers?

As discussed earlier, in California, the cost of housing prisoners far outweighs the cost to educate kids. We must not let this become the norm throughout the U.S. Investing more in children to set them off on the right path—one that leads to fulfilling and productive lives—is a much wiser public expenditure. It has been well documented that children who grow up in and are surrounded by poverty are much more likely to gravitate toward a life of crime or delinquency. If left untreated or cared for, these kids can grow up to be liabilities and could likely endanger the security and quality of life of the rest of society. As has been shown, if inequality is lessened, levels of violence decline.

Ted Kennedy, quoting George Bernard Shaw at his brother Bobby's funeral, said: "Some men see things as they are and say why. I dream things that never were and say, Why not?" Federal, state, and local policies can be changed. As Harvard professor Elizabeth Warren and *New York Times* columnist Charles Blow pointed out, U.S. corporations have thrived because of the decisions that produced publicly educated workers, improved roads, and provided protection in the form of police and fire departments, and safety from international threats. But, as has been shown, many corporations are not paying their share of taxes, even getting away with paying none while our nation's infrastructure is literally crumbling. Furthermore, for those companies that do pay taxes, in 2011, the U.S. corporate tax rate for multinational companies was 35 percent, whereas the global average was 28 percent. As Edward Kleinbard, professor of law at the University of Southern California and former chief of staff of the U.S. Congress' Joint Committee on Taxation, said, "The only feasible solution is to lower the U.S. rate to a level comparable with global norms and to pay for the reduction in part by introducing worldwide tax consolidation for U.S. firms, just as they today consolidate their worldwide operations for financial accounting purposes." What is needed is a mandatory "reinvestment tax" on companies of a certain size that would pay to foster a better environment for startup firms.

When we ignore the conditions listed in Part One and when we are silent in the face of the egregious failures of the system or the sorry state of the nation's infrastructure, we are granting approval. As Bob Herbert of *The New York Times* noted: "We saw how the civil rights movement changed the face of our nation, and again in the women's movement. We saw it long ago in the labor movement, and later in the fight for a cleaner environment. It's tough. It can be dangerous. It requires courage. It can take a long, long time. But it can be done."

In Herbert's same article, he wrote: "If you didn't understand during the fight over welfare reform—when millionaires on the Senate floor stood up and cheered the withdrawal of benefits from poor children—if you didn't understand then that when they finished tearing up the safety net for the poor that they would soon be coming after the middle class, you bear some responsibility. We're all responsible for the state of our society. The banks and the great corporations are always pressing their case in the corridors of power. But who is pounding the table for working people, day in and day out? Who's their advocate?"

Insightfully, Herbert Gans wrote in *The War Against the Poor*: "Today's middle class and working class whites may not be able to imagine it, but only a generation of severe and persistent downward mobility is enough to produce children and grandchildren who could develop the same poverty-related behavior patterns found among today's poor. Some will become school dropouts, unmarried mothers, and street criminals reacting with the same despair and anger, and many others will be accused of departing from mainstream ways even if they have not done so." Is that the future we want for our families, our neighbors?

Crisis has a funny way of bringing opportunity. Speth, of Vermont Law School, wrote, "America's gaping social and economic inequality poses a grave threat to democracy ... our country's senior political scientist Robert Dahl believes it is 'highly plausible' that 'powerful international and domestic forces [could] push us toward an irreversible level of political inequality that so greatly impairs our present democratic institutions as to render the ideals of democracy and political equality virtually irrelevant.'" Yet, "Dahl also believes that an alternative, hopeful outcome is also 'highly plausible,'" Speth wrote. We can decide this future.

As outlined in this book, a society can maintain individual freedom and great wealth even while improving the lives of others. Public policies and laws can be implemented to minimize harmful effects on the environment, even while ensuring freedom and liberty. We define patriotism as love or devotion to one's country, and we invoke it when we seek to defend our country from outside threats. We've sacrificed thousands of our young men and women and resources for the good of democracy, to preserve it for our children. Yet, somehow we ignore the call of duty when we are threatened from within. Our "inside" threats of poverty, segregation, inequality, environmental deterioration, waste, and inefficiency cannot continue indefinitely. Perhaps a new patriotism can be acted on to benefit our children and future generations, a patriotism that includes love of neighbor, quality communities, and sustainability for future generations. The ancient Greek citizens were required to be directly involved in politics, justice, military service, religious ceremonies, intellectual discussions, athletics, and artistic pursuits. If more of our citizens were engaged in such a way, our communities would improve, and positive change could occur. This classical Greek culture and philosophy is the foundation of our modern Western culture. We ought to get back to our roots.

Rohatyn, the author and investment banker, wrote that "market capitalism is the best economic system ever invented; but it must be fair, it must be regulated, and it must be ethical" because "only capitalists can kill capitalism." To support capitalism to the detriment of democracy would be self-defeating. "The business of this country is business," President Calvin Coolidge once said. That is still true, but it requires that business and the political leadership remember that the basis of our democracy is fairness. A successful democratic market economy must be seen as fair to the majority of its citizens. As an earlier president, Theodore Roosevelt, warned, "A great democracy must be progressive or it will soon cease to be great or a democracy." It should not be forgotten that capitalism and democracy are two distinct philosophies and at times are in direct opposition to each other. As author William Deresiewicz wrote in *The New York Times* in May 2012: "Capitalist values are also antithetical to democratic ones. Like Christian ethics, the principles of republican government require us to consider the interests of others. Capitalism, which entails the single minded pursuit of profit, would have us believe that it's every man for himself." Striking a balance between capitalism and democracy can be a challenge but is essential for national success. Otherwise, profit-seeking and placing a dollar value on everything can go too far. Harvard professor Michael Sandel expressed this concern in his 2012 book *What Money Can't Buy*. When money takes the place of moral value, we lose dignity, freedom, and social solidarity. Sandel wrote, "We live at a time when almost everything can be bought and sold ... We need to ask whether there are some things money should not buy," otherwise, "the more money can buy, the more affluence (or the lack of it) matters." As a society we cannot sacrifice our ideals for dollar value.

At this time, conclusive and consistent social science, environmental science, or economics alone may not be enough to spur citizen action. That is OK. After all, the United States is a nation built not only on reason, but on faith. As such, here are some key quotes from my—and many Americans'—moral guidebook, the Holy Bible: In Deuteronomy 15:7, God tells the Israelites, "If there be among you a needy man, one of thy brethren, within any of thy gates...thou shalt not harden thy heart, nor shut thy hand from thy needy brother." And in Matthew 25:35, 40, Jesus said: "For I was hungry and you gave me food, I was thirsty and you gave me drink, I was a stranger and you welcomed me ... Truly, I say to you, as you did to one of the least of these my brethren, you did it to me."

In December 2011, Pope Benedict XVI, holy leader of 1.1 billion Catholics and countless other spiritual people, in a message delivered for the World Day of Peace 2012, grieved that "some currents of modern culture, built upon rationalist and individualist economic principles, have cut off the concept of justice from its transcendent roots, detaching it from charity and solidarity." As a society, as a democracy, we can do more. Keep in mind that our science, our religion, and our understanding of challenges change and evolve over time.

According to Speth, only 14 percent of American workers believe they have secured the American Dream. What does that mean? Langston Hughes described a dream deferred like no other:

> *What happens to a dream deferred?*
> *Does it dry up*
> *Like a raisin in the sun?*
> *Or fester like a sore –*
> *And then run?*
> *Does it stink like rotten meat?*
> *Or crust and sugar over*
> *Like a syrupy sweet?*
>
> *Maybe it just sags*
> *Like a heavy load.*
>
> *Or does it explode?*

Wouldn't you love to leave the world a better place for your children and others? Native Americans did. The timeless and ancient wisdom provided through the Great Law of the Iroquois Confederacy said that "in our every deliberation we must consider the impact of our decisions on the seventh generation." Perhaps we can adopt those words.

American surveys consistently say that society is not focused on the right priorities, that people are too focused on shopping and spending, that we are too materialistic, and that excessive materialism is causing harm to the environment. If these surveys are close to being correct, then there is a powerful base on which to build.

References

Abrams, Paul. "Prescription for Progressive Politics: I Am A PreAmbler, Will You Join?" *Huffington Post*. October 23, 2007. http://www.huffingtonpost.com/paul-abrams/prescription-for-progress_b_69619.html (accessed 2010).

Allard, Scott. *Strained Suburbs: The Social Service Challenges of Rising Suburban Poverty.* Metropolitan Opportunity Series, Number 8, Washington DC: Brookings Institution, 2010.

Anderson, Kurt. "Madman Theory." *New York Times*, August 5, 2011.

Armario, Christine and Dorie Turner. "Shocking: Nearly 1 in 4 High School Graduates Can't Pass Military Entrance Exam." *Huffington Post*, December 21, 2010.

Babbitt, Bruce. *Cities in the Wilderness.* Washington DC: Island Press, 2005.

Bader, Richard. "Are You Smarter Than a Fifth Grader?" *Albany, NY Times Union*, June 20, 2011.

Baker, Dean. "Compromise on Social Security and Medicare? Why My Center Left Friends Are Wrong." *Huffington Post*. November 22, 2010. http://www.huffingtonpost.com/dean-baker/compromise-on-social-secu_b_786763.html (accessed November 2010).

Barnes, Bill. "Emerging Issues: Putting Poverty in Places." *National League of Cities*, November 18, 2010.

Barnes, Peter. *Capitalism 3.0: A Guide to Reclaiming the Commons.* San Francisco: Berrett-Koehler, 2006.

Baum, Deborah. "John Logan: Census Shows Integration has Slowed to a Standstill." *Brown University*. December 20, 2010. http://today.brown.edu/articles/2010/12/logan (accessed December 20, 2010).

Benfield, Kaid. "How History Killed the Suburb." *The Atlantic*, April 25, 2011.

Benjamin, Gerald and Richard Nathan. *Regionalism and Realism: A Study of Governments in the New York Metropolitan Area.* New York: Brookings Institution Press, 2001.

Berensson, Markus. *City Mayors.* April 1, 2011. www.citymayors.com.

Berry, Thomas. *The Dream of the Earth.* San Francisco: Sierra Club Books, 1988.

Bishop, Russell. "Are We Wasting Money on the Arts?" *Huffington Post*. November 29, 2010. http://www.huffingtonpost.com/russell-bishop/are-we-wasting-money-on-t_b_788475.html (accessed November 29, 2010).

Bittman, Mark. "Don't End Agricultural Subsidies, Fix Them." *New York Times*, March 1, 2011a.

—. "Sustainable Farming Can Feed the World?" *New York Times*, March 8, 2011b.

—. "Guns, Butter and Then Some." *New York Times*, August 9, 2012.

Blackwell, Angela Glover and Radhika K. Fox. *Regional Equity and Smart Growth: Opportunities for Advancing Social and Economic Justice in America*. Coral Gables: Funders' Network for Smart Growth and Livable Communities, 2004.

Blow, Charles. "The Decade of Lost Children." *New York Times*, August 5, 2011.

Bock, Kenneth. *Human Nature Mythology*. Champaign: University of Illinois Press, 1994.

Boehlert, Sherwood. *Washington Post*, November 22, 2010.

Bornstein, David. "For Children At Risk." *New York Times*, October 7, 2011.

Briggs, Xavier de Souza. *The Geography of Opportunity: Race and Housing Choice in Metropolitan America*. Washington DC: The Brookings Institution, 2005.

Brinkley, Douglas. *The Wilderness Warrior: Theodore Roosevelt and the Crusade for America*. New York: HarperCollins, 2009.

Brooks, David. "The Materialist Fallacy." *New York Times*, February 14, 2012.

—. "The Splendor of Cities." *New York Times*, February 8, 2011.

Buik, Elise and Manuel Pastor. "Split Down the Middle." *Los Angeles Business Journal*, 2010.

Carbone, June and Naomi Cahn. "Family Values? Conservative Economics Have Shredded Marriage Rates." *Huffington Post*. August 9, 2011. www.huffingtonpost.com (accessed August 9, 2011).

Carter, Jimmy. "Call Off the Global Drug War." *New York Times*, July 17, 2011.

Cass, Julia. *Held Captive: Child Poverty in America*. Washington DC: The Childrens Defense Fund, 2010.

Center for American Progress. *From Poverty to Prosperity*. Task Force Report, Washington DC: Center for American Progress, 2007.

Center for Clean Air Policy. *Growing Wealthier: Smart Growth, Climate Change and*

Prosperity. Washington DC: Center for Clean Air Policy, 2011.

Center for Local, State and Urban Policy. *Regional Planning in Michigan: Challenges and Opportunities of Intergovernmental Cooperation.* Policy Report Number 3, Ann Arbor, MI: University of Michigan, 2005.

CNA. *Powering America's Defense: Energy and the Risks to National Security.* Alexandria, VA: CNA, 2009.

Cohen, Patricia. "Culture of Poverty Makes a Comeback." *New York Times*, October 17, 2010.

Collins, Gail. "Waiting for Somebody." *New York Times*, September 30, 2010.

Cowie, Jefferson. *Staying Alive: The 1970s and the Last Days of the Working Class.* New York: The New Press, 2010.

Creamer, Robert. "Why Growing Inequality Is Bad for America." *Huffington Post.* October 27, 2009. www.huffingtonpost.com (accessed October 27, 2009).

Dahl, Robert A. *On Political Equality.* New Haven and London: Yale University Press, 2006.

Denvir, Daniel. "10 Most Segregated Urban Areas in America." *Salon*, March 29, 2011.

DeParle, Jason. "Harder for Americans to Rise From Lower Rungs." *New York Times*, January 4, 2012.

DeSouza, Mike. "Avoiding Urban Sprawl Could Reduce Pollution, Boost Economy." *Postmedia News.* May 5, 2010. http://www.questcanada.org/documents/Avoidingurbansprawlcouldreducepollutionboosteconomy_report.pdf (accessed June 2010).

Diamond, Jared. *Wikipedia.* 2011. http://en.wikipedia.org/wiki/Collapse:_How_Societies_Choose_to_Fail_or_Succeed (accessed 2009).

Dickinson, Tim. "How the GOP Became the Party of the Rich." *Rolling Stone*, November 9, 2011.

Dukakis Center for Urban and Regional Policy. *Maintaining Diversity in America's Transit Rich Neighborhoods: Tools for Equitable Change.* Boston: Northeastern University, 2010.

Edelman, Marian Wright. "A Thanksgiving Prayer to End Poverty in Our Lifetime." *Huffington Post.* November 23, 2009. www.huffingtonpost.com (accessed November 2009).

—. *The Measure of Our Success.* New York: HarperCollins, 1992.

—. "The Threat of Persistent Poverty." *Huffington Post.* November 16, 2010. www.huffingtonpost.com (accessed November 2010).

—. "Voting Rights Under Attack." *Huffington Post.* May 13, 2011. www.huffington-post.com (accessed May 13, 2011).

Edelman, Peter. *Searching for America's Heart: RFK and the Renewal of Hope.* New York: Houghton Mifflin Company, 2001.

Edwards, Chris. "Ten Reasons to Cut Farm Subsidies." *Examiner.* June 28, 2007. www.examiner.com (accessed August 2011).

Ehrenreich, Barbara. "On Turning Poverty into an American Crime." *Huffington Post.* August 10, 2011. www.huffingtonpost.com (accessed August 10, 2011).

Environmental Law Institute, *Improving Economic Health and Competitiveness Through Tax Sharing,* An Environmental Law Institute Issue Paper, April 2008.

Environmental Protection Agency. *Partnership for Sustainable Communities: A Year of Progress for American Communities.* Washington DC: Federal Environmental Protection Agency, 2010.

Feighery, Ellen and Todd Rodgers. *Building and Maintaining Effective Coalitions.* Palo Alto, CA: Stanford Health Promotions Resource Center, Guide No. 12, 1989.

Finley, William E. *Curing Urbanitis.* Florida: Partners for Community Building, Inc, 2008.

Fischer, Claude S., Michael Hout, Martin Sanchez Jankowski, Samuel R. Lucas, Ann Swidler, and Kim Voss. *Inequality by Design.* Princeton: Princeton University Press, 1996.

Fishman, Robert. *1808-1908-2008: National Planning for America.* New York: Regional Plan Association, 2007.

Florida, Richard. "The Metro Story: Growth Without Growth ." *Creative Class.* April 6, 2011. www.creativeclass.com (accessed April 6, 2011).

—. *Who's Your City?* New York: Basic Books, 2008.

Folbre, Nancy. "In Equality We Trust." *New York Times,* April 25, 2011.

Franken, Bob. "Number of 'Them's That Got' Keeps Shrinking." *Times Union.* November 13, 2010. www.timesunion.com (accessed November 13, 2010).

Freemark, Yonah. *Next American City.* October 10, 2010. http://americancity.org/columns/entry/2670/.

Friedman, Thomas. "Rising Above the Gathering Storm Revisited: Rapidly Approaching Category 5." *New York Times*, October 27, 2010.

Froomkin, Dan. "If Prison Is the Disease, Not the Cure, How Do You Treat It?" *Huffington Post*, March 8, 2012.

Galbraith, John Kenneth. *The Affluent Society.* Boston: Houghton Mifflin, 1958.

Gans, Herbert J. *The War Against the Poor.* New York: Basic Books, 1995.

Geoghegan, Thomas. "Get Radical: Raise Social Security." *New York Times*, June 20, 2011.

Gerard, Leo. "One Damning Report." *Huffington Post*, July 30, 2012.

Glaeser, Edward. "A Level Playing Field for Cities." *Boston Globe*, February 29, 2008.

—. *Do Regional Economies Need Regional Coordination? The Economic Geography of Megaregions.* Keith Goldfield, ed. Princeton: Policy Research Institute for the Region, 2007.

Goetz, Edward. "The Reality of Deconcentration." *National Housing Institute: Shelterforce Online.* November/December 2004. http://www.nhi.org/online/issues/138/deconcentration.html (accessed 2010).

Goldman, David. *Most Firms Pay No Taxes.* August 12, 2008. www.cnnmoney.com (accessed March 2011).

Goodman, Peter. "Highly Concentrated Poverty." *Huffington Post*, November 3, 2011.

Gottlieb, Roger S. *Religion and the Environment.* New York: Routledge, 2010.

Gottman, Jean. *Megalopolis: The Urbanized Northeastern Seaboard of the United States.* New York: Twentieth Century Fund, 1961.

Greenlining Institute. "Corporate America Untaxed: Tax Avoidance on the Rise," 2011.

Hahn, A., Coonerty, C., and Peaslee, L. *Colleges and Universities as Economic Anchors: Profiles of Promising Practices.* Baltimore, MD: Annie E. Casey Foundation, 2002.

Hamilton, Clive. *Growth Fetish.* London: Pluto Press, 2004.

Hindery, Leo Jr. "Management Responsibility to Employees Demands the Proposed NLRB Rule Change, Not its Rejection." *Huffington Post.* July 8, 2011. www.huffingtonpost.com (accessed July 8, 2011).

Herbert, Bob. "Fast Track to Inequality." *New York Times*, November 1, 2010a.

—. "The Corrosion of America." *New York Times*, October 26, 2010b.

—. "This Raging Fire." *New York Times*, November 16, 2010c.

Jackson, Jesse. "Cutting Exceptional Poverty Should Be Nation's Top Priority." *Huffington Post*. December 1, 2010. www.huffingtonpost.com (accessed December 2010).

Jackson, John. "US No Longer Leader of the Free World." *Huffington Post*. June 28, 2011. www.huffingtonpost.com (accessed June 28, 2011).

Johnson, Curtis. "Paradigm Lost: Can Americans Change Course?" *Washington Post Writers Group*. April 17, 2011. www.citiwire.net (accessed April 17, 2011).

Kambitsis, Jason. "Transportation as a Civil Rights Issue." *Wired Magazine*. July 26, 2011. www.wired.com (accessed July 2011).

Katz, Alyssa. "The Reverse Commute." *The American Prospect*. July 15, 2010. http://prospect.org/cs/articles?article=the_reverse_commute (accessed July 15, 2010).

Keynes, John Maynard. *Essays in Persuasion*. New York: W.W. Norton, 1963.

Khimm, Suzy. "Why affordable housing is a myth." *Washington Post*, March 19, 2012.

Kleinbard, Edward D. "The Global Tax Avoidance Dance." *Huffington Post*. March 31, 2011. www.huffingtonpost.com (accessed March 2011).

Knafo, Saki. "U.S. Child Poverty Second Highest Among Developed Nations: Report ." *Huffington Post*, May 31, 2012.

Kocieniewski, David. "G.E.'s Strategies Let It Avoid Taxes Altogether." *New York Times*, March 24, 2011.

Koehler, Robert. "The Sacred and the Dead." *Huffington Post*. April 28, 2011. www.huffingtonpost.com (accessed April 28, 2011).

Kristof, Nicholas. "A Hedge Fund Republic." *New York Times*, November 18, 2010a.

—. "End the War on Pot." *New York Times*, October 28, 2010b

—. "How Chemicals Affect Us." *New York Times*, May 2, 2012a.

—. "Persistent Poverty is America's Great Moral Challenge, but It's Far More than That." *New York Times*, February 9, 2012b.

—. "Taxes and Billionaires." *New York Times*, July 6, 2011.

Krugman, Paul. "Money and Morals." *New York Times*, February 10, 2012.

—. *The Conscience of a Liberal*. New York: W.W. Norton, 2007.

Langdon, Davis. *The Cost of Green Revisited.* Industry, AECOM, 2007.

Learsy, Raymond. "The Arts, Our Government Respect, and the Aspen Institute." *Huffington Post.* July 7, 2010. http://www.huffingtonpost.com/raymond-j-learsy/the-arts-our-governments_b_638314.html (accessed July 7, 2010).

Lee, Mike. "Study Shows Urban Sprawl Threatens Genetic Diversity." *San Diego Union Tribune*, September 22, 2010.

Lehrer, Jonah. "A Physicist Solves the City ." *New York Times*, December 22, 2010.

Leopold, Les. "Why the Idiocy About Unemployment." *Huffington Post*, July 9, 2010.

Lerner, Sharon. "Segregation Nation." *The American Prospect.* June 20, 2011. www.prospect.org (accessed June 20, 2011).

Lincoln Institute for Land Policy. *The Great Housing Reset.* February 4, 2011. http://atlincolnhouse.typepad.com/weblog/2011/02/the-housing-reset.html (accessed February 2011).

Lu, Max. "Rural Regionalism." *Planning magazine*, July 2010.

MacKaye, Benton. *The New Exploration, A Philosophy of Regional Planning.* (Harcourt, Brace and Company, 1928)

Massey, Douglas and Gregory Squires. "Segregation: The Invisible Elephant in the Foreclosure Debate." *Huffington Post*, November 1, 2010.

Mauer, Marc and David Cole. "Five Myths About Americans in Prison." *Washington Post*, June 17, 2011.

Maurrasse, David. *Beyond the Campus: How Universities and Colleges form Partnerships with their Communities.* New York, NY: Routledge, 2001

McKibben, Bill. "Reversal of Fortune." *Mother Jones*, March-April 2007: 39-40.

McLean, Bethany. "Who Wants a Thirty Year Mortgage?" *New York Times*, January 5, 2011.

McMahon, Edward T. "A Long Hot Summer: Climate Change and Extreme Weather." *Washington Post Writers Group.* August 12, 2011. www.citiwire.net (accessed August 2011).

McNamara, Robert. *Albert Gallatin's Report on Roads, Canals, Harbors, and Rivers.* 2011. http://history1800s.about.com/od/canals/a/gallatinreport.htm (accessed 2011).

McNeill, J.R. *Something New Under the Sun: An Environmental History of the Twentieth Century World.* New York: W.W. Norton, 2000.

Milken Institute. *Best Performing Cities: Where America's Jobs Are Created and Sustained.* Available from http://bestcities.milkeninstitute.org/. 2004.

Mitchell, Stacy. "Survey Finds "Buy Local" Message Benefitting Independent Businesses." *New Rules.* January 26, 2011. http://www.newrules.org/retail/news/survey-finds-buy-local-message-benefitting-independent-businesses (accessed January 2011).

Morley, David . "Is Growth a Prerequisite for Long-Term Community Health and Prosperity?" *APA's Sustaining Places Blog,* March 21, 2012.

Mortensen, Greg, and David Oliver Relin. *Three Cups of Tea.* New York: Viking Penguin, 2006.

Moyers, Bill. *Bill Moyers Journal.* April 2, 2010. http://www.pbs.org/moyers/journal/04022010/transcript2.html (accessed April 2010).

Mumford, Lewis. *The City in History.* New York: Harcourt Inc, 1961, 53.

Muro, Mark. *Metropolitan Business Plans: A New Approach to Economic Growth.* Washington DC: Brookings Institution, Metropolitan Policy Program, 2011.

Myers, David. "What is the Good Life?" *Yes! A Journal of Positive Futures,* 2004: 15.

Nasser, Haya El. "How will the USA cope with unprecedented growth?" *USA Today,* October 27, 2006: 2006.

—. "Megapolitan Areas Compete Globally." *USA Today,* November 17, 2011.

National League of Cities. *Using Poverty Simulations to Build Support for Poverty Reducion Initiatives.* Municipal Action Guide, Washington DC: National League of Cities, 2008.

Newsom, Mary. *On Earth.* April 18, 2011. http://www.onearth.org/article/triumph-of-the-city.

Noah, Timothy. "The Great Divergence." *Slate.* September 3, 2010. www.slate.com (accessed September 3, 2010).

Nocera, Joe. "The Limits of School Reform." *New York Times,* April 26, 2011.

Pagano, Michael. "Ways to Reuse Vacant Lots." *New York Times,* March 28, 2011.

Peirce, Neal.

—. "Britain's Budget Lesson for Ascendant GOP/Tea Party." *Citiwire.* October 29, 2010. www.citiwire.net (accessed October 29, 2010).

—. "Combating Youth Violence - Intervene Early, Decisively." *Washington Post Writers Group.* November 16, 2009. www.citiwire.net (accessed November 16, 2009).

—. "Curbing the Prison Boom - If Not Now, When?" *Washington Post Writers Group.* January 14, 2011a. www.citiwire.net (accessed January 2011).

—. "Fast Net, Slow Food: Chattanooga's New Formula." *Washington Post Writers Group.* July 10, 2011b. www.citiwire.net (accessed July 2011).

—. "Fighting Traffic Deaths: Incomplete Without Smart Growth." *Washington Post Writers Group.* August 12, 2011c. www.citiwire.net (accessed August 2011).

—. "Green Community Aids Prove Their Political Mettle." *Washington Post Writers Group.* April 29, 2011d. www.citiwire.net (accessed April 2011).

—. "Money's Not Everything: Surprise City Poll Results." *Citiwire.* November 25, 2010b. www.citiwire.net (accessed November 25, 2010).

—. "State Fighting Poverty: Time to Get Serious." *Washington Post Writers Group.* August 18, 2008. www.citiwire.net (accessed August 2008).

—. "The Just City - For America Soon?" *Washington Post Writers Group.* July 24, 2011e. www.citiwire.net (accessed July 24, 2011).

—. "Unsung Villain of the Budget Struggles." *Citiwire.* April 17, 2011f. http://citi-wire.net/post/2633/.

Perlstein, Rick. "America's Forgotten Liberal." *New York Times,* May 27, 2011.

Philips, Kevin. *Boiling Point: Democrats, Republicans and the Decline of Middle Class Prosperity.* New York: Harper Collins, 1994.

Pimentel, David. "Pollution Causes 40 Percent of Deaths Worldwide." *Human Ecology,* 2007.

PolicyLink. *Shared Prosperity, Stronger Regions: An Agenda for Rebuilding America's Older Core Cities* by, 2nd Edition 2006.

Ozment, Steven. "German Austerity's Lutheran Core." *The New York Times.* August 11, 2012.

Repetto Robert, William Magrath, Michael Wells, Christine Beer, Fabrizio Rossini. *Wasting Assets: Natural Resources in the National Accounts.* Washington DC: WRI, 1989.

Rhodes, Jean E. "Youth Mentoring in Perspective." *Encyclopedia of Informal Education.* 2001. http://www.infed.org/learningmentors/youth_mentoring_in_perspective.htm (accessed November 30, 2011).

Rigg, Kelly. *Huffington Post.* June 20, 2011. www.huffingtonpost.com (accessed June 20, 2011).

Robinson, Eugene. "People Causing the Burn." *Washington Post*. August 11, 2012.

Rohatyn, Felix. *Bold Endeavors: How Our Government Built America, and Why It Must Rebuild Now.* New York: Simon & Shuster, 2009.

Rusk, David. *Cities Without Suburbs.* Baltimore: The Johns Hopkins University Press, 2003.

—. *Inside Game Outside Game.* Washington DC: Brookings Institution Press, 1999.

Sachs, Jeffrey. "Stop This Race to the Bottom." *Huffington Post*. March 29, 2011. www.huffingtonpost.com (accessed March 2011).

Salkin, Patricia E. "Supersizing Small Town America: Using Regionalism to Right-Size Big Box Retail." *Vermont Journal of Environmental Law* , 2004-2005: Volume 6.

Sanders, Bob Ray. "Locking Up One Generation Dooms the Next." *Times Union, Albany, NY*, October 7, 2010.

Schliveck, Louis. *Man in Metropolis.* Garden City, NY: Doubleday, 1965.

Sciammacco, Sara. *Environmental Working Group.* June 2011. http://www.ewg.org/farmsubsidies (accessed June 2011).

Shank, Michael. "New Study Shows Violence Costing America Over $460 Billion ." *Huffington Post*, April 24, 2012.

Shutkin, William. *The Land That Could Be: Environmentalism and Democracy in the Twenty-First Century.* Cambridge, MA: MIT Press, 2000.

Simril, Renata. "Transit Oriented Development Doesn't Just Happen." *The Planning Report.* June 23, 2010. http://www.vwwv.planningreport.com/2010/06/23/transit-oriented-development-doesnt-just-happen (accessed July 2010).

Sklar, Holly. *Let Justic Roll.* July 2011. www.letjusticeroll.org (accessed July 2011).

Slaper, Timothy, and Tanya Hall. "The Triple Bottom Line: What Is It and How Does it Work?" *Indiana Business Review*, Spring 2011.

Smart Growth America and Taxpayers for Common Sense. *Transportation Spending Strategies to Save Taxpayer Dollars and Improve Roads.* Washington DC: Smart Growth America, 2011.

Sorensen, Theodore C. *Why I Am a Democrat.* New York: Henry Holt and Company, Inc, 1996.

Speth, James. *The Bridge at the Edge of the World.* New Haven and London: Yale University Press, 2008.

Stiglitz, Joseph. *Christian Science Monitor*, 2006.

—. "What Must Be Done To Restore the American Dream?" *Slate Magazine*, June 10, 2012.

—. "Of the 1%, by the 1%, for the 1%." *Vanity Fair*, May 2011.

Sugrue, Thomas J. "A Dream Still Deferred." *New York Times*, March 26, 2011.

Taylor, Paul. "The Old Are Outpacing the Young." *New York Times*, November 9, 2011.

Times Union Editorial Board. "Still Failing After All these Years." *Albany, NY Times Union*, June 19, 2011.

Tough, Paul. *Whatever It Takes*. New York: Mariner Books, Houghton Mifflin Harcourt, 2008.

United Nations. *Our Common Future*. New York: United Nations, 1987.

Urban Land Institute. *Urban Land Institute*. 2011. http://www.uli.org/Community-Building/UrbanPlan/UrbanPlan.aspx.

U.S. Department of Housing and Urban Development, *The Power of Partnership with Colleges and Universities: Celebrating Ten Years - 1994-2004 - Community Outreach Partnership Centers*. Washington, D.C.: U.S. Department of Housing and Urban Development, 2005.

Venkatesh, Sudhir. "How To Understand the Culture of Poverty." *St Petersburgh Times*, March 16, 2009.

Walker, Charlotte Zoe. *Sharp Eyes: John Burroughs and American Nature Writing*. Syracuse, NY: Syracuse University Press, 2000.

Warren, Elizabeth. "America Without a Middle Class." *Huffington Post*. December 3, 2009. www.huffingtonpost.com (accessed December 2009).

White, Jane. "The Social Security Fix: End Corporate Welfare." *Huffington Post*. March 28, 2011. www.huffingtonpost.com (accessed March 28, 2011).

Wikipedia. *Environmental Vegetarianism*. http://en.wikipedia.org/wiki/Environmental_vegetarianism#cite_note-6 (accessed August 1, 2011).

Wilkinson, Richard and Kate Pickett. *The Spirit Level: Why Greater Equality Makes Societies Stronger*. New York: Bloomsbury Press, 2009.

Wilson, William Julius. *The Truly Disadvantaged*. Chicago: University of Chicago Press, 1987.

Wright, Thomas. "Celebrating the Mayors Institute on City Design." *Washington*

Post Writers Group. May 6, 2011. www.citiwire.net (accessed May 2011).

—. *Land Development and Growth Management in the United States: Considerations at the Megaregion Scale.* Briefing Papers for America 2050: Innovations for an Urban World: a Global Urban Summit, 8-13 July 2007. Bellagio, Italy: Regional Plan Association and the Rockefeller Foundation.

Y, Mr. *A National Strategic Narrative.* Washington DC: Woodrow Wilson International Center for Scholars, 2011.

Zeitz, Joshua. "Why Did America Explode in Riots in 1967?" *History News Network.* July 23, 2007. http://hnn.us/node/41259 (accessed May 2010).

Zelman, Joanna. "Are We Living Out The Lorax?" *Huffington Post.* April 29, 2011. http://www.huffingtonpost.com/2011/04/29/arbor-day-2011-wwf-living-forests-report_n_854613.html (accessed 2011).

Zhang, Ming, Frederick Steiner and Kent Butler. *Connecting the Texas Triangle: Economic Integration and Transportation Coordination. Megaregions in California: Challenges to Planning and Public Policy.* Conference Proceedings for: The Healdsburg Research Seminar on Megaregions. Healdsburg: Regional Plan Association and the Lincoln Institute of Land Policy, 2007

Zimmer, Carl. "Multitude of Species Face Climate Threat." *New York Times*, April 5, 2011.

Zimmerman, Jess. "Grist." February 4, 2011. www.grist.com.

Index

A

B

C

Cahn
 Naomi, 69
Canada
 Geoffrey, 53, 157, 170
capitalism, 31, 32, 39, 62, 171, 176
Carbone
 June, 69
Cavanaugh
 Mayor Jerome, 49
Center for American Progress, 54
Center for Clean Air Policy, 147, 154
Center for Community Change, 66
Center for Environment and Population, 21
Center on Budget and Policy Priorities, 61
Centers for Disease Control, 98
Century Foundation, 71
chamber of commerce, 137, 159, 161
Chesapeake Bay, 16, 19
Children's Defense Fund, 57, 98
Churchill
 Winston, 4, 155
Cicero, 4, 8
Cities in Transition, 131
city, 22, 23, 24, 25, 26, 27, 28, 35, 44, 45, 48, 50, 51, 54, 61, 62, 63, 65, 67, 68, 95, 99, 100, 105, 107, 115, 117, 122, 125, 128, 129, 130, 131, 132, 134, 136, 137, 138, 139, 140, 144, 145, 146, 147, 152, 154, 155, 157, 158, 159, 160, 162, 163, 169

civic environmentalism, 127
Civil Rights Act, 77
Clark
 Dr. Kenneth B., 50
Climate Change, 11, 12, 13, 14, 15, 16, 23, 93, 101, 102, 103, 104, 144, 147, 149, 153
Clinton
 Hillary, 103
Cobbs
 John, 41
Cohen
 Patricia, 52, 53, 99
Coleman
 James, 70, 71
College of Nanoscale Science and Engineering
 CNSE, 140
community benefit agreement
 CBA, 159
Community loan funds, 159
Community Reinvestment Act of 1977, 27
Constitution, 8, 9, 10, 134, 172
Cowie
 Jefferson, 77, 78, 87, 90, 91
Crow
 Jim, 49, 65
Currie
 Elliott, 97

D

Dahl
 Robert, 175
Daly
 Herman, 41
Danziger
 Sheldon, 45
Decentralization, 28, 63, 122
Declaration of Independence, 74
deforestation, 11, 12, 17, 21, 153
deindustrialization, vii, 65,
Delbanco
 Andrew, 9
democracy, 8, 9, 10, 32, 33, 54, 62, 74, 151, 155, 175, 176, 177

Denvir
 Daniel, 65
DeParle
 Jason, 46, 47
Deresiewicz
 William, 176
Dewey
 John, 90
Diamond
 Jared, 11
Dickinson
 Tim, 86
Dionne, Jr.
 E.J., 83

G

H

I

J

K

L

M

N

S

T

U

V

W